Postcolonial Theory and Autobiography

Cultural theory has often been criticized for covert Eurocentric and universalist tendencies. Its concepts and ideas are implicitly applicable to everyone, ironing over any individuality or cultural difference. Postcolonial theory has challenged these limitations of cultural theory, and *Postcolonial Theory and Autobiography* addresses the central challenge posed by its autobiographical turn.

Despite the fact that autobiography is frequently dismissed for its Western, masculine bias, David Huddart argues for its continued relevance as a central explanatory category in understanding postcolonial theory and its relation to subjectivity. Focusing on the influence of post-structuralist theory on postcolonial theory and vice versa, this study suggests that autobiography constitutes a general philosophical resistance to universal concepts and theories.

Offering a fresh perspective on familiar critical figures like Edward W. Said and Gayatri Chakravorty Spivak, by putting them in the context of readings of the work of Jacques Derrida, Gilles Deleuze, and Alain Badiou, this book relates the theory of autobiography to expressions of new universalisms that, together with postcolonial theory, rethink and extend norms of experience, investigation, and knowledge.

David Huddart is Assistant Professor in the Department of English at the Chinese University of Hong Kong. He is the author of *Homi K. Bhabha* (Routledge, 2005). His research interests cover postcolonial literature, literary theory, and the history of English languages.

POSTCOLONIAL LITERATURES

Edited in collaboration with the Centre for Colonial and Postcolonial Studies, University of Kent at Canterbury, this series presents a wide range of research into postcolonial literatures by specialists in the field. Volumes will concentrate on writers and writing originating in previously (or presently) colonized areas, and will include material from non-anglophone as well as anglophone colonies and literatures. The series will also include collections of important essays from older journals, and re-issues of classic texts on postcolonial subjects. Routledge is pleased to invite proposals for new books in the series. Interested authors should contact Lyn Innes or Rod Edmond at the Centre for Colonial and Postcolonial Studies, University of Kent at Canterbury, or Routledge's Commissioning Editor for Literature.

The series comprises three strands.

Routledge Research in Postcolonial Literatures is a forum for innovative new research intended for a specialist readership. Published in hardback, titles include:

1 *Magical Realism in West African Fiction: Seeing with a Third Eye* by Brenda Cooper
2 *The Postcolonial Jane Austen* edited by You-Me Park and Rajeswari Sunder Rajan
3 *Contemporary Caribbean Women's Poetry: Making Style* by Denise deCaires Narain
4 *African Literature, Animism and Politics* by Caroline Rooney
5 *Caribbean–English Passages: Intertextuality in a Postcolonial Tradition* by Tobias Döring
6 *Islands in History and Representation* edited by Rod Edmond and Vanessa Smith
7 *Civility and Empire: Literature and Culture in British India, 1822–1922* by Anindyo Roy
8 *Women Writing the West Indies, 1804-1939: 'A Hot Place, Belonging To Us'* by Evelyn O'Callaghan
9 *Postcolonial Pacific Writing: Representations of the body* by Michelle Keown
10 *Writing Woman, Writing Place: Contemporary Australian and South African Fiction* by Sue Kossew
11 *Literary Radicalism in India: Gender, Nation and the Transition to Independence* by Priyamvada Gopal
12 *Postcolonial Conrad: Paradoxes of Empire* by Terry Collits
13 *American Pacificism: Oceania in the U.S. Imagination* by Paul Lyons
14 *Decolonizing Culture in the Pacific: Reading History and Trauma in Contemporary Fiction* by Susan Y. Najita
15 *Writing Sri Lanka: Literature, Resistance and the Politics of Place* by Minoli Salgado
16 *Literature of the Indian Diaspora: Theorizing the Diasporic Imaginary* by Vijay Mishra
17 *Secularism in the Postcolonial Indian Novel: National and Cosmopolitan Narratives in English* by Neelam Srivastava
18 *English Writing and India, 1600–1920: Colonizing Aesthetics* by Pramod K. Nayar
19 *Decolonising Gender: Literature, Enlightenment and the Feminine Real* by Caroline Rooney
20 *Postcolonial Theory and Autobiography* by David Huddart
21 *Contemporary Arab Women Writers* by Anastasia Valassopoulos

Postcolonial Literatures makes available in paperback important work in the field. Hardback editions of these titles are also available, some published earlier in the *Routledge Research* strand of the series. Titles in paperback include:

Postcolonial Studies: A Materialist Critique by Benita Parry
Magical Realism in West African Fiction: Seeing with a Third Eye by Brenda Cooper
The Postcolonial Jane Austen edited by You-Me Park and Rajeswari Sunder Rajan
Contemporary Caribbean Women's Poetry: Making Style by Denise deCaires Narain

Readings in Postcolonial Literatures offers collections of important essays from journals or classic texts in the field. Titles include:

1 *Selected Essays of Wilson Harris* edited by Andrew Bundy

Postcolonial Theory and Autobiography

David Huddart

Routledge
Taylor & Francis Group

LONDON AND NEW YORK

First published 2008
by Routledge
2 Park Square, Milton Park, Abingdon, OX14 4RN

Simultaneously published in the USA and Canada
by Routledge
270 Madison Avenue, New York, NY 10016

Routledge is an imprint of the Taylor & Francis Group, an informa business

Typeset in Baskerville by Keyword Group Ltd
Printed and bound in Great Britain by Biddles Ltd, King's Lynn

British Library Cataloguing in Publication Data
A catalogue record for this book is available from the British Library

Library of Congress Cataloging in Publication Data
Huddart, David (David Paul)
Postcolonial theory and autobiography / David Huddart.
    p. cm. – (Postcolonial literatures)
Includes bibliographical references and index.
    1. Autobiography. 2. Postcolonialism. 3. Postcolonialism
in literature. 4. Biography as a literary form. I. Title.
CT25.H83 2007
809'.93592–dc22   2007018253

ISBN10:.0-415-35342-4 (hbk)
ISBN10: 0-203-30657-0 (ebk)

ISBN 13: 978-0-415-35342-7 (hbk)
ISBN 13: 978-0-203-30657-4 (ebk)

Contents

Acknowledgments

This book builds on ideas explored in my doctoral thesis, and so I would like to offer my thanks to Geoffrey Bennington, who supervised me during my three years at the University of Sussex. In addition, there are other people from Sussex who probably remain unaware of their importance to this project, so I will take this opportunity to thank Jonathan Tiplady, Jennifer Huyn, Rafe Hallett, and Ben Roberts. In addition, the comments of Willy Maley and Laura Marcus were important in framing this book's argument in an appropriate way. Some of these ideas developed during my studies at Goldsmiths' College in London, and for their teaching and advice I would therefore like to thank Helen Carr, Bart Moore-Gilbert, and Gareth Stanton. I have benefited from the efforts of various people at Routledge, particularly Liz Thompson, James Whiting, and Polly Dodson.

The project has been written in various locations, beginning in London, moving on to Tokyo, with an interlude in Bath, before completion in Hong Kong. I would like to thank the staff and students in the various institutions in which I've worked, particularly David Ewick, Bernard Wilson, James Quan-Nicholls, Richard Stamp, Fiona Peters, and David Parker. Finally, for invaluable assistance during the final stages of this book's writing, I would like to thank Huiwen Shi and Chloe Li.

Not all demonstrations are exhibitions of how to do things.

Gilbert Ryle

1 Postcolonial theories of autobiography and autobiography in postcolonial theory

Postcolonial theories of autobiography

I want to begin with Charles Taylor's *Sources of the Self,* in which he famously argues that, 'We are selves only in that certain issues matter for us'. My self, alongside similar selves, takes shape in relation to things defined as important, things accepted if not defined as important by me as an individual: 'these things have significance for me, and the issue of my identity is worked out, only through a language of interpretation which I have come to accept as a valid articulation of these issues.' Languages of interpretation do not take shape once there are selves existing to shape them, but themselves frame the taking shape of selves: 'To ask what a person is, in abstraction from his or her self-interpretations, is to ask a fundamentally misguided question, one to which there couldn't in principle be answer.' Indeed, it might seem to be a strictly impossible question. Be that as it may, Taylor continues to make the central point that, 'we are selves only insofar as we move in a certain space of questions, as we seek and find an orientation to the good'.[1]

Certain things about me form a limit to what I want to describe, consciously or not, through my talking or writing about myself. I can insist that I have five legs, but this re-description or textual performance has no efficacy – at least not the kind I might seem to desire. By contrast, as Taylor reminds us, I say things about my social, cultural, or ethical identity within a context or framework of questions. These questions are no less real, it might be argued, than biological facts, but these questions are also variable across space and time. There's little point in discussing Shakespeare and Mao as if they shared absolutely a sense of what it is to be a self, what it means to lead a good life, or what it is to be an individual. Here there is an element of cultural relativity. Communities of interpretation imagine selves in their own specific ethical terms. Following Taylor, David Parker has adapted this understanding of ethical orientation in order to re-cast the study of life writing generally.[2] Parker insists that insofar as Taylor's account is about 'necessary frameworks' and 'transcendental conditions', about ethical orientations that we cannot *not* want, then 'it is not specific to Western culture'.[3] This is why the term *moral,* to the extent that each moral system is culturally specific, is less helpful than *ethical.* If we talk in terms of ethics then we can suppose that certain kinds of good inescapably structure our sense of who we are and how we live our lives, even if they are not always the same kind of good. Different cultures require different forms of thick description in order to capture their different ethical orientations. Accordingly, it is possible to imagine that the forms of writing that accompany this kind of self-imagination are also culturally relative. This possibility delivers an immediate problem, and perhaps one that is more than merely terminological. I seem to want to set certain conceptual tools to work on a context that has at least challenged the validity of those tools, sometimes even rejecting them outright. Postcolonial theory does not always think about selves in a way that fits the discourse of autobiography, or so it might seem, and so this book's title intuitively requires some explanation.

Over the last twenty five years there has been an explosion of interest in what now needs to be called life writing. One of the reasons it needs to be called that, rather than autobiography, is that the latter term privileges one particular way of writing a life, a way that for many critics is simultaneously too abstract, too masculine and Western. As an example, Anita Rupprecht asserts that, 'Born from Enlightenment secular humanism, [autobiography] denotes the narrative inscription of an abstract and unique individual agent moving through time and space'.[4] Further, Linda Anderson suggests that, 'Insofar as autobiography has been seen as promoting a view of the subject as universal, it has also underpinned the centrality of masculine – and, we may add, Western and middle-class – modes of subjectivity.'[5] Of course, as Anderson implies, this is not the only way of seeing autobiography. Nonetheless, it has been a dominant understanding, and so the genre has its canon, its claims made about the construction of the modern subject, and all of this institutionalised authority has tended to exclude any other way of imagining life writing, for example forms that give expression to collective subjects. Accordingly, Sidonie Smith and Julia Watson report that,

> a growing number of postmodern and postcolonial theorists contend that the term *autobiography* is inadequate to describe the extensive historical range and the diverse genres and practices of life narratives and life narrators in the West and elsewhere around the globe.[6]

We cannot restrict ourselves to a narrowly ethnocentric and paternalist model of life writing, and if that is what autobiography tends to designate, then we might do better using other terms to describe the most general tendencies.

Now, it is true that there has been renewed interest in the father figures of Western autobiography, for example Augustine, Montaigne, and Rousseau. It is impossible simply to dismiss what they stand for, or the complexities of their writings. Nonetheless, the searching questioning of Western autobiography is something that needs to be taken into account here, precisely because as has already become clear such questioning is, in one form, a postcolonial questioning. So already there is a problem with my title: it could be argued that it ought to read *Postcolonial Theory and Life Writing*. But this problem is one which will be considered, directly or indirectly, throughout the book. Also, it is well to remember that *autobiography* and *life writing* are often enough used interchangeably, and that there might be important reasons why this is so, beyond simple theoretical confusion. Indeed, various critics have already begun to explore the convergence of postcolonial theory and autobiography as having positive consequences. For example, Hornung and Ruhe see the term autobiography as an expedient genre for certain political purposes: 'Autobiography in its widest definition seems to provide a convenient genre to embrace the crossroad cultures from East and West and to launch an emancipatory political and cultural program'.[7] Now, it seems clear from the context (wide-ranging French and English edited collections bringing together postcolonialism and autobiography) that they are using autobiography as synonym for life writing, and they seem unfazed by critiques levelled at this gesture. What is it that they find in this convergence?

To answer this question requires some sense of the resources to be found in concepts of autobiography. The term, broadly understood or not, can seem imprecise, but it has been persuasively argued that this imprecision is actually rather useful, and is an apparent weakness that can be converted into a strength.[8] It may be understood as a concept, tendency, or genre. Here it is used to designate what challenges universalized notions of subjectivity, and in this usage it must be understood sometimes consecutively and sometimes simultaneously as concept, tendency, *and* genre. That this general usage lacks specificity hopefully does not indicate insufficient rigour, and related dispersals are a central operation of postcolonial theory. Laura Marcus, in her general consideration of autobiography, suggests that, 'Contemporary debates in feminist and post-colonial theory have made autobiography a central topic, but it is now a centre which disperses towards its margins and its borders'.[9] Dispersal is an appropriate way of describing many operations in contemporary cultural practice, and may be celebrated as conceptually and politically inclusive or dismissed for lack of conceptual and political rigour. Thus already autobiography's implication in fundamental theoretical and political questions is beginning to emerge. Not every writer on these matters is convinced that autobiography can have much to offer, particularly if it becomes the marker of a constitutively hazy disruptiveness. Any such designation needs justification, which it will receive.

Matching doubts about the definitional rigour are concerns about the practical outcomes of autobiographical practice. It is not clear that autobiographical criticism offers much in the way of a response to neo-colonial structures. Of course, in answer to such an objection it is necessary to recall that this criticism is not advocated as sufficient in itself. Aram Veeser makes this clear when he asserts that, 'Autobiographical criticism shapes itself within larger

critical projects, but the larger projects continue in force'.[10] Autobiographical
practice is a contribution to the awareness of the necessity of transforming
textual practices. In the related context of the shared concerns of anti-racist
and feminist critical practices, for example, Nancy K. Miller writes the
following:

> In the face of the visible extremes of racism or misogyny, or the equally
> violent silences of theoretical discourses from which all traces of embodi-
> ment have been carefully abstracted, the autobiographical project might
> seem a frivolous response. How can I propose a reflection about an ethics
> in criticism (an ethics requires a community) from these individualistic
> grounds? But the risk of a limited personalism, I think, is a risk worth run-
> ning – at least the movement of a few more degrees in self-consciousness –
> in order to maintain an edge of surprise in the predictable margins of
> organized resistances.[11]

We might actually argue that the autobiographical transformation of
postcolonial theory is concerned with transforming notions of universal subjectivity that themselves disrupt the possibility of the community to which
Miller refers. Miller's reference to a *limited* personalism perhaps distracts us
from the extent to which such practice tries to transform the polarity between
personalism and communalism. But how does autobiographical practice work
to transform this apparently rigid opposition? Postcolonial theory, in displacing universalized subjectivities associated with Western thought, wants
to emphasize how one universalization of subjectivity has always excluded
other modes of subjectivity. In other words, it wants to show how at best other
subjectivities are admitted to consideration in order to bolster sameness. Postcolonial suspicion of this universal subjectivity does not, however, coincide
with the absolute dismissal of subjectivity. There remain debts to ideas of subjectivity and authorship that postcolonial theory ought to acknowledge. Sean
Burke, for one, wonders if this questioning is fully worked out in postcolonial
theory or remains incomplete:

> Postmodern emphases on locality, on little narratives, on singularity; neo-
> ethical concerns with respecting the Otherness of the Other; postcolonial
> specifications of the subaltern, of national and historical contexts – all
> these drives within contemporary critical discourse pass from the text to
> its histories without properly acknowledging that an authorial life and its
> work allow such a passage to be made.[12]

To give context to text, without acknowledging that most insistent of contexts, the authorial life, is certainly a peculiar gesture and one that is only
partly explicable as a reaction against the absolute privileging of authorial intention. Indeed the omission of the authorial context must derive
from assumptions within the new critical orientations connecting texts and

contexts. In fact, Burke suggests elsewhere that the incompleteness of the postcolonial transformation of subjectivity derives from an incompleteness of its questioning of post-structuralism:

> [T]he concerted return to context which we have recently witnessed in the discourses of New Historicism, Cultural Materialism and Post-colonialism suggests the restoration of a working concept of authorship if only to provide a point of access to historical, cultural and colo-nial contexts. Quite often, in fact, these discourses proceed covertly through the author while disclaiming the author with an embarrass-ment which presumably stems from too heavy and reactive an invest-ment in modernity's characterisation of authorship as autonomous agency.[13]

For Burke, then, contemporary criticism wants to scorn traditional forms of authorship, because of a rather simplistic and one-dimensional under-standing of how it has been imagined. David Parker has recently argued the related point that, 'the thin third-person languages of post-Saussurean theory are inadequate for many first person life purposes'.[14] Laura Marcus observes the polarization in critical approaches towards universal subjectivity in a similar way:

> Although autobiography – as concept or as a body of texts – is undoubt-edly a crucial site for explorations or constructions of selfhood and identity, the focus on universal subjectivity, or the denial, resulted in a neglect of ethnic and gender diversity and differential subjectivities, and a highly abstract concept of identity[15]

For Marcus, feminist and postcolonial discourses fill the lack of concern with the concepts that will succeed ideas of universal subjectivity. Like Burke, Marcus implies that modernity's critique of the universal subject wanted to dispense with subjectivity altogether. Burke, however, further argues that postcolonial and feminist approaches, with their investment in post-structuralism, continue to neglect important resources that can be found in past notions of authorship. Such a criticism could only be levelled at some theorists associated with post-structuralism and postcolonialism. As we will see, time and again postcolonial theory not only questions but also performs the tasks Burke demands.

Autobiography in postcolonial theory

Adapting Valéry, Leigh Gilmore makes the following point: 'Every autobiog-raphy is the fragment of a theory'.[16] If the fictive qualities of autobiography have been blurred ever more productively, its theoretical qualities have also come in for increased exploration. The same is true of the autobiographical

quality of theory to the point at which the blurring works to make both categories problematic in a productive way. So, in terms of the second half of
this chapter's title, it is possible to state that autobiographical moments have
become very common in postcolonial theory, along with other forms of literary and cultural theory. The question of what functions such moments are
designed to perform, or perform in spite of design, will be a major focus.
Suffice to say, right now, that such moments can be related to identity politics. But this is something which will be discussed later, and the relation is
not as simple as it can seem. However, the question of whether or not they
should be expected to perform any function at all might be considered here,
specifically in terms of what academic discourses can be expected to do. So,
in *The Intimate Empire*, Gillian Whitlock asks an important question about the
efficacy of autobiography: 'When does autobiography become active in the
politics of identity? A discursive threshold must be reached before autobiographic writing appears as an agent. This is clearly not the case for each
individual autobiographic act'.[17] Whitlock's point must be taken into account
in the very different context of academic writing in cultural and literary theory. When is the discursive threshold reached, in that context? Measurement
is clearly impossible, but the impressionistic import of the wealth of teaching and researching in both life writing and postcolonialism tells its own
tale. And yet perhaps matters are not so simple. There is more than volume at work, and authority of academic writing is clearly marked by the
so-called star system. Linda Anderson, in discussing the personal in critical writing, asserts that, 'What is at stake is who speaks or rather who is
authorized to speak'.[18] To some extent, we need to see this in Foucault's
terms, as Whitlock invites us to do, remembering that a discursive threshold does not refer us to copies sold or prescribed in reading lists. Foucault
writes that, 'We know perfectly well that we are not free to say just anything,
that we cannot simply speak of anything, when we like or where we like;
not just anyone, finally, may speak of just anything'.[19] By that he means
that, for example, not just anyone can pronounce upon medicine, only those
with the elements that mark them as medics. However, within that, we will
want to hold onto the capital accruing to certain practitioners, giving them
an elevated authority. So, if we look again at Anderson's terms, we need to
accept that not every theoretical writer can get away with an autobiographical
moment.

   Furthermore, as Whitlock points out, not every act does what it seeks to do,
or does anything at all. Otherwise, we might further argue, there would be
no readability at all. Indeed, when autobiographical writing is understood as
being performative, it is vital to remember the questions posed to J. L. Austin
by Jacques Derrida and, through him, Judith Butler. Moments of apparently
skewed reading are what enable reading in general. Indeed, autobiographical
turns in cultural and literary theory might so easily be written off as more
academic self-obsession, an obsession deriving from the general postmodern
atmosphere of humanities writing. According to this criticism, the staging

of the self precludes the development of a practical form of theory. Janet Harbord summarizes this judgment:

> A contentious development, writing the 'self' into narratives of cultural explication has come to represent the cul-de-sac of contemporary thought; caricatured as endlessly reflexive, autobiography is read as the aporia of postmodernism, knowingly playing at the edges and reproducing only the retracted limits of a theoretical project.[20]

It is not possible to simply write off this reading as skewed: we ought always to look for the sources of a misreading in the *mis-read*, and in this case we should look at the question of readership or audience. When Whitlock refers to a discursive threshold, the relatively limited market for theory must be recalled: we need to ask who reads theoretical writing. Some might suppose that it is destined to remain extremely distant from the lived realities of most people, toiling masses and non-toiling intelligentsia (as Terry Eagleton might say) alike.

This might particularly be the case if the autobiographical subject's textuality is emphasized, prompting Adriana Cavarero to mischievously suggest that,

> [T]he whole affair about the centrality of the text, which reduces the existence of the living to a *status* of extra-textuality, depends on the well-known tendency of intellectuals to represent the world in their own likeness and image.[21]

Yet not all theory wants to reduce subjects to being textual, although we might want to say that subjects are constituted by text-effects, which is a very different matter. And not all autobiographical theory undermines its own efficacy through an obsession with the textual limitations of the subject it constructs. Harbord suggests the following way of understanding autobiographical theory:

> Autobiography is never simply about the constitution of a stable, knowable self, even if that is the desire in the writing. The writing of the self involves an engagement with the various cultural resources available, forms which are recognizable to institutions, publishers and audiences. Such conventions do not repress the potential text of the 'self' but constitute its possibilities. The emergence of autobiography in academic work marks a different way of thinking through the relationship of writers to audiences, of negotiating public forms of rhetoric, and of making interventions into the debate about the role of intellectuals. To dismiss it as an intrinsically private activity, signaling a retreat from either public communication or narratives of broader social application, is to miss the point, and to reinstate the tired polarities of public and private, abstract

versus embodied knowledge, the political subject versus the narcissist: the ineluctability of othering each other.[22]

We might even say that there is a need to write this kind of theory, in order to re-think some of these relationships. The very idea of a *public intellectual* rather obviously depends on the relationship between intellectual and public, and autobiographical theory is one way that relationship is being re-imagined at a time when it really does require re-imagination. Indeed, if relationality is a key idea for *all* manner of contemporary critical perspectives,[23] it is intriguing to find that autobiographical theory is actually a contribution to its exploration rather than its implicit denial through narcissistic neologism.

There are many examples that begin to demonstrate the need for autobiographical theory, a need that can be understood in terms of the critical margins revising apparent centres. Jane Gallop's *Anecdotal Theory* pursues a questionable, although understandable, argument that runs together debates about clarity, literary/critical style, and the autobiographical turn in theoretical writing.[24] In particular, she chooses to interpret Barbara Christian's *The Race for Theory*[25] as a call for a more literary style of theoretical writing, a style that Gallop herself then attempts to create, in her own singular fashion. Christian, it will be remembered, understands the prevalent theoretical bent of literary criticism as both ugly and unnecessary. First, it is ugly in that, for writing that is supposed to be sensitive to the subtleties of literary language, it displays an alarming propensity to be tone-deaf in both its treatment of that language and its presentation of its findings. In other words, it does not really care for the challenge of *literature as language*, and its interpretations are really quite difficult to read in their embarrassing word-play and hopeless jargon. Christian writes: '[A]s a student of literature, I am appalled by the sheer ugliness of the language, its lack of clarity, its unnecessarily complicated sentence constructions, its lack of pleasurableness, its alienating quality.' Second, it is unnecessary because the kind of theory that is on offer (at the beginning of the 1990s) is simply only one option, with other kinds of theory being created all the time at the margins of critical debate. Christian again: '[P]eople of color have always theorized – but in forms quite different from the Western form of abstract logic.' Against the theory that she sees as so much abstract Western verbiage, Christian poses a criticism alive to the experience of reading literature that, she rightly points out, is one of *surprise*:

> [M]y language is very much based on what I read and how it affects me, that is, on the surprise that comes from reading something that compels you to read differently, as I believe literature does. I, therefore, have no set method, another prerequisite of the new theory, since for me every work suggests a new approach. As risky as that might seem, it is, I believe, what intelligence means – a tuned sensitivity to that which is alive and therefore cannot be known until it is known.[26]

According to Christian, and in 1990 she had a point, theory as disseminated led to a methodological rigidity entirely at odds with truly sensitive literary criticism. Respect for the specificity of the literary work demands that we treat each work, or even each instance of reading, as an experience of the other, and, as we might say in a different critical idiom, we must respect the otherness of the other. To do this, Christian asserts, we have to stop writing in a rigid, mechanistic style, which is really a style betraying a rigid and mechanistic attitude to literature. Gallop is quite right, then, that Christian is really calling for a new form of critical writing. However, I imagine that Gallop's own approach to this task is quite distant from that which Christian had in mind. Gallop puts post-structuralist theory to work as a central element of her anecdotal theory. Indeed, it is one of the key justifications for writing such theory at all. Surprise, as Christian says, is perhaps the nature of the experience of literature, although as we know surprise only makes sense in the contexts of structure, predictability, and genre. As we might then go on to argue, surprise is actually one of the very things that theory has been concerned to theorize – the ways in which there are excesses above and beyond system, things that elude our desire for mastery. In fact, it can be argued that the autobiographical turn in theoretical writing is a development rather than rejection of theory. Candace Lang makes this point:

> [T]he most essential component of what I consider to be theoretical activity is the reflexive (self-reflective) moment in which the critic attempts to define her own presuppositions, methodological tools, and the consequences of these choices. Thus it seems to me that the recent trend toward autobiographical or personal criticism is a necessary development in the evolution of critical theory, a further elaboration of the self-reflexive moment of theory through a move beyond the ostensibly 'rational' determinants of reading, in order to identify some of the highly specific, localized (both spatially and temporally), empirical factors affecting the critical agent.[27]

Many writers might wonder if this component is really 'the most essential' aspect of theory – unless theory is strictly sequestered from the practice of criticism, as might be put to work in reading a poem, photograph, or social network. Such writers might see this emphasis as yet more academic navel-gazing. We have already briefly mentioned that particular kind of argument, and it will be considered again later. According to Lang, as I read her argument, we need to guard against the idea that post-structuralist theory repressed the critical subject (along with other subjects), and that autobiographical theory therefore marks the triumphant return of that subject. She sees theory as the necessary condition for the more thorough inventory of contemporary theory. So, for Lang, what *precedes* the moment of theory has been the object of previous consideration, but only apparently more objective ('rational') determinants have been analyzed. The autobiographical turn provides us with still further analysis of the determinants of theory. And, appropriately, given the emphasis of much theory on excess, autobiographical theory gathers in that which exceeds thematization, that which is 'highly specific, localized' – we might say singular. A key word in Lang's paragraph is 'attempts', in that autobiographical theory is no more a full inventory of presuppositions than any other autobiographical writing is a complete laying bare of a self. Indeed, given the inevitable emphasis on the blurred division between the factual and fictive elements in autobiography, it should be said that autobiographical theory is itself an invention, a re-construction or re-staging that must be other than the truth of the presuppositions, methods, etc. of a theory. Sven Lindqvist's autobiographical exploration of European imperialism in Africa, *Exterminate all the brutes*, makes the point explicitly in relation to writing a doctoral thesis:

> Even in the most authentic documentary there is always a fictional person – the person telling the story. I have never created a more fictional character than the researching 'I' in my doctorate, a self that begins in pretended ignorance and then slowly arrives at knowledge, not at all in the fitful, chancy way I myself arrived at it, but step by step, proof by proof, according to the rules.
> [...]
> As a reader, as soon as I see the word I used (or avoided, for even avoidance is a way of using it) I know I have a fictional character in front of me.[28]

We might want to say *especially* when it is avoided, except of course that it rarely is avoided by now. And of course this fiction in scholarly writing is in some sense necessary. For one thing, as James Clifford suggests in the specific context of anthropology, 'One could hardly count on being awarded a Ph.D., or finding a job in anthropology department, for autobiographical research'.[29] In another essay, 'On Ethnographic Authority',[30] Clifford uses Bakhtin's notion of *heteroglossia* to think about how ethnographical interpretation and self-interpretation now take place in multiple idioms. Clifford Geertz, meanwhile, states that ethnography is all about persuading us that the 'offstage miracle' of the ethnographer 'having actually penetrated (or, if you prefer, been penetrated by) another form of life' has actually taken place.[31] Geertz is well known for his adaptation of the notion of *thick description* from Gilbert Ryle, a notion capturing the essence of anthropological description of other cultures, which we can also see as capturing the essence of the ethnographic act itself.[32] Thick description is the act but it is also the description of itself, its own process, and its own result, in all of which there is an ethnographic self orienting itself in what we might now see as ethical terms. Ethnographic research and its writing appear to be all about the autobiographical inflection of a social science, and that inflection is something often explicitly staged. And yet it is clear, as Clifford implies, that some contexts require that the heteroglossic and autobiographical multiplicity be reduced to a singular and probably quite familiar idiom, which we might assume is a rather traditional idiom of scholarly impersonality. I am sure that this would be the case for the humanities generally, their autobiographical turn notwithstanding. Not just anyone can write a book of or about anecdotal theory, or not just anyone can expect to get such a book published anyway.

In any case, there is a further reason that this fiction is necessary, and it is one regarding an impossibility in the idea of questioning the questioning subject. Terry Eagleton makes the point with admirable clarity, when he writes:

> A human subject who could be known would be a determinate object, and so not a subject at all. The free subject, the founding principle of the whole enterprise, cannot itself be represented in the field which it generates, any more than the eye can capture itself in the field of vision. The subject is rather the incalculable element or out-of-place factor which allows that field to emerge into existence in the first place. What our knowledge tells us is that we are beyond its reach.[33]

For those who find the autobiographical moment in postcolonial theory evidence of an unseemly self-obsession, a slightly trashy urge to stage the personal, or even an unwarranted assertion that the personal is always political, it would be useful to recall Eagleton's point. Full disclosure is never as full as it appears, in the sense that its disclosure always marks a constitutive gap, the absence deriving from the impossibility of grasping ourselves, even as we seem to desire full frankness. David Simpson draws out the practical implications of this point when he writes that, 'no one fully wishes to be what they say they are, because what is enabling at one moment might become a liability at another'.[34] The autobiographical moment might seem to demonstrate the inflection of theories by the contingency of individual lives, but just as much brings forth the fact that such contingencies come to existence against implacably objective structures, and, importantly, these are structures that change. We might then think about the temporary objectivity of *situations*.

Postcolonial theory as situated knowledge

Simpson's book *Situatedness* traces through law, literature, philosophy, etc., the widespread use of what he calls the *azza* sentence: 'as a straight white male …' or similar beginnings. In the book, he does not explicitly discuss the use of such sentences in theoretical writing – indeed, such use of that particular sentence may be rare enough. However, Simpson does consider the equivalent rhetorical tics and methodological assumptions in an earlier essay called 'Speaking Personally'. Here he sees that autobiographical theory might provide the beginnings of what he calls a *critical historicism*, which 'would seek to be at once objective and unfinal'.[35] In extremely simplified terms, such a criticism would be objective but open to 'future objectivities'. In *Situatedness*, Simpson points out that, 'The invocation of Situatedness draws heavily on the habits of Culturalism, but also leaves open an option for other, more classically materialist, accounts of what we are'.[36] A critical historicism, or an autobiographical theory, is not necessarily always on its way to culturalist identity politics, and might always be an important part of a materialist cultural criticism, postcolonial or otherwise.

In any case, Simpson does not discuss critical historicism in his later book, and the name was perhaps a little misleading. Indeed, of course there was already a name for this kind of criticism in contemporary cultural theory. As is well known, Donna Haraway calls it *situated knowledge* and describes it as follows:

> [T]he alternative to relativism is not totalization and single vision, which is always finally the unmarked category whose power depends on systematic narrowing and obscuring. The alternative to relativism is partial, locatable, critical knowledges sustaining the possibility of webs of connections called solidarity in politics and shared conversations in epistemology. Relativism is a way of being nowhere while claiming to be everywhere equally. The 'equality' of positioning is a denial of responsibility and critical enquiry. Relativism is the perfect mirror twin of totalization in the ideologies of objectivity; both deny the stakes in location, embodiment, and partial perspective; both make it impossible to see well[37]

This characterization is by now extremely familiar, and despite the common association of Haraway's work with critiques of natural sciences, it also helps us to think about social science and humanities writing. From one perspective, this book can be understood as an investigation of postcolonial theory as a form of such knowledge. Once again, this would bring postcolonial theory into a relationship with other forms of critical theory like feminism. Like feminism, postcolonial theory can be understood as a situated knowledge both because such situatedness is a simple fact of knowing, and also because this situatedness makes it in important ways particularly valuable. Certain perspectives, it has been argued, give inherently more useful knowledge about a situation than do others. Particular standpoints are the ones to which we should turn when we really want to know that which is unsaid in a situation, or that which is denied and perhaps disavowed by a society. For the unsaid or the disavowed we need to look to situated knowledge. Lynette Hunter clearly explains its importance for contemporary critical discourse, in discussing standpoint theory:

> Standpoint theory argues that knowledge articulated from the standpoint of those excluded from ruling relations of power is particularly important. Because of the exclusion, the knowledge that is offered from that

excluded position is quite different to that current within the ethical ideological systems of a society and its culture, and is therefore a sou. of assessment and potential change and renewal. The theory is concerne with articulating situated knowledge, with retaining a concept of the rea. in the sense of critical rather than naïve realism, and with re-defining the 'individual' to account for people who are not subjects, or to account for the not-subjected of people's lives.[38]

In terms of knowledge about a social system, for example, situated knowledge can be argued to be the most valuable form of knowledge, identifying the gaps that constitute the system and are as such unthinkable to that system. Most often, the standard ways of conceptualizing any system pretend to have no situation, and no tendency whatsoever. Whether consciously or not, then, such conceptualizations will be unlikely to offer us new ways of thinking about the system, ways that will point to any weaknesses needing to be addressed.

Situated knowledge is, then, a form of standpoint theory, and as such is one (albeit particularly controversial, given its arguments about the natural sciences) version of a more general theoretical attitude that attaches particular value to voices that have not been heard: it is another version of privileging the margins. Standpoint theory, as a theory of knowledge, contributes to the construction of forms of oppositional consciousness.[39] In terms of feminism, it arose as a way of explaining the importance of a political programme in the context of knowledge production. But, and as Hunter's emphasis on *rhetoric* makes clear, there is a need to mark standpoint textually. Indeed, this can be seen as the logic of standpoint: that apparently neutral bodies of knowledge have failed to textually mark standpoint, and have thereby retained this apparent neutrality. From yet another critical perspective, we can accordingly see the value of autobiographical forms of theory. But as Hunter asserts, there needs to be a real appreciation of what is going on in any such theory, because, 'Without an understanding of rhetorical stance and the situatedness of textuality, standpoint can and has been dismissed as identity politics'.[40] Once again, the simple autobiographical statement of identity and location cannot be enough, and certainly in no way guarantees the achievement of any political or critical position whatsoever.

Cases against autobiographical theory: culturalism and identity politics

As Hunter warns, there is a danger that situating gestures become simply assertions of identity and its privilege. Therefore, familiar criticisms of postmodern identity politics might be applicable to some autobiographical theory. Indeed, the whole idea of postcolonial identity politics has been dismissed as another form of postmodern academic self-obsession, an obsession that on occasion even becomes a little dishonest. Some of these criticisms focus on 'postcolonial', following up many of the important points that have been made about that imprecise term. For example, insisting on the difference between real historical postcolonialism and its apparently dislocated, disconnected cultural theorization in Western university departments, Terry Eagleton jokes that there must be a secret handbook of postcolonial studies that stipulates that its practitioners, 1) must write incomprehensibly, and 2) must immediately distance themselves from the term 'postcolonial':

> All kosher postcolonial critics are deeply suspicious of the idea of post-colonialism, just as, back in the palmy days of sixties' high structuralism, it was as difficult to stumble upon a structuralist who confessed to the title as it was to find someone who habitually referred to themselves as 'asshole'.[41]

It is hardly coincidental that Eagleton uses structuralism as an example, also remarking on Jacques Derrida's ambivalence towards 'deconstruction'. The various names of theory (and 'Theory' itself) are often unwelcome to their apparent originators. In any case, Eagleton's point is clear: academics need to be a little more circumspect when identifying their practices with those of actual anti-colonial activists. No one may want to be called a postcolonial critic, but many critics seem to be quite happy to trade on the ersatz glamour associated with the idea.

This particular criticism of postcolonial theory is exemplified by Eagleton's argument. However, it is explored in more detail by Aijaz Ahmad,[42] Arif Dirlik,[43] and Benita Parry.[44] In brief, it argues that postcolonial criticism, in common with other supposedly radical versions of academic criticism, neglects the hard analysis of global capitalism in favour of simplistic claims to identity. This neglect derives from the class position of postcolonial theorists, seen as upwardly mobile beneficiaries of global capitalism in the university sector. Elleke Boehmer expresses this position clearly, writing that, 'not only the work, but also the biographies of post-colonial writers, many or whom are émigrés or exiles, appear to enact [hybrid] minglings. Their lives are distinguished by cultural clash, linguistic collision, and transnational movement'. However, this emphasis is enabled by the 'social position of migrant writers': 'Though there may be extremely valid reasons for many writers' relocation or migration to the West, it is important to note that in a number of cases access to former colonial metropolises like London and Paris has been buttressed by class position, educational background, and other social connections carried over from the home country'.[45] In fact, it might be argued that such privileges are both criticized and disavowed in postcolonial theory. Rey Chow, in comparable fashion, identifies a process of *self-subalternization* in academic cultural studies, which has unfortunate consequences: 'What these intellectuals are doing is robbing the terms of oppression of their critical and oppositional import, and thus depriving the oppressed of even the vocabulary of protest and rightful demand'.[46] A comparable point is made, with particular reference to postcolonial theory, by Kenneth Parker: '[T]he position from which the critic speaks has, once again, become crucial. [...] [I]t is precisely that awareness of the speaking position adopted by the critic which is sometimes neglected in discussions of [postcolonial] theories'.[47] For Parker, this unwillingness to self-scrutinize is specifically an unwillingness to interrogate economic determination, and this unwillingness also translates itself into a cavalier attitude towards the historical and economic conditions that are supposed to be under consideration. E. San Juan Jr. makes the point even more straightforwardly when he writes that, 'Loss of critical reflexivity is the price one pays for fetishizing discourse and the deterritorialized psyche'.[48] For him, if you generalize your specific critical position to the absurd degree evident in postcolonial theory, then you really lose all specificity and all critical perspective whatsoever. Of course, the choice of 'deterritorialized' here is a reference to Deleuze and Guattari, something I will return to later; however, his criticism would seem to cover all varieties of postcolonial theory.

To summarize, according to this criticism postcolonial theory is a form of postmodern identity politics and therefore has serious insufficiencies for the tasks facing criticism today. Globalization requires more than an emphasis on discourse and a vague recourse to generalized exile, and these are all postcolonial theory really has to offer. To return to Eagleton's argument, it seems that the difference between real postcolonialism and its unreal, scare-quoted accompaniment 'postcolonialism', is dependent on precisely the gesture he is initially mocking, which views the name postcolonialism sceptically. That would not be Eagleton's point, of course, as what he really wants to say is that *in spite of* these initial critical gestures towards the term 'postcolonialism', those privileged postcolonial critics immediately override their own disclaimers by making increasingly elaborate *culturalist* claims for their critical practices: '"Postcolonialism" has been on the whole rather stronger on identity than on the International Monetary Fund, more fascinated by marginality than by markets.'[49]

Eagleton's argument coincides with and generalizes the increasingly widespread sense that postcolonial studies are rather too literary, confining themselves to the 'merely cultural'. Eagleton also makes this general argument about postcolonial studies in the 'Afterword' to the second edition of his *Literary Theory*, condensing Aijaz Ahmad's criticisms of 'literary postcoloniality'. Postcolonial studies are *culturalist*, inflating the significance of cultural matters and neglecting the monumental facts of neo-colonial political and economic determinations. Accordingly, it has been a central feature of materialist critiques of postcolonial studies that they re-introduce economic determinations, and in particular the economic determinations of the Western university's employees, who are elevated by an academic variation of a more general capitalist star system, commodified for the apparent radical marking granted by their 'race', ethnicity and nationality, etc. Culturalism and identity politics go together, and according to its critics, postcolonialism as a phenomenon of the Western university system (particularly, then, postcolonial critics and theorists) is exemplary of the exaggerated focus on culture and identity.

So it would seem that postcolonial criticism concerns the historical and cultural forms of colonialisms and their resistance; however, postcolonial criticism is itself exemplary of neo-colonial extensions and consolidations of global capitalism. In this situation some critics have felt that it is time to undermine pretensions to radicalism. Stephen Slemon, for example, is disarmingly frank in his assessment of postcolonial criticism, and also concerning the aims of his discussion:

> [A]s the field of post-colonial studies is becoming professionalized as an institution for social critique and as an apparatus for producing cultural knowledge, it is beginning to perform within itself a regulating operation which has no necessary relation to, or investment in, a politics of anti-colonialism. This article, consequently, is an attempt to carry out some (ideological) refereeing in this structure of professionalized or disciplinary regulation: I want to address the question of who gets to play on the post-colonial field, who is asked to sit on the bench, who plays on the first team, how and when a player is, or ought to be, called 'out'.[50]

Immediately acknowledging the clear problems with professing to *referee* a 'game' that everyone seems to be playing, Slemon goes on to mark his discussion as strategic: '[F]or the purposes of this exercise, I want to pretend to stand somehow outside the "field".'[51] Slemon's extension of the field metaphor turns postcolonial criticism into a game, and this in itself is revealing. Slemon later summarizes postcolonial debates concerning agency as follows: 'the question of agency can be restated as a question of who or what acts oppositionally when ideology or discourse or psychic processes of some kind construct human subjects'.[52] The economic is markedly not on the list. Slemon suggests that, from his privileged refereeing position, it is possible to find a critical practice of polarization, one which he finds symptomatic of unresolved tensions around this practice's institutional location.

> The general tenor of the rhetoric in this pattern of accusation and counter-accusation – the figurations by which basic methodological differences are subject to disciplinary policing strategies – is peculiar to post-colonial studies, and I think it is significant: the Other is always neo-colonialist: the voice of the colonizer in renewed function and in institutionalized form.[53]

Slemon's focus on the tone of postcolonial criticism is welcome, again bringing us back to the question of how critical texts are autobiographically marked. In this case, however, the marking is rebarbative. In similar terms, Ihab Hassan signals his dismay at the tone of postcolonial criticism: 'the tone, in America at least, repels thought'.[54] Hassan's piece mimes an autobiographical mode in order to argue that such a mode, in the service of an identity politics, reduces the individual to an abstraction: 'personhood, personality, even a personal name, are all challenged in favor of some human abstract called "gender", "class", "race", or most frequently "cultural identity".'[55] Yet such a theory is, despite the apparent reduction of the individual in a total system, desperately incomplete: 'Valéry considered every theory a fragment of autobiography. In the present instance, autobiography has led us only to a fragment of theory'.[56]

I have discussed Hassan alongside Slemon to emphasize the similarities in their positions. Hassan explicitly positions his comments alongside critiques of 'cultures of complaint', as Robert Hughes would say;[57] however, this 'neo-liberal' position makes the same criticism as the Marxist critique, that in postcolonial criticism cultural identity becomes the sole horizon of judgment. For Hassan, the critique operates in terms of a demand for an aesthetics of multiculturalism. The Marxist critique operates to demand an analysis of postcolonialism within neo-colonial relations. So, it is clear that, for Slemon, if we could set ourselves outside the field, we would find that these rhetorical gestures merely conceal the deeper and common neo-colonial complicities of nominally opposed versions of postcolonial criticism. Postcolonial criticism's state of permanent dissensus would be a way of not talking about the common determinations, determinations that are final and that make the pretensions of culturalist criticism appear problematic at best, and dishonest at worst.

Although Slemon is apparently concerned with both materialist and textual postcolonial approaches, arguing that more tolerance of contrasting positions is required, it is clear that there is a certain privilege given to that materialist analysis able to comprehend postcolonial theory's complicity in neo-colonial structures. Accordingly, it is important to consider one example of this materialist critique in more detail, the work of Aijaz Ahmad. Ahmad's exemplary work insists not only on postcolonial theory's neo-colonial complicity, but also features his infamous tendency toward the *ad hominem*[58] discussion of writers like Edward Said and Salman Rushdie, a tendency that accompanies a general suspicion of literary and cultural theory. Ahmad's *In Theory* begins as it ostensibly means to continue, by putting literature in its proper place: the opening chapter is titled (with my emphasis) 'Literature *among* the Signs of Our Time'. Obviously, being *among* signs is not quite as decisive as being *the* sign. This works for both of the main implicit readings of this title: that literature is a sign of everything that is wrong about our time, or that literature might be in some way beneficial for our time. The stress on *our* time is important: this is undoubtedly an inclusive *our*. Relatedly, this is most definitely a *singular* time: no one can be consigned to the margins of history by allochronic discourses.[59] In any case, literature as an institution is not what is in question for Ahmad: what is in question is literary *study*, by which we might also understand *textualism* or *theory*. As soon as we narrow our focus in this way it is clear that literature is a *bad sign*. Theory, for Ahmad, is constantly working, 'to displace an activist culture with a textual culture'.[60] This displacement is of Marxism, and occurs most comprehensively *within* literary studies: what is in question is a professionalized activity, and this designation is in itself a judgment.

So, for Ahmad, we should be wary of this textualized academic culture, but we should simultaneously acknowledge its irrelevance. This double gesture is signalled clearly by his adopted focus. He wishes to consider a limited number of 'seminal' positions (e.g. Foucault and Said). What he argues is that post-structuralism has unduly elevated reading, which is a strange charge to make in the context of a discussion of literature. Ahmad has widened the debate immediately, implicitly acknowledging the general claims that literary theory has on our attention. Yet this generalized set of claims (around questions of 'textuality') is precisely what Ahmad is concerned to disavow: such claims are only *among* the signs of our time. He acknowledges that there is a Marxist philosophical reading of Marx, supposedly divorced from questions of political economy, yet this seemingly more abstract level of reading is immediately linked to a heterogeneity of literary theory: 'eclecticism of theoretical and political positions is the common ground on which radical literary theory is, on the whole, constructed'. The clear point is that Marxism, in contrast to theory (literature), is not among the signs of our time, but is instead *the* sign of our time.

This structure apparently puts Marxism in a strange position. One might imagine that Marxism was analyzing the signs, but in this structure Marxism is the central sign all the while orbited by lesser signs, like literature. Of course it is not inconceivable that Marxism might be both sign and its reader, but this would be a peculiarly narcissistic structure, and might just be that, 'ironic self-referentiality and self-pleasuring' Ahmad ascribes to 'post-structuralism'. And this might also remind us, in passing, that Marxism is necessarily a (neo-)colonial discourse itself, although what that means is not clear-cut, and nor could it be. Ahmad considers this point on occasion, but it seems to frequently come up for other critics, often when other forms of postcolonial criticism are under consideration. For example, Benita Parry claims that,

> [F]ar from failing to break away from the 'grammar of colonial culture' [...] the texts of decolonization to which Marxism was central (see the writings of Césaire, Fanon and Cabral), had deconstructed colonialism's ideology and teleology long before western theory got round to it.[61]

As already mentioned, it is difficult to argue that Marxism is not 'Western theory' itself. Relatedly, it is not clear that the writers in question can be construed as having absolutely non-Western subject-positions. Further, there is a narrative of deterioration that accompanies these criticisms, in which it is becoming increasingly difficult to give appropriate attention to neo-colonialism. In this narrative, theory can be dismissed as Western, textualist, and idealist, and importantly as the product of a specific class position. So, Ahmad writes of theory's material determinations, insisting on 'the objective determination of the theory itself by these material co-ordinates of its production, regardless of the individual agent's personal stance towards these locations and co-ordinates'.[62] There is little mention of economy as the final determinant here, for all individual attempts to wrestle theory away from such determination are overridden. But that is not the only form of determination at issue, and the economic is here sliding into identity politics. Theory is being determined and there is nothing the theorist can do about it. So, Marxist analysis of postcolonial theory is drawn into arguing not only in terms of the economic determinations on which it insists, but also in terms of cultural or identitarian determinations, i.e. the very terms in which postcolonial study often conducts itself.

Autobiographical postcolonialism

Against the materialist critique of postcolonial theory, it is possible to find autobiographical re-writings of theory that resist not only the exclusionary (and illusionary) universal subject, but also a Marxist insistence on always final economic determinations. Foucault argues that Marxism is structurally analogous to the bourgeois economics it challenges, and accordingly to all the other bourgeois systems of thought that accompany that economics. Insofar as a certain postcolonial theory seeks to displace all totalizing Western forms of subjectivity, it is unsurprising that this displacement is extended to the *investigating* subject: the philosopher, the sociologist, the historian, the anthropologist, etc. Further, this displacement is accompanied by a suspicion of the boundaries between the various disciplines of the human sciences. This displacement and suspicion is expressed by situated, autobiographical, discipline- and genre-mixing texts that resist totalizing urges of all kinds, seeing epistemological totalization as analogous to ethnocentrism. A quick way of understanding these texts is to see them as marked by a kind of postcolonial self-reflexivity.

However, such situating gestures can seem to be beside the point, especially when made by the so-called Western critic. It might seem that some self-reflexive or autobiographical critics are anxious not only to avoid speaking for others, but also to distance themselves from the very subjectivities they are supposed to be staging and interrogating. Asha Varadharajan makes this point very forcefully, when discussing the self-reflexivity of the so-called Western critic:

> Since the Western critic is inevitably implicated in the history of colonization, any intervention on behalf of the other, it could be argued, will be contaminated by that history and therefore futile. The process of self-scrutiny would then translate itself into consolation for the wrongs of the past and into paralysis in the present.[63]

However, this argument seems perhaps dependent on the class-blindness diagnosed by Ahmad and others. Presumably the 'Western' here would have to extend further than Varadharajan seems to want, for it to make any sense at all. And if it does not, then a sharper sense of class differentiation is required, because the invocation of what we would now call globalization might be argued to challenge all postcolonial theory, written by Western or non-Western critics alike, whatever those terms might mean. Nonetheless, Varadharajan is making a serious point: the self-reflexive critical gesture must not be allowed to take up all critical energies, leading to an overall lack of critical activity. Putting the investigative subject in question still implies that the subject will get round to doing some investigating, sooner or later.

Granted, however, that we will sometime move on (even if our self-situation can *never* be over), it is important to understand how the suspicion of the universal theory works, and how it is discussed. Importantly, we can find examples of autobiographical transformation's thematisation and expression in the work of what Robert Young has famously, if perhaps ambivalently, named the 'Holy Trinity' of postcolonial theory[64]: Homi Bhabha, Gayatri Chakravorty Spivak, and Edward Said. It may be objected that it is both politically and theoretically unfortunate to consider these predictable critics yet again, but there are fresh ways of thinking about their work that justify this approach. Of course, there are other places where postcolonial theoretical autobiography can be found,[65] for example in the work of critics like bell hooks, Henry Louis Gates, Jr., and Sara Suleri, which both theorizes and demonstrates variations of autobiographical practices; all three have additionally published straightforwardly autobiographical books.[66–69] Yet it will be at least as illuminating to look again at the canonical critical figures. Gates writes in terms of an *autocritography*, and there is a great deal of suggestive material on this general feature of postcolonial criticism in Bhabha, Spivak, and Said. Their various and extensive engagements with the works of Foucault and Derrida allow me to consider differing modes of autobiography, particularly the extent to which certain modes refuse simplistic celebrations of difference. Bhabha's notions of *hybridity* and *mimicry* imply a 'textualized' theory of subjectivity particularly open to transformation through specific textual practices. Bhabha finds that critical prose has recently become less jargonistic, and that, 'we are asked to face the full frontal reality of the idea of "Culture" itself';[70] his slightly rueful tone may imply a nostalgia for the days of 'high' theory, but elsewhere Bhabha has formally and thematically developed this textual potential.[71,72] Spivak, meanwhile, is well-known for the neologistic and syntactic difficulty of her autobiographical critical writing, and I will argue that such difficulty is constitutive of specific critical aims rather than symptomatic of academic obscurantism. Meanwhile, the example of Edward Said provides me with the clearest demonstration of the political stakes involved in these issues.

Said, of course, is explicit about the motivations behind his critical practice: 'In the end, I am moved by causes and ideas that I can actually choose to support because they conform to values and principles that I believe in'.[73] *Orientalism*, both demonstrates the immensity of the discourse of orientalism, overriding individual intention or sentiment, and simultaneously implies by its very existence that the techniques of its production can be radically revised. It operates to demonstrate that belief is irreducible in supposedly objective critical practice, proposing a general analysis of representation that in Said's other texts extends specifically to questions of memory both personal and political:

> Memory and its representations touch very significantly upon questions of identity, of nationalism, of power and authority. Far from being a neutral exercise in facts and basic truths, the study of history, which of course is the underpinning of memory, both in school and university, is to some considerable extent a nationalist effort premised on the need to construct a desirable loyalty to and insider's understanding of one's country, tradition, and faith.[74]

Said has elaborated this operation in the specific case of Palestinian issues, and in this context the stakes around questions of the authority and veracity of personal recollection and situated subjectivity have been clearly demonstrated. Prior to the publication of Said's memoir, *Out of Place*,[75] *Commentary* magazine published an article by Justus Reid Weiner[76] arguing that Said had over time misrepresented his past, and accordingly had no right to present himself as Palestinian. Weiner's research was motivated by the fact that, 'There can be no doubt that a great deal of the moral authority accruing to Edward Said derives as much from his personal as from his intellectual credentials'. He asserts that, 'in retelling the facts of his own personal biography over the years, he has spoken anything *but* the plain, direct, or honest truth'. Weiner suggests that many aspects of Said's supposed biography are inconsistent, and that he is therefore not entitled to call himself Palestinian. A generous interpretation, Weiner suggests, would see Said's self-representation as a *parable*; however, he concludes, 'the parable itself is a lie. An artful lie; a skillful lie; above all, a very useful and by now widely accepted lie – but a lie'. In response to Weiner's article, it can be noted that *Out of Place* is marked by the scrupulous reconstruction of Said's early life, emphasizing the limits of his own knowledge about his background, and not in fact making the claims that Weiner sets out to discredit.[77] However, we should also note Weiner's privileging of a specific kind of absolute identity, the kind of identity that very few can ever claim. In important ways, such a privileging can be found in Aijaz Ahmad's very different questioning of Said's credentials to oriental subjectivity.[78] That such different attitudes can coincide in ungenerous discussions of biography and critical authority alerts us to the delicacy of the issues, and demands an effort of critical generosity.

References

1. Taylor, *Sources of the Self* (Cambridge MA: Harvard University Press, 1990), p.34.
2. See Parker, *The Self in Moral Space: Life Narrative and the Good* (Ithaca NY: Cornell University Press, 2007), esp. pp.15-19.
3. Taylor, *Sources of the Self* (Cambridge MA: Harvard University Press, 1990), p.19.
4. Rupprecht, 'Making the Difference' in Jan Campbell and Janet Harbord (eds.) *Temporalities: Autobiography and Everyday Life* (Manchester: Manchester University Press, 2002), p.35.
5. Anderson, *Autobiography* (New York and London: Routledge, 2001), p.3.
6. Smith and Watson, *Reading Autobiography: A Guide for Interpreting Life Narratives* (Minneapolis: University of Minnesota Press, 2001), p.4.
7. Hornung and Ruhe, (eds.) *Postcolonialism and autobiography. Michelle Cliff, David Dabydeen, Opal Palmer Adisa.*, Amsterdam and Atlanta GA, Rodopi, 'Preface', p.3.
8. See, for example, Robert Smith's *Derrida and Autobiography* (Cambridge: Cambridge University Press, 1995).
9. Marcus, *Auto/Biographical Discourses: Theory, Criticism, Practice* (Manchester: Manchester University Press, 1994), p.294.
10. Veeser, 'Introduction: The Case for Confessional Criticism' in Veeser (ed.) *Confessions of the Critics* (London: Routledge, 1996), p.xix.
11. Miller, *Getting Personal: Feminist Occasions and Other Autobiographical Acts* (London: Routledge, 1991), p.xiv.
12. Burke, *The Death and Return of the Author: Criticism and Subjectivity in Barthes, Foucault and Derrida* [2nd Ed.](Edinburgh: Edinburgh University Press, 1998), p.203.
13. Burke, 'Reconstructing the Author', in Burke (ed.) *Authorship: From Plato to the Postmodern – A Reader* (Edinburgh: Edinburgh University Press, 1995), pp.xxvii–xxviii. He elaborates: 'What is true for feminism in this context would also apply to the postcolonial challenge to the "universal position" which has reified its own European pre-occupations into a global model of subjectivity. Furthermore, the second-order post-colonial critique of a hypostasised colonial subject would imply as its positive counter a defence of the specificity of the subject, the grounding of the text in the irreducible personal and cultural experiences of its author. In each case, a rigorous rejection of the universal subject must imply a reassertion of the subject in his/her particularity' (xxviii).
14. Parker, *The Self in Moral Space*, p.37.
15. Marcus, *Auto/biographical Discourses*, p.183.
16. Gilmore, *The Limits of Autobiography: Trauma and Testimony* (Ithaca and London: Cornell University Press, 2001), p.12.
17. Whitlock, *The Intimate Empire* (London and New York: Cassell, 2000), p.146. She returns to questions of cultural authority and testimonial empowerment in her discussion of 'minority' genres in *Soft Weapons: Autobiography in Transit* (Chicago: Chicago University Press, 2007).
18. Anderson, *Autobiography* (New York and London: Routledge, 2001), p.123.
19. Foucault, 'The Discourse on Language' in *The Continental Philosophy Reader* (New York & London: Routledge 1996), p.340.
20. Harbord, 'Platitudes of Everyday Life' in Jan Campbell and Janet Harbord (eds.) *Temporalities: Autobiography and Everyday Life* (Manchester: Manchester University Press, 2002), p.24.
21. Cavarero, *Relating Narratives* (London and New York: Routledge, 2000), p.76.

22. Harbord, 'Platitudes of Everyday Life', pp.32–33.
23. David Parker insists on its centrality to life writing studies, even referring to a 'relational turn'. See Parker, 'Inhabiting Multiple Worlds: Auto/Biography in an (Anti-)Global Age', *Biography* 28(1), 2005, p.vi.
24. Gallop, *Anecdotal Theory* (Durham and London: Duke University Press, 2002), pp.1–2.
25. Christian, 'The Race for Theory', in Padmina Mongia (ed.) *Contemporary Postcolonial Theory: A Reader* (London: Hodder Arnold, 1996), p.152, 149.
26. Christian, 'The Race for Theory', p.156.
27. Lang, 'Autocritique', in Veeser (ed.) *Confessions of the Critics* (London and New York: Routledge, 1996), pp.43-44.
28. Lindqvist, *'Exterminate all the brutes'*, trans. J. Tate (London: Granta, 1997), p.104.
29. Clifford, *Routes: Travel & Translation in the Late Twentieth Century* (Cambridge, MA: Harvard University Press, 1997), p.88.
30. In Clifford, *The Predicament of Culture: Twentieth-Century Ethnography, Literature, and Art* (Cambridge, MA: Harvard University Press, 1988), pp.21–54.
31. Geertz, *Works and Lives: the Anthropologist as Author* (Oxford: Blackwell, 1990), p.4.
32. For more on *thick description*, see Geertz, *The Interpretation of Cultures* (New York: Basic Books, 1973), esp. pp.3–30. David Parker borrows this idea, via Bernard Williams, in *The Self in Moral Space*, to capture the way in which life writing makes sense of lives through recourse to thickly descriptive ethical languages.
33. Eagleton, *Sweet Violence: the Idea of the Tragic* (Oxford: Blackwell, 2003), p.214.
34. Simpson, *Situatedness, or, why we keep saying where we're coming from* (Durham: Duke University Press, 2002), p.107.
35. Simpson, 'Speaking Personally: the Culture of Autobiographical Criticism' in Veeser (ed.) *Confessions of the Critics* (London & New York: Routledge, 1996), p.89.
36. Simpson, *Situatedness*, p.6.
37. Haraway, *Simians, Cyborgs, and Women: the Reinvention of Nature* (London: Free Association Books, 1991), p.191.
38. Hunter, *Critiques of Knowing* (New York and London: Routledge,1999), p.2.
39. See the argument of Chela Sandoval (2004), 'U.S. Third World Feminism: the Theory and Method of Differential Oppositional Consciousness' in Sandra Harding (ed.) *The Feminist Standpoint Theory Reader* (New York and London: Routledge), pp.195–209.
40. Hunter, *Critiques of Knowing*, p.7.
41. Eagleton, 'Postcolonialism and "Postcolonialism"', *Interventions* 1(1), (1998), p.24. Eagleton is pleased with this joke, and repeats it in 'In the Gaudy Supermarket', *London Review of Books* 13 May 1999, pp.3–6.
42. Ahmad, *In Theory: Classes, Nations, Literatures* (London: Verso, 1992).
43. Dirlik, 'The Postcolonial Aura: Third World Criticism in the Age of Global Capitalism', *Critical Inquiry* 20 (Winter 1994), pp.328–356.
44. Parry, 'Signs of Our Times: Discussion of Homi Bhabha's *The Location of Culture*', *Third Text* 28/29, pp.5–24.
45. Boehmer, 'Post-Colonial Literary Studies: A Neo-Orientalism?' in C. C. Barfoot and Theo d'Haen(eds.) *Oriental Prospects* (Amsterdam: Rodopi, 1998), pps.241, 242.
46. Chow, *Writing Diaspora* (Bloomington: Indiana University Press, 1993), p.13.

47. Parker, 'Very Like a Whale: Post-Colonialism Between Canonicities and Ethnicities', *Social Identities* 1(1) (1995), p.155.
48. San Juan Jr. (2002) *Racism and Cultural Studies: Critiques of Multiculturalist Ideology and the Politics of Difference* (Durham: Duke University Press, 2002), p.249.
49. Eagleton, 'Postcolonialism and "Postcolonialism"', p.26.
50. Slemon, 'The Scramble for Post-Colonialism' in Tiffin & Lawson (eds.) *De-Scribing Empire: Postcolonialism and textuality* (London: Routledge, 1994), p.15.
51. Slemon, 'The Scramble for Post-Colonialism', p.16.
52. Slemon, 'The Scramble for Post-Colonialism', p.22.
53. Slemon, 'The Scramble for Post-Colonialism', p.29.
54. Hassan, 'Counterpoints: Nationalism, Colonialism, Multiculturalism, etc., in Personal Perspective', *Third Text* 41 (Winter 1997-98), 3–14, p.4.
55. Hassan, 'Counterpoints: Nationalism, Colonialism, Multiculturalism, etc., in Personal Perspective', p.11.
56. Hassan, 'Counterpoints: Nationalism, Colonialism, Multiculturalism, etc., in Personal Perspective', p.5.
57. See Hughes, *The Culture of Complaint* [new Ed.](London: Panther, 1999).
58. Lewis R. Gordon explicitly applauds Ahmad's *ad hominem* tendencies; in *Fanon and the Crisis of European Man* (London: Routledge, 1995), p.101.
59. On the *allochronic*, see Johannes Fabian, *Time and the Other* (New York: Columbia University Press, 1983), for example p.143.
60. Ahmad, *In Theory*, p.1.
61. Parry, 'Post-Colonial Ambiguity', *New Formations* 33, 1998, p.152.
62. Ahmad, *In Theory*, p.1.
63. Varadharajan, *Exotic Parodies: Subjectivity in Adorno, Said, and Spivak* (Minneapolis: University of Minnesota Press, 1995), p.xvi.
64. See Young, *Colonial Desire: Hybridity in Culture, Theory, and Race* (London: Routledge, 1995), p.163.
65. See, for example, Ien Ang's 'On Not Speaking Chinese', *New Formations* 24 (Spring 1994), pp.1–18. Ang writes that, '[W]hat I hope to substantiate in staging my "Chinese identity" here - or better, my troubled relationship to "Chineseness" – is precisely the notion of *precariousness* of identity which has preoccupied cultural studies for some time now. [...] I should confess that there is considerable, almost malicious, pleasure in the flaunting of my own "difference" for critical intellectual purposes' (p.4).
66. See hooks, *Wounds of Passion* (London: Women's Press, 1998).
67. hooks, *Bone Black* (London: Women's Press, 1997).
68. Gates, *Colored People* (London: Penguin, 1995).
69. Suleri, *Meatless Days* (London: Flamingo, 1991).
70. Bhabha, 'Culture's In Between' in D. Bennett(ed.) *Multicultural States* (London: Routledge, 1998).
71. Bhabha writes, on the first page of 'DissemiNation: time, narrative, and the margins of the modern nation' (in *Nation and Narration* (London: Routledge, 1990)), that, 'I have lived that moment of the scattering of the people that in other times and other places, in the nations of others, becomes a time of gathering' (291).
72. See also 'Unpacking my library ... again' in Curti & Chambers (eds.) *The Postcolonial Question* (London: Routledge, 1996).
73. Said, *Representations of the Intellectual* (London: Vintage, 1994), p.65.
74. Said, 'Invention, Memory, and Place', *Critical Inquiry* 26 (Winter 2000), p.176.

75. Said, *Out of Place: A Memoir* (London: Granta, 1999).
76. Weiner, '"My Beautiful Old House"and Other Fabrications by Edward Said'; accessed at http://www.commentarymagazine.com/9909/weiner.html on January 19 2001.
77. Said notes in 'Defamation, Zionist-style' (in *Al-Ahram*), that Weiner allows, 'himself the preposterous claim that my memoir (begun in 1994 and completed in 1998) was written to refute him in 1999'; accessed at http://www.ahram.org.eg/weekly/1999/444/op2.htm on February 25 2001.
78. See Ahmad, 'Orientalism and After', in *In Theory*.

2   De-defining autobiography

Exile and the writing-thing

The urge to deconstruct autobiography can be difficult to resist. I might want to make the point that the self, with its apparently obvious pre given self-identity, is enabled by iterability, an open-ness to citation that undoes this self-sameness. To make such an argument would by now be rather predictable, and even if the argument was granted, I might be requested to re-define autobiography in some way, my refusal met by exasperation. Instead for the moment I will *de*-define autobiography, and I will do this by de-defining some of the theories that have seemed so hostile to ideas of self and therefore autobiography.

If I am going to explore the situated investigator in postcolonial theory, it is of course necessary to develop a complex sense of the relationship between subjectivity and critical project. It is so commonly assumed that French theory, Continental Philosophy, or whatever we want to call it, is dismissive of the subject, that it can be quite a surprise to find theoretical writings influenced by such thought that place the subject right back in the centre of the theoretical text. Such theoretical writings are motivated by the urge to situate through a kind of thick description far distant from their reputed arid theoreticism. We need a much more nuanced sense of what these writings put forward, even though this will certainly involve some confirmation of the everyday views about the death of the author and the like. Trying to undermine some of the more simplistic ideas about and within post-structuralist writings, this section will examine the relevance of an idea of de-definition for the writing of Edward Said.

Said's criticism is often extremely impatient with theory, even postcolonial theory, displaying frustration and contempt for its neologism and philistine lack of concern for the art which is supposed to be its object. And yet it can be argued that again and again he explores the implications of theory's lessons, for example in his more autobiographical writings. Whatever he might have written about theory, works like *Beginnings*[1] and of course *Orientalism*[2] put theory to work, test its limits, and make it travel. Theory travels through locations, of course being transformed, and therefore has its biographies; perhaps it even 'speaks' me.

Returning to our biography of theory, it is a pronounced feature of much so-called post-structuralist thought that it decentres the subject. This much everyone at least thinks they know. Nonetheless, the exact meaning of this decentring is not as obvious as it seems, and it is certainly not any form of destruction or dismissal of the subject. Nor does this decentring necessarily entail a sense that the subject is in any way *simply* an effect of textuality,[3] or its equivalent, an idea that might lead to its rejection. Many of the writers associated with post-structuralism or postmodernism demand a rethinking of subjectivity, rather than its dismissal. These points must be acknowledged by theories of life writing. Nonetheless, it is reasonable to seek the sources of mis-readings in the misread texts, and of course there is a widespread emphasis on textual subjects by many writers. But it is not obvious what this textual quality really entails. The example of Hélène Cixous will help give a clear sense of what is meant by textuality in this kind of context. Although she has written theoretical texts, they are now often cast as dated, writing to a past moment, perhaps slightly dogmatic: accordingly she focuses on the literary staging and production of otherness. Additionally, Cixous's work performs and, in its theoretical statements, thematises a complication of presumed autobio-graphical self-evidence, and this complication is suggestive in the context of postcolonial criticism's autobiographical turn. In what follows I have quoted lengthy passages from Cixous's theoretical writings, interviews,[4] and fiction, to try to give some sense, even in translation, of the form of her writing.[5]

In Cixous's writing there *were* various clear propositions regarding the nature of language and writing. For example, there are arguments made in support of a kind of constitutive foreignness in language, a foreignness that transports it from its apparently proper or natural location. To write in a strong sense is to hold on to this foreignness: Cixous writes that, 'even if [language] seems to be native or national, it happily remains foreign to those who write. Writing consists first of all in hearing language speak itself to our ears, as if it were for the first time'.[6] In her work there is a certain privileged connection between this foreignness of language and a particular foreign perspective on French and French-ness; for example, Cixous suggests that,

> My inner feeling has always been a feeling of foreignness. I have never felt, never, that I wasn't foreign. And I even felt guilty since I admit-ted I was integrated in society with my French passport and my status as a civil servant. Sometimes I even felt as if was a liar. By and by I was pacified when I realised that in the so-called French 'nation' 75% of the French are not 'pure' French. Those who claim that they are French-French are deceived. Eventually I gave up my feeling of guilt and adopted the nationality *foreign*, which I think is really a very good thing. I recom-mend it to everyone. But then woman, is she foreign or not? I think the feeling of being a woman, *womanbeingness* – let us forge this word womanbeingness – is foreignness. All women are foreign in society and if they don't feel foreign it is because they have abolished their reality,

which they so often do in France. A number of women imagine they are adopted when they marry because suddenly they have a French roof, ie. the roof of their husband's name. It's as if they were crossing the border under the husband. But they lie to themselves: they remain foreign, they remain women.[7]

The question of *womanbeingness* reminds us of some of the critical convergences between postcolonialism and feminism (and others) that I discussed earlier; the question reminds us further of the contexts of globalisation and the international division of labour. Here Cixous refers to two kinds of foreignness: simply, if not a little reductively, they seem to be a literal and a metaphorical foreignness, although the point is exactly that the former is always collapsing into the latter, despite all efforts to guard against this collapse. So, Cixous puts herself forward as not-quite-French-French, a French citizen with a trace of the foreign. This foreignness is something she has initially felt as a guilty secret, and has been something that seemed to compromise her apparently pure official French identity. However, she further suggests that this pure identity is a fiction, and that her position as an Algerian Jewish woman puts her in an exemplary relation to the constitutive foreignness at the heart of every self-proclaimed pure identity. Elsewhere she is more explicit about the various determinations of her identity, determinations that never quite determine anyone's identity. In fact, she finds France itself to be exemplary of this condition. France, she writes, is 'a country which always seemed to me to manifest a porosity [...] a travelled, passed-through, invaded, crossbred country, a country with ports, and not interned or withdrawn. I rejoiced in French passporosity'.[8]

Passporosity, of course, cancels any self-sufficient identity symbolised by a passport per se: that is the point of the traversed and traversing qualities Cixous associates with France. So, having established certain qualities in Cixous's autobiographical presentation, it is also important to stress that she finds ideas and practices of autobiography, as it is classically understood, to be a hindrance to the kind of writing she wants to produce. Cixous finds self-identical proclamation of difference without (self-)difference to be a crime against hospitality. Further to the *passporosity* of France that she mentions in 'My Algeriance', Cixous elaborates carefully on the 'paradox of this passport'. For her to assert Frenchness would be 'a lie or a legal fiction'. But to deny Frenchness would be 'a breach of courtesy. And of the gratitude due for hospitality. The stormy, intermittent hospitality of the State and of the Nation. But the infinite hospitality of the language'.[9] Any claims to permanence of identity, particularly perhaps French identity, violate a kind of open-ness that is found in both the French language and in France's geography, if not consistently in its laws (of course, the distinction between the two kinds of hospitality is clearly important). In a way comparable to Derrida's consideration of Europe's autobiography in *The Other Heading*,[10] here Cixous poses the question of France's autobiography, and the autobiography enabled by the French language. But it is autobiography not quite sure of itself, a France with porous borders, uncertain limits; and this autobiographical conscious-ness (which is not the right word, although places, nations, and even theories have autobiographies, and perhaps then consciousness of a kind) is exem-plarily produced by the experience of the Jews of Algeria, their French-ness a legal and cultural uncertainty.[11]

So, Cixous suggests that, 'in the end a certain writing is engendered that does not settle in, it does not inhabit its house, it escapes, it goes off without turning back ...'.[12] Further, referring to a 'quasi-original detachment', she writes that, 'The possibility of living without root was familiar to me. I never call that exile'.[13] She suggests that, 'in an originary way for me I am always passing by, in *passance*'.[14] Nowhere does Cixous explicitly generalize this position, and it clearly is one of relative privilege – the kind of privilege Albert Memmi ascribes to his position in Tunisia under French colonialism, for example. However, as in her interview with Sophia Phoca, where she explicitly recommends this 'nationality of foreignness' to 'everyone', there is a sense in which this kind of quasi-identity is being elevated. I write *quasi*-identity because of the clear ambivalence Cixous demonstrates towards identity, which in its classical form appears precisely to encompass the kinds of purity she dismisses as fiction – and bad fiction, at that. Cixous seems else-where ambivalent about 'subjectivity' as a term, at least as it has been blurred into a kind of individualism. For example, she writes the following:

> It seems – you have heard this as well as I – that there are fashionable proceedings, especially in the English-speaking world, on the theme of subjectivity. The trend, the code, the 'canon,' are in themselves tools for thought (I do not mean 'modern,' for whatever is 'code' is already outmoded and ready to fall into disuse). Now the fashionable code, these days, holds subjectivity, which is confused (unwittingly or not) with individualism, in suspicion: there is confusion – and this is a pity for everyone – between the infinite domain of the human subject, which is, of course, the primary territory of every artist and every creature blessed with the difficult happiness of being alive, and stupid, egotistic, restric-tive, exclusive behaviour which excludes the other. Whereas subjectivity is the wealth we have in common and, by definition, the subject is a non-closed mix of self/s and others; the human subject who, in the Bible for example, calls himself our like. No I without you ever or more precisely no I's without you's. I is always our like. When I explore I – I take as object of observation a human sample. There is no true art which does not take as its source or root the universal regions of subjectivity.[15]

Cixous's point is implied by the difference between 'qui sont-je?' and 'qui suis-je?'. The first is untranslatable, 'who are I?', as opposed to 'who am I?'. Elsewhere, introducing *Stigmata, or Job the Dog*, she writes that, 'It is an autobiographical narrative, which does not mean very much, because an autobiographical narrative is at the same time a creation'.[16] This basic sentiment conveys the sense in which autobiography is not privileged access to truth, but often obscures the force of that question, 'who are I?'. The story *Stigmata* itself very precisely presents the multitudinous autobiographical practice that for Cixous must engulf classical autobiography. The story additionally presents this theme in a specific context, that of Algeria. It again exemplifies the structures of exemplarity that Cixous's texts thematise and enact, in ways familiar from Derrida's writing.

Stigmata is, then, a kind of *de*-definitional text, rather than a *re*-definitional one, which might imply the permanence and consequent and necessarily unavoidable stagnation of the new definition. Cixous resists producing stable texts, texts that recommend single 'official' interpretations of themselves: her comments about her own theoretical texts (that they are dogmatic, etc.) are perhaps a little mischievous, as those texts are clearly not models of dogmatic clarity as usually understood. And, 'Cixous' as a text 'herself' also strives to confound the definitional moment. Accordingly, if autobiography classically understood tries to offer such a self-definitional moment, Cixous's autobiographical texts produce similar de-definitional effects; in an interview with Sophia Phoca, she makes the following comments on a specific text that appears to be an autobiographical assertion of identity:

> A young student from New York 'wrote to me' making a remarkable analysis of his own circumstances, biographical circumstances, mother, father, etc. Everything that was surrounding him, defining him as a black student. He was *de-defining* himself through relating to what I have written. It was a paper in the form of a letter addressed to me, Hélène Cixous. He spoke to me in the letter although *it was never addressed to me in reality*, which I thought was also a way of displacing the whole scene. It was incredibly imaginative. I received it because somebody was in his class quite accidentally and sent the virtual letter to me. This is really what a writer can wish. To have become a pure writing-being and not to be re-appropriated as a person 'in reality' which is very dangerous and totally deceptive. I'm always extremely wary in this regard. So I'm happy when people treat me as a text, which I think is closer to the truth.[17]

The point she is drawing out is related again to that iterability of the self that I mentioned at the beginning of this chapter, and that I suggested might seem rather predictable. The question that might be asked is to what extent every other self is so happy to be treated as a text. As I mentioned near the beginning of this book, Adriana Cavarero has suggested that the textual self becomes central to the extent that academics take their own situatedness as equivalent to that of others.[18] Accordingly, it should be pointed out immediately that Cixous's very example puts in question her model of becoming or at least being treated as a writing-thing, at least to the extent that her addresser himself conceives his letter as a kind of narrative of orientation.

Of course she is using this example to show a self-defeating self-definition, but that already implies other kinds of definition. There is a quite classical valorisation of breaking free from constraints on one's identity, particularly perhaps political constraints. Indeed, what Cixous is drawing out through this example is the extent to which the assumptions of identity politics are every bit as constraining as the projected assumptions they reject. In the language recommended by David Parker,[19] we might argue that one kind of good is being substituted for another, and that we would do well to be as explicit as possible about the nature of the substitution taking place.

The kind of good structuring this thought relates to the desirability of a kind of exiled self. Cixous seems to desire becoming a kind of word-thing or - machine, to be in *passance*, as she says in 'My Algeriance'. To be more specific, she exults in being in this continual state of non-arrival. This state is one to which we are all subject, in the sense of the *entredeux*, that space of inbetween-ness so powerfully evoked by her writing but also argued through and about, in ways familiar from postcolonial theory, if only the most obvious examples like Homi Bhabha. It is a space between life lived and life yet unlived, a space in fact of a kind of nothingness; in a passage from *Rootprints*[20] discussed below it is described as an unfamiliar 'space-time' into which we are propelled when our domesticity is interrupted, and this description puts it in a before/after scheme. However, this way of describing it is displaced elsewhere, and in another register the *entredeux* is a space of permanent exile, of being exiled even when one is at home.

This state of being between two points in time or space is of course at one with Derrida's sense of the new International and messianicity, outlined in particular in *Specters of Marx*.[21] For Derrida, the messianicity in which he's interested is a waiting for an arrival that will never take place in any future present, something that will never be a full presence, and will therefore never be over and done with. Cixous alludes to such a thought in 'My Algeriance', writing the following:

> To depart (so as) not to arrive from Algeria is also, incalculably, a way of not having broken with Algeria. [...] I want arriv*ance*, movement, unfinishing in my life. It is also out of departing that I write. I like the phrase: *j'arrive* (I'm coming, I manage, I arrive...), its interminable and subtle and triumphant messianicity. The word *messiance* comes to me from Algeria.[22]

No arrival will ever fully take place, and be over and done with, on this view. Cixous writes that from an early age she knew she would leave Algeria: her experience of Algeria has been one of privileged access to the de-definitional moment, from the laws that produced the de-definition of Jews, to the refusing look of the Algerian population. However, as she indicates here, this leaving does not imply an arrival: it does not imply an arrival in France, or of course an arrival in a self-secure identity. The leaving of Algeria is a leaving of such self-security or self-definition – and it is one that requires highly circumspect generalization, *if* it is going to be generalized at all. But still, for Cixous *messiance* has come 'from' Algeria – as for Derrida, as perhaps can be discerned in his *Monolingualism of the other*.[23] I will for now quote Cixous further to give a sense of her *messiance*, which is by definition the de-definitional:

> Human beings are equipped for daily life, with its rites, with its closure, its commodities, its furniture. When an event arrives which evicts us from ourselves, we do not know how to 'live'. But we must. Thus we are launched into a space-time whose coordinates are all different from those we have always been accustomed to. In addition, these violent situations are always new. Always. At no moment can a previous bereavement serve as a model. It is frightfully all new: this is one of the most important experiences of our human histories. At times we are thrown into strangeness. This being abroad at home is what I call an *entredeux*. Wars cause *entredeux* in the histories of countries. But the worst war is the war where the enemy is on the inside; where the enemy is the person I love the most in the world, is myself.[24]

This constitutive foreignness in the heart of the self is the *worst*, Cixous says, and this is not a thought that comes so easily. This foreignness is the worst in the sense that the best entails the worst. It must be said that the *entredeux* is not an experience that we could simply celebrate, just as postcolonial theory has to be cautious that descriptions of inbetween-ness do not become celebratory or even prescriptive. This caution comes from the inherent qualification of each generalization, that is, each translation of a singularity. 'Being abroad at home' is not a general description of many specific cases, which are all equivalent if we simply studied them carefully. That is why Cixous's comment about exile is not generalized, although others have come to a comparable understanding of exile, as my reading of Edward Said will suggest. Yet there is a generalization at work here: it is that the worst war ensues upon discovery that the presumed self-sufficiency one had relied upon is compromised and has always been compromised from within. Cixous, with her interest in the uncanny and Freud in general, of course writes through this sense of compromise. Said, as we will see, explores this sense, in one particular text by reading Freud's *Moses and Monotheism*.[25] It is fitting that thinkers of exile should constantly think through this thought of permanent exile, a thought that travelled and was in its own way exiled.

Roots and routes: the biography of a theory

There are various well-worn themes drawn from Said's work, and that of travelling theory is perhaps more worn than most. However, it is a vital theme when bringing together the idea of exile and the kind of critical writing in which we should be, according to Said, engaged. The idea of travelling theory helps us to formulate Said's self-situation, and to understand the performative power of his writing. This is something on which Timothy Brennan for one insists, writing that,

> If the field is to be the work of being from a place, with recognizably foreign names or an alien look, then Said's identity as a Palestinian is paramount to his performance. The colored subject enters theory, and a new field is born.[26]

In this article, Brennan insists on a 'site-specific Americanness' to *Orientalism*, but he also acknowledges that from its publication that book's reception has made it travel a considerable distance in many directions. *Orientalism*, with its use of Gramsci and Foucault, is an exemplary instance of travelled and travelling theory. As I mentioned, it is well known that Said has a certain investment in travelling theory,[27] however open to misappropriation such a formulation might appear, but let's not assume we know exactly what that means because of the straightforward name. Said identifies four stages in a theory's travel: 1) its origin, 'or what seems like one' (WTC,226); 2) the distance it travels; 3) the conditions of its acceptance; and 4) its transformation in its new context.

Said illustrates his argument with the example of Lukacs' theory of *reification*, followed through Lucien Goldmann, and on into the work of Raymond Williams. From Hungary to Cambridge, the theory of reification becomes more academic, but also becomes more stretched, and so its inherent limitations are exposed. Theories have origins, routes, and destinations, and none of these are ever final. Certainly Said consistently wants to interrogate the position from which the intellectual speaks; he writes that a critical consciousness is, 'a sort of spatial sense, a sort of measuring faculty for locating or situating theory'(WTC,241). Said insists on situating both his own theories and theory more generally. Every theory has an itinerary, even if we would normally say that of a theorist. The sense of movement and temporary location is a key fact for Said, particularly for example in his distinction between filiation and affiliation, the latter being a question of travel compared with the former's rootedness. Theories themselves, we might argue, become exiled when they are appropriated and transformed in the work of later critics, or re-contextualized in radically dissimilar theoretical contexts.[28] And of course Said puts significant emphasis on the category of exile, but an emphasis that we need to be careful not to misunderstand.

A particularly important example of the intellectual exile, for Said, is Erich Auerbach, with Said focusing on the context of his *Mimesis*,[29] around which Said elaborates his notion of a *secular* criticism.[30] Against the backdrop of Julien Benda's accusation of the *trahison des clercs*, Said reacts to the increasing professionalisation of literary criticism with an injunction to be between, and proximate to, culture and totalizing systems of thought. As is often the case in Said's writing, he provides us with an example of this position, rather than ever quite giving a definition of it. The example is Auerbach, particularly this passage from the 'Epilogue' to *Mimesis*, his study of representation from biblical narrative to *To the Lighthouse*:

> I may also mention that the book was written during the war and at Istanbul, where the libraries are not well equipped for European studies. International communications were impeded; I had to dispense with almost all periodicals, with almost all the more recent investigations, and in some cases with reliable critical editions of my texts. Hence it is possible and even probable that I overlooked things which I ought to have considered and that I occasionally assert something which modern research has disproved or modified. I trust that these probable errors include none which affect the core of my argument. The lack of technical literature and periodicals may also serve to explain that my book has no notes. Aside from the texts, I quote comparatively little, and that little it was easy to include in the body of the book. On the other hand it is quite possible that the book owes its existence to just this lack of a rich and specialized library. If it had been possible for me to acquaint myself with all the work that has been done on so many subjects, I might never have reached the point of writing.[31]

Auerbach, as Said notes, only briefly gestures toward the reasons behind his time in Istanbul, instead focusing on the strangely enabling difficulties of the book's composition. Yet this deflection of interest towards apparently less historically important matters is not merely reversed by Said. Auerbach, for Said, becomes exemplary of a kind of enabling isolation or ultimately exile. But this exile is significant not only for Auerbach's displacement or alienation from Western culture (the culture that is his object of study) but also for that very displacement from the techniques saturating the discourse of comparative literary studies (the theory of that study). So, for Said, *Mimesis* is a disarming gesture of 'cultural survival', and the identification of its place (Istanbul) is highly symbolic, immediately calling to mind an entire set of Orientalist attitudes, particularly for someone in Auerbach's field of research. Exile is, then, converted from risk to a positive condition. In fact, perhaps we might say that the two coexist, or rather that the possibility of one is the possibility of the other. *Perfectus vero cui mundus totus exilium*, as Hugo of St. Victor expresses it in his *Didascalion*.[32] *Mimesis* affirms Occidental culture by way of its alienation from that culture. But Said implies, and this argument will be given its fullest expression in *Orientalism*, that such alienation cannot only be alienation from place. The supposed 'technical difficulties' experienced by Auerbach (lack of all the usual apparatus of scholarly research) actually allow him to produce a work that is not merely a confirmation of its culture. Auerbach becomes exemplary of a certain privilege given to exile, accidentally fulfilling the ideal role of the intellectual.

Removed from a context that takes in research practices and rules, pedagogical techniques, hegemonic incorporation (or indeed ideological performance in service of the State, whatever the revolutionary content), the exiled intellectual is able to break the patterns of filiatory repetition, and to construct new patterns of affiliation. Said identifies such a shift as characteristic of Modernism generally, but argues that the shift toward affiliation is only a shift toward a restored order, in which familial bonds are replaced by cultural bonds. So, if the university has been insistent on filiatory bonds, the genetic repetition of all that is great about the Western tradition through pedagogical techniques predicated on clear and consistent demarcation of role, subject, and method, it is not enough merely to reverse the value bestowed upon different kinds of bond. But again, one cannot renounce bonds completely. The critic (who is the ideal intellectual) has two possibilities: either to reside in 'organic complicity', in a filiatory and exclusive cultural model, or to distinguish each time between filiation and affiliation. In fact, in the latter case the critic must place him- or herself in that in-between place, between culture and totalising system. As already recalled, the name that Said gives to the criticism that hopefully will emerge from this in-between place is secular criticism. Being in such an in-between location is really of course to be constantly becoming 'other', and that goes for the theory as much as the theorist or critic. Said's specific example in the essay 'Travelling Theory' certainly can be understood as questioning the fixing of this becoming: he is, of course, discussing Georg Lukács' theory of reification. Reification is the freezing of flow under capitalism, and the transformation of time into space: in other words, a movement of quantification of things. In Said's terms, regarding subjectivity, there is, 'the increasing retreat of the subject into passive, privatized contemplation' (WTC,231) in 'modern bourgeois thought': the atomization of facts tends toward the fragmentation of system. In Said's presentation of Lukács, theorization constitutes the coming to class consciousness, and the re-introduction of the temporal; this concentration of transformations sees an at least projected reconciliation of subject and object, and the production of a critical consciousness where there had been a passive consciousness. So, in Said's understanding the movement of theoretical totalization produces a de-quantification of thought, to the extent that simple equivalence of facts is denied, even if measurement still continues.

In Said's presentation, there is a large measure of coincidence between Lukács' understanding of the modern bourgeois subject and the later reflections of Barthes and Foucault, at least to the extent that there appears to be a certain necessary critical transformation. However, of course, Foucault's objection to Marxism focuses precisely on the kind of totalizing gesture that constructs proletarian consciousness, and to that extent Marxism must appear to Foucault the substitution of one system of equivalence for another.

In fact, Said agrees with Foucault on this point. Writing against a generalized fixation on necessary misreading, Said insists that we must measure different misreadings, and to that extent the apparently appropriatory (and progressively less politicized) gestures made by Goldmann and Williams test the limits and inherent dangers of Lukács' notion of totality. Goldmann's work, for Said, constitutes the scholarly application of Lukács, pushing the formal correspondences of totality into a more brutally formal reading of textual constellations as expressions (however indirect and ingeniously derived) of base. Goldmann's apparently less activist work produces the reduction that is in some sense inherent in Lukács. Said follows this reading to an apparently paradoxical conclusion in his assertion that Williams, who assimilates the insurrectionary force of Lukács via Goldmann to the revitalization of moribund English studies at Cambridge University, follows the vicissitudes of the idea of totality more fully than either Goldmann or Lukács himself. Williams is the most attentive, in Lukács' notion of totality of reduction, to the necessary possibility of codification, and repetition. In Said's itinerary of the idea of totality from Lukács to Williams, the sense of place (even the apparently 'bad' place) is what grants the possibility of distance, reflection and transformation. Just as in the example of Auerbach in Istanbul, there is a privilege granted to a metaphorical thought of exile.

The further consequence of Said's concerns about bad totalities (substituting one kind of absolute measurement for another, forcing heterogeneous elements into unfortunately repetitive systems) is the identification of a certain convergence between the over-totalization of Lukács and the apparently claustrophobic notion of power elaborated in later Foucault.[33] For Said (and this point it evident throughout *The World, the Text, and the Critic*, where he frequently argues that Foucault obliterates agency) Foucault has twin epistemological deficiencies: first, he has an inadequate notion of subjectivity; and secondly, in Foucault there is an apparent of immovability of power.[34] When I say that for Said these constitute *epistemological* deficiencies, I do not mean to elide Said's concern with adequacy to anti-colonial resistance, but I do want to shift emphasis onto Said's self-positioning. As he argues in 'Roads Taken and Not Taken in Contemporary Criticism':

> A genetic hypothesis admits the notion of human agency into the work—not a daring idea in itself. But the obligation to rational interpretation along these lines goes further to include as part of the dialectic the critic's own shaping awareness of what he or she is doing. (WTC,156–7)

This reference to the dialectic is perhaps not as informal as it appears, especially in the context of Foucault's engagement with modes of dialectical thinking, and Said's attempts to think about the writing of Derrida *with* Foucault. I will return to this point about Foucault and Said in the context of Said's essay 'Criticism Between Culture and System'. Despite praising the self-situating elements in Derrida's 'Structure, Sign and Play', Said ignores that essay's concluding warnings about a choice between the two interpretations of interpretation. Rather Said seems to settle for a denuded sense of this insufficiency of choice, in which we need to hold on to aspects of both ideas of interpretation. So, he argues in 'Roads Taken and Not Taken in Contemporary Criticism' for a kind of non-confirmational dialectical thought, making reference, after Poulet, to an 'I that is not mine'. He suggests that, 'The critical identity is the presentational device for certain, formally determined matters in language' (WTC,148). A little later he suggests that, 'Pedagogically, there is every good reason for regarding the choice of a subject and its formulation as being not only the beginning of a critical project but also the critical project itself' (WTC,153). The argument about the dangers of over-totalization needs to be understood in terms of exile again, this time through the necessary flaw inherent in every identity. This brings together the critic's role and the general structures of identity, to be sure, but also situates these things in the context of Said's political concerns, specifically of course the question of Palestine.

The consistency of identity: Freud

It has been said (he said it himself, more or less seriously) that Edward Said was the last Jewish intellectual, and this suggestion is more than cavalier or even insulting misunderstanding. When Said makes his own brief return to Freud in *Freud and the Non-European*, he finds more than an argument, but also the demonstration of a certain intellectual position of exile. To be sure, there is an argument that Said draws from Freud's *Moses and Monotheism*, in which the prophet is of course speculated to have been Egyptian. In that argument, Said reads Freud demonstrating the inherent limits of Jewish identity, in that this identity cannot be a *single* identity at all. Said writes that, 'identity cannot be thought or worked through itself alone; it cannot constitute or even imagine itself without that radical originary break or flaw which will not be repressed'.[35] This limit, which is of course the limit of any identity according to Freud and many that have followed, is symbolized by the figure of Moses. The radical break, symbolized by the imagined murder of Moses and his elevation to prophet-hood, enables the identity. Said continues to write the following:

> This is a necessary psychological experience, Freud says, but the problem is that he doesn't give any indication of how long it must be tolerated or whether, properly speaking, it has a real history – history being always that which comes after and, all too often, either overrides or represses the flaw.[36]

According to Said, of course, Zionism has repressed the necessary flaw in its consistent and absolute self-imagination. Indeed, explicitly following Said,

Jacqueline Rose extends this analysis even further, writing that,

> Zionism is more than one thing. But in the ascendant today is a vision of the Jewish nation that is, I believe – precisely because it has, as it so fervently desired, made itself master of its own destiny – in danger of destroying itself.[37]

According to Rose, then, the thing that Zionism seemed to want most is what endangers its very existence, in that a tolerance for strangeness and the foreign is wiped from its mental map.

As already indicated, using Freud to think about identity in this way is, of course, not confined to thinking about Zionism. We can explore this through the work of Kristeva, who reads Freud in order to think about immigration in Europe in her *Strangers to Ourselves*, in which she writes that,

> In the fascinated rejection that the foreigner arouses in us, there is a share of uncanny strangeness in the sense of the depersonalization that Freud discovered in it, and which takes up again our infantile desires and fears of the other – the other of death, the other of woman, the other of uncontrollable drive.[38]

The foreigner has an uncanny effect upon us because he or she brings out the ghostly mark of our infantile identity formation, something that we might think had better have remained hidden, but which we had in fact better recognize in the political contexts that Kristeva, like Rose, is discussing. There is something else that is significant in the way Kristeva talks about this uncanniness: the way she theorizes the urge to order and limit is strikingly similar to her analysis of the urge to theorize, given very clear expression in *Powers of Horror*.[39] There Kristeva reads anthropologist Mary Douglas's *Purity and Danger*. Douglas's main argument, operating in a classical ethnographical mode in its construction of self-consolidating otherness, is that rites of purity and impurity offer structure and coherence to experience:

> In chasing dirt, in papering, decorating, tidying we are not governed by anxiety to escape disease, but are positively re-ordering our environment, making it conform to an idea. There is nothing fearful or unreasoning in our dirt-avoidance: it is a creative movement, an attempt to relate form to function, to make unity of experience. If this is so with our separating, tidying and purifying, we should interpret primitive purification and prophylaxis in the same light.[40]

Douglas relates this apparent structuring of experience to the social construction of and adherence to 'danger-beliefs' that threaten the social transgressor or outsider, thereby producing a coherence of society. Douglas summarizes this in the following way: 'These danger-beliefs are as much threats which one man uses to coerce another as dangers which he himself fears to incur by his own lapses from righteousness. They are a strong language of mutual exhortation'. Later Douglas notes that, 'It is only by exaggerating the difference between within and without, above and below, male and female, with and against, that a semblance of order is created.' Although Douglas has returned to the nominal objects of her study, specific societies from various contexts, she has just been admitting her own methodological expediency: 'I admit to having made society sound more systematic than it really is. But just such an expressive over-systematising is necessary for interpreting the beliefs in question'.[41] So, there is a certain analogy between the purification that societies perform in constructing their coherence, and the systematisation that characterizes the objectification of societies, in other words the production of a society as knowledge.[42] In Kristeva's reading of *Purity and Danger*, she develops her initial general remarks on the improper/the unclean, drawing out the sense in Douglas that the improper is in some sense a necessary possibility of the proper: 'It is [...] not lack of cleanliness or health that causes abjection but what disturbs identity, system, order. What does not respect borders, positions, rules. The in-between, the ambiguous, the composite'.[43] What will not fully belong is apparently necessary to full belonging, not least because otherwise the notion of belonging could be given no meaning, but also because non-belonging and impropriety haunt the proper. In Kristeva's reading of Douglas, such a characterization of the symbolic order both transcends specific expression and is each time rooted in a time and place, being therefore open to endless transformations:

> [W]hen I speak of *symbolic order*, I shall imply the dependence and articulation of the speaking subject in the order of language, such as they appear diachronically in the advent of each speaking being, and as analytic listening discovers them synchronically in the speech of analysands. I shall consider as an established fact the analytic finding that different subjective structures are possible within that symbolic order, even if the different types presently recorded seem subject to discussion and refinement, if not reevaluation.[44]

Kristeva's reading wants, then, to hold onto both a universal system (the symbolic order itself, and Douglas's necessary systematization) and messy contingency (instances of the symbolic order, and what falls outside the objectification of a society). It is not that Douglas' analysis, and her putting to work of the theoreticism she is describing, are things that we could realistically abjure, and so get to the reality of other cultures, specific instances, or even the unique particular. For a theory to be a theory at all, it needs to be something like the universal system that we assume in our everyday talk about theory. And yet the level of contingency coexists and cannot be denied by that theoretical drive. This is all the more true for the exiled theorist, or better the travelled and travelling theory, forced to recognize and be recognized as in process and therefore incomplete, however universal they seem. The identity of a theory might seem clear, so that we ask about what it proposes, what it hopes to explain, the context of its elaboration, and its authors. But a theory has no more (and no less) identity than a culture, for example, and we cannot hold on to the sense of a self-present theory any more than to that of a self-present culture, even as the urge to hold on to these things is irreducible.

Against such a vision (for *any* identity, although picking on Zionism is of course necessarily and endlessly controversial) of regular and consistent identity, Said of course elaborates a notion of privileged exile, as we have already recalled with the example of Auerbach, and already introduced through Cixous' own sense of the exile that is writing in general. This sense of exile is both something that has everyday reality and something that is to do with writing, what writing is and does. The first (everyday, literal reality) is rather controversial in Said's case, given his class position and the difficulties we encounter in identifying him with the Palestinian community in general. However, it should be said that these are difficulties that he hardly discounts in his own writing, and often rather foregrounds, so they're not something that can somehow be used against him in order to discredit his writing. The second (metaphorical, written reality) is something that Said explores in a sustained manner through many of his shorter critical works, and is something given a further twist in his identification of a general 'late style'.[45] In fact, he did not consistently link the thought of exile with political or critical privilege, something suggested by its association with music, so clearly the model for the work on late style. In, for example, *Musical Elaborations*,[46] Said seems to imagine a rather separate world for music. In contrast to Adorno, cited throughout the work, Said remains ambivalent about music's sociality.[47] This contrast with Adorno (and Said invites the comparison himself) is obvious and instructive; as Rose Rosengard Subotnik suggests, 'whereas Adorno describes a balance between art and popular musical traditions, Said conjures up the possibility of music that breaks free of all ties to the social world'.[48] But as Subotnik herself implies, this conjuration is brief and unfulfilled, and the exilic status associated with music is never quite the exorbitant phenomenon it appears, and its privilege is uncertain or at best temporary, as we will see.

In the celebrated essay 'Reflections on Exile', Said makes a case for some kind of privilege in the experience, although it must be said that he explicitly denies that he sees it as a privilege, instead seeing it as a form of alternative to mass politics: 'I speak of exile not as a privilege, but as an *alternative* to the mass institutions that dominate modern life.'[49] There is a literature of exile, and its resources (Said's own memoir included) can offer vital ways of thinking about identity beyond those of the collective, particularly the nation: 'The exile knows that in a secular and contingent world, homes are always provisional.'[50] The consolations of the mass politics of nationalism are unavailable to the honest exile, it seems, and this brings a measure of clear-eyed apprehension that ought to be valued. The solitude of the exile, so distinct from the group-feeling that disfigures contemporary cultures, is both deprivation and privilege, from this perspective. The privilege is an unavoidable awareness of suspension between locations. Said writes that, in a language familiar from elsewhere in his work, 'Most people are principally aware of one culture, one setting, one home; exiles are aware of at least two, and this plurality of vision gives rise to an awareness of simultaneous dimensions, an awareness that – to borrow a phrase from music – is *contrapuntal*.'[51] The deprivation, meanwhile, derives from the sense of need to transcend the solitude of such a suspension, a solitude because each case of suspension is its own example. The question Said asks most insistently is the following:

> Nationalisms are about groups, but in a very acute sense exile is a solitude experienced outside the group: the deprivations felt at not being with others in the communal habitation. How, then, does one surmount the loneliness of exile without falling into the encompassing and thumping language of national pride, collective sentiments, group passions?[52]

This surmounting may be a difficult task, but from Said's perspective the balance that might result can best be achieved by the exiled.

From other perspectives, such an argument is open to the charge that it is an absurd generalization from privileged personal experience. Even when that personal experience is made the explicit topic of discussion, it seems that Said is willing to make the jump between that experience and some more generally desirable structure of intellectual conduct. Not every commentator has been sympathetic to this jump, of course. In the midst of generous discussion, Alon Confino makes the questioning point in the context of Said's memoir *Out of Place* when he writes that, 'The link Said makes between his personality and the definition of the intellectual may be viewed by some critics as self-serving: all intellectuals are exiles, but some are more intellectual and some more exilic than others.'[53] Many critics are less generous than Confino, as they have been about postcolonial theory more generally. Indeed, many of the more central postcolonial theorists have come under attack for apparently dismissive attitudes to nationalism, most obviously Homi Bhabha. This brings us back to the claims I recalled in my introduction, principally that postcolonial theory is the house style of an upwardly-mobile diasporic academic community, and is therefore far removed from the realities of the colonialism it purports to discuss. Said has often been criticised in class-based terms, and his privileging of exile looks like an easy opportunity for those who wish to dismiss his work. However, he is extremely clear about the need to set aside the experiences of exile that come to mind so easily in a literary context:

> [T]o concentrate on exile as a contemporary political punishment, you must [...] map territories of experience beyond those mapped by the literature of exile itself. You must first set aside Joyce and Nakokov and think instead of the uncountable masses for whom UN agencies have been created.[54]

Indeed, Said goes on to assert that the only way really to think about the realities of contemporary exile is to depart from the privileged reflections of the literary writer:

> To reflect on exiled Muslims from India, or Haitians in America, or Bikinians in Oceania, or Palestinians throughout the Arab world means that you must leave the modest refuge provided by subjectivity and resort instead to the abstractions of mass politics.[55]

Nonetheless, there are moments in which it seems that this principled rejection of *easy* continuity and generalization masks a disdain for the abstractions demanded by engagement with mass politics. Said asks the question, '[I]s exile so extreme and private that any instrumental use of it is ultimately a trivialization?'[56] The danger might be suddenly to accord exile a non-relational singularity that would, obviously enough, sequester its resources from a world in need of insights derived from privacy and extremity.

The apparent hesitation between an acknowledgement of exile's uses and an insistence on its private irreducibility can be understood as a case of a *both/and* logic, one which we might more usually associate with someone like Derrida. Yet such a logic is expressed time and again in Said's writing. He insists, for example, that postcolonial writing (principally criticism, in this context) requires some sense of a personal stake that makes it impossible to deny the ongoing presence of the colonial history, its virtual existence in our present moment. As this book argues, postcolonial criticism is not the application of theories that work in the same way for any user at any time. Instead, there is an excess over that repeatability of method, an autobiographical element which, while it must avoid leading to the subjective distortion of the facts, must also recognize the way in which we cannot but be implicated in the object of our study:

> The best post-colonial writing [...] doesn't depend on an easy, repeatable methodology but on a perspective derived from experience, a personal stake. To write well about colonialism you don't have to have had a colonial or imperialist background, but as with any history of a complex experience that involved many actors, the worst thing – even in the name of critical impartiality – is to empty that history of its existential residue in the present: a dangerous temptation in writing about the legacy of empire, which sits like a menacing and metastasising cancer just beneath the skin of our contemporary lives.[57]

We might understand this as a need for autobiographical criticism, for the personal stake made explicit, and for the rejection of dubious objectivity. At the same time, Said is quite clear that the other danger is always there, that of reducing everything to identity. The rejection of spurious objectivity might collapse into the proclamation of an equally spurious self-present identity, according to which the critical perspective has consistency and leverage that cannot be gainsaid by another identity's perspective. If we are to have an autobiographical criticism, it cannot be one that simply delineates a critical standpoint and proceeds to rule out other perspectives purely on the basis of class, race, or other grounds. Such a criticism would accord all too well with present (and widely criticised, of course) trends in culturalist identity politics, tending to reduce everything to clearly defined and stable identities interacting in s somewhat stagnant space of mutual antagonism. Said writes the following:

> Identity as such is about as boring a subject as one can imagine. Nothing seems less interesting than the narcissistic self-study that today passes in many places for identity politics, or ethnic studies, or affirmations of roots, cultural pride, drum-beating nationalism, and so on.[58]

Here again identity is associated with nationalism, and criticised for its self-obsession. The best criticism may require a verve born from personal experience, or at least a sense of personal stake, but the very worst seems to derive from a drive to delineate and defend the personal as a reified form of identity. This kind of identity is, says Said, simply boring.

Boring it may be, in Said's opinion, but his self-definition and the personal stake involved came in for notorious scrutiny several years before his death when Justus Reid Weiner published '"My Beautiful old House" and Other Fabrications by Edward Said' in *Commentary* magazine.[59] In brief Weiner argues that Said defines himself as 'an archetypal exile', and that this self-definition depends upon 'a tissue of falsehoods'. Weiner's conclusion is the following: 'the plain, direct and honest truth is radically at odds with the parable he has been at pains to construct over the decades. That parable, designed to augment the passions that have animated the revanchist program of so many Palestinian nationalists, is a lie'. It would seem by now that Weiner's attack has been discounted as rather transparently and disreputably motivated.[60] Christopher Hitchens, for example, dutifully rebuts Weiner's central points, and points to the exhaustively honest account of the disputed facts that appears in Said's *Out of Place*; Hitchens summarizes Weiner's reaction to that book:

> [Weiner] contends that an exhaustive book commissioned in 1989, begun in 1994 (after Edward had learned that leukemia had set a term to his life) and completed in 1998, was undertaken to rebut a half-baked article in *Commentary* that had not yet been written.[61]

As a media attack, Weiner's articles were potentially extremely damaging, but as scholarship they were never likely to hold up for long. Nevertheless, Weiner's approach raises questions about tensions between conceptions of identity in Said's work, principally because the absolutised identity presupposed as authority in Weiner's work *simultaneously* cuts precisely against Said's general claims about identity, *and* bears striking comparison with certain features of Said's recent work, that are by no means confined to Said's work.

Weiner's investigation of Said operates with an apparently rigorous definition of what constitutes Palestinian identity, but such a definition can only appear ironic given Israel's Law of Return. As is well known, the founders of Israel proclaimed 'the renewal of the Jewish State in the Land of Israel, which would open wide the gates of the homeland to every Jew'. This open-ness is guaranteed by the Law of Return (1950), giving every Jew, wherever he or she may be, the right to enter Israel as an *oleh* and become an Israeli citizen. Under this Law, 'Jew' refers to individuals born of a Jewish mother or who have converted to Judaism. Since 1970 this right of immigration has been extended to the child and the grandchild of a Jew, the spouse of a Jew, the spouse of a child of a Jew and the spouse of a grandchild of a Jew. These extensions aim to ensure the unity of families where intermarriage has occurred. Criteria that might justify exclusion have been specified as 1) engagement in activity directed against the Jewish people; 2) potentially endangering public health or the security of the state; and 3) having a criminal past, or being likely to endanger public welfare.

There is a flexibility to the rigour of identity defined here, but nonetheless it provides a powerful regulatory model for judgment of identity claims in other circumstances, hence Weiner's unquestioning assertion of such a model to judge Said's claims, which do indeed appear to challenge not the model itself but merely its application. Of course, in one way this is more than a simple challenge, but is an extremely important assertion of legal principle, and the demand that law be applied without prejudice. Even in 2000, Said was specifically invoking the Law of Return, in an interview published in *Ha'aretz*. Ari Shavit asks about Said's personal right of return, and that 'beautiful old house', to which Said's cousin has a deed, focuses the answer:

> [T]his is a very specific thing. If you ask me in the abstract, I would say that I have a right to return just as my Jewish colleague has a right under the Israeli Law of Return. But if you ask me specifically, I would affiliate with my cousin, whose father's name is on the deed, and would like to get some recognition that it was taken from him.[62]

Answering in both abstract and specific terms, Said effectively concedes that his class positioning and personal history take him outside the bounds of the regulatory model of absolute identity. But his personal history also ties him into familial identities that are within that identity. These two ways of seeing his identity are held together here in the way that the abstract and the specific answers coincide. Beyond this point, it is interesting that Said's writing practices also attempt to hold these two levels together. In works like

After the Last Sky and *Out of Place* he gives us complex models of the apparently impossible mediation between these levels.

Beyond the discursive threshold: Said the autobiographer

When asked by Jacqueline Rose about writing his autobiography, Said responded by saying that, 'It's not really an autobiography. I've resisted the use of that word. I call it a memoir, because, first of all because I'm not really a public figure [...]. But I felt that I had something to understand about a peculiar past.'[63] This is the kind of suggestion that we might think is rather unrealistic, given the fact of Said's status as one of the last public intellectuals, taking him far beyond the discursive threshold mentioned by Gillian Whitlock. But we can perhaps see what he is getting at, and put aside the inherent interest of the autobiographical writings of such an individual, trying to see what kinds of effects Said's texts produce. In short, Said's non-theoretical writings demonstrate the kinds of complex oscillation between singular and specific that this chapter has considered. *After the Last Sky* and *Out of Place* are examples of a kind of invention[64] of personal and communal beginnings – and it is an invention that, under limitations of various kinds, is undergoing constant denial and is therefore constantly re-starting, repeating itself with variation. At one point in *After the Last Sky*, Said's collaboration with the Swiss-German photographer Jean Mohr, he mournfully diagnoses an attitude toward the present that implies something rather less than being fully present in that moment, but is nonetheless not an object of pity:

> The dynastic sense, the feeling for one's immediate past, the effort of placing ourselves in a living continuum: there is little help to be gotten for such things. The closeness and clutter of the present force us to attend to the details of everyday life. Whenever I look at what goes on in the interior I am always surprised at how things seem to be managed normally, as if I had been expecting signs of how different 'they,' the people of the interior, are, and then find that they still do familiar things. We Palestinians conduct ourselves, I think, with an energetic consciousness that there are still chores to be done, children to be raised, houses to be lived in, despite our anomalous circumstances.[65]

Much of the text implies almost a privilege to the perspective of the Palestinian people, even if it is a privilege born of often extraordinarily harsh situations. It is a fragmented perspective, but one that is transformed in Said's memoir, *Out of Place*, into the motor of his intellectual work, and a genuine inspiration behind his drive for a secular criticism. Yet of course this perspective ultimately aims at self-dissolution, and this is true in terms both of the Palestinian people and Said personally. So, we can see a constantly mutating and re-inventing impulse that does not delude itself with dreams of return and redemption, but an impulse that not so secretly posits a dream of a kind of wholeness. This wholeness is desired in the context of the impermanence that any photograph betokens, given that the photograph structurally does not require for its existence and meaningfulness the thing of which it is a photograph.

Of course it is hardly surprising that Said explores these ideas in this text in particular, and it is instructive to compare *After the Last Sky* with Barthes' *Camera Lucida*, an explicit influence on Said's text. In that book Barthes writes that,

> It is because each photograph always contains this imperious sign of my future death that each one, however attached it seems to be to the excited world of the living, challenges each of us, one by one, outside of any generality (but not outside of any transcendence).[66]

We can follow the implications of this thought by looking at Derrida's reading of Barthes. Following Barthes, Derrida defines the *punctum* (opposed to the *studium*, although this is not quite opposition as usually understood) as 'a point of singularity that punctures the surface of the reproduction – and even the production – of analogies, likenesses, and codes'. There is an originary complication of translation familiar from Derrida's work, yet of course some kind of translation occurs. Derrida continues:

> It pierces, strikes me, wounds me, bruises me, and, first of all, seems to concern only me. Its very definition is that it addresses itself to me. The absolute singularity of the other addresses itself to me, the Referent that, in its very image, I can no longer suspend, even though its 'presence' forever escapes me, having already receded into the past. (That is why the word 'Referent' could be a problem if it were not reformed by the context.) This solitude, which rends the fabric of the same, the networks or ruses of economy, addresses itself to me.[67]

Thematically, Derrida's comments on Barthes seem relevant here, despite their apparent distance from postcolonialism.[68] Indeed, Derrida remarks throughout on how Barthes gives the reader a running commentary on his writing process, and how theories come and go in his writing, puncturing the steady certainties or even orthodoxies at various opportune moments. Yet it would seem that the theory of the *punctum*, which of course resists any description of itself as a theory, is not congenial to any talk of politics: this, after all, is a matter that eludes 'the networks or ruses of economy', comes only to me, and is seemingly strictly untranslatable.[69] However, the reference to economy refers us to Derrida's essay on Bataille titled 'From Restricted to General Economy',[70] in which he examines the apparent opening of restricted onto general economy, always yet gathered in, rhythmically, to that same restricted system.

In the piece on Barthes, Derrida writes:

> Ghosts: the concept of the other in the same, the *punctum* in the *studium*, the completely other, dead, living in me. This concept of the photograph *photographs* every conceptual opposition; it captures a relationship of haunting that is perhaps constitutive of every 'logic'.[71]

This given concept at this given time is made exemplary of concepts generally. Discussing postcolonial translation, it is possible to argue that within given limits this translation is also a question of reproduction or iteration of theories. Derrida continues:

> [I]t is the modern possibility of photography [...] that combines death and the referent in the same system. It was not for the first time, and this conjugation of death and the referent did not have to wait for the Photograph to have an essential relationship to reproductive technique, or to technique in general, but the immediate proof given by the photographic apparatus or by the structure of the *remains* it leaves behind are irreducible events, ineffaceably original. It is the failure, or at any rate the limit, of all that which, in language, literature, and the other arts seemed to permit grandiose theories on the general suspension of the Referent, or of what was classified, by a sometimes gross simplification, under that vast and vague category. By the time – at the instant – that the *punctum* rends space, the reference and death are in it together in the photograph. But should we say reference or referent? Analytical precision must here be equal to the stakes, and the photograph puts this precision to the test: in the photograph, the referent is noticeably absent, suspendable, vanished into the unique past time of its event, but the reference to this referent, call it the intentional movement of reference [...] implies just as irreducibly the having-been of a unique and invariable referent.[72]

The structure in question is not uniquely produced by photography, although photography is for various reasons at this moment (that of Barthes' text, and also Derrida's, and perhaps even mine) the best example of what is at stake. If what Derrida identifies in Barthes is attributable to concepts generally, then what is argued here about reference is important for the question of conceptual movement in general. Generality would be the kind of totality we ought to resist, transcendence the kind we cannot ignore because it is a necessary desire, a kind of structural wholeness that cannot ever be fully present, and thereby forgotten. This wholeness might be called a desirable totality, although we should resist simplistically reading off Said's theory from his autobiography, or vice versa.

At least, we should perhaps follow such a reading to the same extent as Said himself. First, we need to consider *After the Last Sky* in more detail. It is a text that attempts to be adequate to the photographs it accompanies, and the lives they record and produce. Early in the text Said gives the following justification for its forms:

> Since the main features of our present existence are dispossession, dispersion, and yet also a kind of power incommensurate with our stateless exile, I believe that essentially unconventional, hybrid, and fragmentary forms of expression should be used to represent us. What I have quite consciously designed, then, is an alternative mode of expression to the one usually encountered in the media, in works of social science, in popular fiction. It is a personal rendering of the Palestinians as a dispersed national community – acting, acted upon, proud, tender, miserable, funny, indomitable, ironic, paranoid, defensive, assertive, attractive, compelling. (ALS,6)

This fragmentary mode of expression matches not only the fragmentary experience of the Palestinians, but is a suitable mode for capturing what is a personal vision rather than an attempt to give an encyclopaedic history,[73] particularly so, despite what Aijaz Ahmad claims in an admittedly different context, because Said is quite aware of the specificity of his perspective.[74] One example of this fragmentary invention is given later on the same page, when Said details his use of pronominal shifts to convey the Palestinian sense of foreignness within: this text is one which actually aims at confusing the 'we' with the 'I', and even with the 'you'.[75] So, although it is not an objective book, as Said points out, it strives to be adequate to its object, which is also of course in a way its subject. Said conveys the exemplariness of the Palestinian perspective as gift-as-poison, simultaneously disabling and enabling:

> To be on the inside, in this sense, is to speak from, be in, a situation which, paradoxically, you do not control and cannot really be sure of even when you have evolved special languages – sometimes evasive, always idiosyncratic – that only you and others like you can understand. The structure of your situation is such that being inside is a privilege that is an affliction, like feeling hemmed in by the house you own. Yes, an open door is necessary for passing between inside and outside, but it is also an avenue used by others to enter. Even though we are inside our world, there is no preventing others from getting in, overhearing us, decoding our private messages, violating our privacy. (ALS,52–3)

So, the privilege of this fragmentary perspective is also an affliction. Or we might say the best the chance of the worst. The historical implications of this general structure in this specific context are constantly made clear by the full force of Said's text, for the Palestinians do not exist as fragmented in a featureless realm or even void, but are constantly next to the Israelis in various senses. So, Said juxtaposes the fragmented nature of the Palestinian culture, history, and ultimately social organisation with the order of Israeli culture, history, and social organisation.[76] Although on an intellectual and perhaps even a spiritual level, the total nature of Israeli organisation and self-identity may appear problematic to the secular intellectual, Said is constantly lamenting what he sees as the inadequacy of a fragmented Palestinian response to comprehensive military and political systems: 'The contrast between their urge to record and systematize and our passive, scattered incoherence comes up again and again in our history' (ALS,96). From this perspective, it is not only the practical success of the Israeli state that excites envy and dismay, but also its apparently self-contained consistency. Of course, as we have already seen, Said reads Freud's *Moses and Monotheism* to demonstrate an originary flaw in this consistent identity, so that it is not quite as consistent as it seems. But then, as Jacqueline Rose points out, it has continued to seem consistent, however damaging such consistency might be. And, according to Said, this consistency is something that the Palestinians *cannot not want*.

This paradox often becomes central in Said's work, because even the binational state solution he more or less consistently advocated entails a de-definitional movement on the part of Israel, and some proper definitional work on the part of Palestinians.[77] Such a paradox surely relates to the following clear if overly simple criticism of Said (and also Foucault): that the comprehensive aspect of discursive regularity seems to leave little room for challenge, qualification, or transformation. Indeed, Said implies this context when he writes of the Palestinians as almost *discursive effects* of Israel:

> What I have been saying is that we ourselves provide not enough of a presence to force the untidiness of life into a coherent pattern of our own making. At best, to judge simply from my own case, we can read ourselves against another people's pattern, but since it is not ours – even though we are its designated enemy – we emerge as its effects, its errata, its counternarratives. Whenever we try to narrate ourselves, we appear as dislocations in *their* discourse. (ALS,140)[78]

Such a notion of Palestinian excess over the official narratives of US–Israeli discourses of course relates quite specifically to the non-totalizing modes of thought that Said so often elevates as critical practice. The parallel makes quite clear what is worrisome in the over-literalisation of dialectical vision, for the *Aufhebung* is in part the annihilation of terms, which in a philosophical register might seem neutral. If we shift to socio-political terms, this annihilation clearly requires a great deal of comment, particularly in this context, as the annihilation of a cultural identity, even in assimilationist discourses, is at least extremely controversial.

In this situation, we might argue yet again that what is required is a double gesture. On the one hand, one's fragmentary perspective is not simply dissolved, explained away, and in other words sublated into another's historical vision. On the other, the fragment cannot be positioned as an absolute end in itself, for it will always be an embattled and anxious form of identity and organization. Said translates this double gesture into more recognizably everyday words when he summarizes what is necessary for the Palestinians at this moment, rather than in some barely conceivable future:

> A part of something is for the foreseeable future going to be better than all of it. Fragments over wholes. Restless nomadic activity over the settlements of held territory. Criticism over resignation. The Palestinian as self-consciousness in a barren plain of investments and consumer appetites. The heroism of anger over the begging-bowl, limited independence over the status of clients. Attention, alertness, focus. To do as others do, but somehow to stand apart. To tell your story in pieces, *as it is.* (ALS,150)

This is a kind of realism that is adequate to the fragmented nature of the identity that is its object. And yet it is a realism that it would be desirable not to employ, given that its fragmented object can only inspire an urge to make whole. Said's summary here plays on various modernist and exilic themes yet again. But these themes are central to Said's work, in so many varied contexts. Indeed the same structure binds together Said's memoir *Out of Place*, an autobiographical text written, as autobiography structurally must be, from within the pretence of death, but also from within the death sentence of chronic lymphocytic leukaemia, with which Said was diagnosed in 1991. The postponed metaphysics of return can be postponed no longer: 'So many returns, attempts to go back to bits of life, or people who were no longer there: these constituted a steady response to the increasing rigors of my illness'.[79] A little later he writes that, 'This memoir is on some level a reenactment of the experience of departure and separation as I feel the pressure of time hastening and running out' (OP,222). It is too easy to straightforwardly read Said's focus on 'late style', for example, as symptomatic of a state of mind, however well-documented or significant; however, Said's own attempts to give consistency to life and work have a consistency in this text. For example, he writes the following of a history that is both personal and communal (if not absolutely and equally shared within that community, clearly):

> To me, nothing more painful and paradoxically sought after characterizes my life than the many displacements from countries, cities, abodes, languages, environments that have kept me in motion all these years. Thirteen years ago I wrote in *After the Last Sky* that when I travel I always take too much with me, and that even a trip downtown requires the packing of a briefcase stocked with items disproportionately larger in size and number than the actual period of the trip. Analyzing this, I concluded that I had a secret but ineradicable fear of not returning. What I've since discovered is that despite this fear I fabricate occasions for departure, thus giving rise to the fear voluntarily. The two seem absolutely necessary to my rhythm of life and have intensified dramatically during the period

I've been ill. I say to myself: if you don't take this trip, don't prove your mobility and indulge your fear of being lost, don't override the normal rhythms of domestic life now, you certainly will not be able to do it in the near future. (OP,217–8)

In Derrida's *Monolingualism of the other*, he discusses an imperative governing the invention of the originary language. Derrida writes that, 'One would have to construct oneself, one would have to be able to *invent oneself* without a model and without an assured addressee'.[80] To have assurances about the destination of your inventive identity would be to think in terms of guaranteed filiation. However, here Derrida makes clear that we cannot be satisfied with de-definition alone, but must work toward affiliation through the writing. Similarly, in *Out of Place* Said writes of an imperative to de-define identity, to grasp affiliation rather than filiation. The filiatory is the assumed and the unquestioned identity, the apparently self-sufficient and well-defined identity. Even in the heart of his family, Said finds the filiatory drive to be short-circuited and inadequate. Suggesting that families necessarily invent themselves, their children, and their identities, he writes that,

> There was always something wrong with how I was invented and meant to fit in with the world of my parents and four sisters. Whether this was because I constantly misread my part or because of some deep flaw in my being I could not tell for most of my early life. Sometimes I was intransigent, and proud of it. At other times I seemed to myself to be nearly devoid of any character at all, timid, uncertain, without will.[81]

So, there is an apparent necessity to invention and even fabrication, or perhaps reading and misreading, an idea he introduces explicitly here. You can never be who you are supposed to be, according to your familial or cultural authorities, because even if they know who they want you to be, and even if you are inclined to fit in to their definitions, there is a necessary element of more or less violent misreading built in to this reading of a part and playing of a role. Indeed, then, perhaps we could say that filiation is always on its way to being affiliation, if only we would recognize this fact. Be that as it may, it is this *recognition* that is important, and affiliation must be made as a choice rather than revealed as logically necessary: it must therefore be an active process. Affiliation requires an act of de-definition, perhaps personal, but also broadly cultural and political. Said's personal de-definition, carried out so thoroughly in *Out of Place*, is a necessary step, but it is not his step only.

Indeed, personal though it may be, Said grants this imperative to de-define a certain generality by his reference back to *After the Last Sky*, in which he discusses his luggage habits as an instance of Palestinian repetition compulsion: 'It is as if the activity of repeating prevents us, and others, from skipping us or overlooking us entirely' (ALS,56). Again there is the strange sense that this 'us' stands on both sides of an only apparent divide. Such a sense if given its most concise expression in the following passage, one that emphasises the mobility of the *contrapuntal* in his work:

> I occasionally experience myself as a cluster of flowing currents. I prefer this to the idea of a solid self, the identity to which so many attach so much significance. These currents, like the themes of one's life, flow along during the waking hours, and at their best, they require no reconciling, no harmonizing. They are 'off' and may be out of place, but at least they are always in motion, in time, in place, in the form of all kinds of strange combinations moving about, not necessarily forward, sometimes against each other, contrapuntally yet without one central theme. A form of freedom, I'd like to think, even I am far from being totally convinced that it is. (OP,295)[82]

This passage from the concluding pages confirms the centrality of a metaphorics of music in Said's work: it is a cautious recommendation of a kind of 'atonal' identity. Rather, Said finds virtue in necessity for Palestinian identity, and simultaneously highlights the privilege of his own position, a position from which the benefits of such an identity can be felt without also its very real afflictions. Said does not romanticise the communality of Palestinian identity, and does not bemoan his distance (by that time, no longer meaningfully *enforced*) from one community of which he considers himself a part. So, Said gives a finely modulated account of an individual experience of identity, thematising and demonstrating the act of invention that must constantly if unequally and provisionally ground any identity. The relationship between his own experience of being Palestinian and a projected general Palestinian identity stages the relationship of exemplarity between that Palestinian communal identity and postcolonial identity, which in turn stages the relationship between postcolonial identity and identity in general. *Staging* refers to acts that are sometimes intentional, but often not intentional, as I suggested by arguing that filiation is always collapsing into affiliation, but that this collapse must be acknowledged and made explicit.

In any case, in the specific instance of *Out of Place* there is a clear oscillation between a sense of Said being emblematic of the experience of identity and the sense that his case is so specific as to be beyond generalization. Alon Confino, again, makes the point that the memoir often seems to stand as a parable (that word again, as used by Weiner, although of course this time more neutrally) of postmodern life; he suggests that, '[Said] would like his life story to be of universal meaning, but he wants also to present it as singular'.[83] There is then an impossible combination of individual representation and general representativeness. This is all the more impossible because of the difficulty in identifying Said with some Palestinian collective. At bottom, though, it seems to be a conceptual impossibility. Moving beyond this apparent dichotomy, Ioana Luca suggests that *Out of Place* inhabits, 'a third space of continuous becoming, the space of the Deleuzian "AND".'[84] The question of how Said might feel about inhabiting this space is perhaps beside the point, but we will certainly come back to the question of the relational nature of such a Deleuzian space, and through that its political qualities. If Luca is right, however, then Said has moved far beyond the banality and boredom of identity politics. Indeed, this space is more radical even than that which Luca derives from, 'the complex metamorphoses and changing parameters of autobiography.'[85] There is a real doubt over whether we should still be calling this autobiography, but in any case this new autobiography needs sharper definition and extension, and resources for such extension can be found not only in Deleuze but also in Derrida. The space of the 'AND' is a space of writing, in Derrida's sense, and this writing will help us understand Said's work and the complexities of its reception, as we will explore in the following chapters.

This chapter has pursued varied comments on and demonstrations of the place of autobiography or identity in Said's work, suggesting that it plays a rather complex role in that work. We can get a clearer sense of this complexity, at least as far as academic criticism goes, by looking back to see the kinds of decision Said makes about critical models from Foucault, who famously is chosen above Derrida. Said may later have shown great impatience with theory in general, but that hardly alters the fact that it shapes everything he writes, not only *Orientalism*. He cannot simply wish it away, and from the examples I've considered in this chapter, that is not even something he wanted to do. His writings show a constant engagement with ideas that can be found in a more explicit form in the postcolonial theory that he ushered in but distanced himself from. To see this engagement for what it is, we should look at the more explicit forms of his own theoretical writing, and get a sense of the ideas he was writing against, and the ideas he was extracting and developing, again not only in *Orientalism* but also the rest of his work, however implicitly. And the fact is that in looking to Foucault, Said is picking a particular kind of reading of the modern subject and its production of knowledge. The choice is important, and one that is open to challenge from many different perspectives: for example, the understanding of Descartes put forward by Foucault, and extended so dramatically in *Orientalism*'s assaults on the illusion of disinterested scholarship, in challenged by theory itself, for example that of Slavoj Žižek or Alain Badiou. More notably, in the context of Said's own theoretical choices, there is a rather more complex sense of subjectivity to be found in Derrida's writing than is usually assumed, an understanding that is clearly present in his earliest writings.

References

1. Said, *Beginnings: Intention and Method*, New York: Columbia University Press, 1975).
2. Said, *Orientalism: Western Conceptions of the Orient*, (New York: Basic Books, 1978).

3. Mary Besemeres, for example, argues that Derrida thinks the self is textual, and she rejects this idea in the name of agency; see *Translating One's Self* (Bern: Peter Lang, 2002), p.12.

4. Interviews are, for Spivak, 'a wonderful way of "othering" oneself', a suggestive comment in the context of this book; see *The Post-Colonial Critic* (London: Routledge, 1990), p.36.

5. Spivak argues, in 'French Feminism In an International Frame', that 'Cixous seems often to identify the Derridian mode of writing about writing with merely the production of prose and verse'; *In Other Worlds: Essays in Cultural Politics,* (London: Routledge, 1987), p.147. However, of course this is not all Cixous understands by writing, even if the privilege she gives literature is clear.

6. Cixous, preface to Susan Sellers (ed.) *The Hélène Cixous Reader* (London: Routledge, 1994), p.xix.

7. 'Hélène Cixous in conversation with Sophia Phoca', *Wasafiri* 31, Spring 2000, p.13.

8. Cixous, 'My Algeriance' in *Stigmata* trans. E. Prenowitz (London: Routledge, 1998), p.155.

9. Ibid., p.155.

10. Derrida, *The Other Heading: Reflections on Today's Europe*, trans. P.-A. Brault and M. B. Naas (Indianapolis: Indiana University Press, 1992).

11. She refers to, 'That French nationality granted to the Jews of Algeria by the Crémieux decree and which was a true *Gift* an example of the gift-poison of which Jacques Derrida has recounted the perversities'; *Stigmata,* p.162. For Derrida, like Cixous, this example is also exemplary.

12. Cixous, *Stigmata* p.163.

13. Cixous, *Stigmata* p.167.

14. Cixous, *Stigmata* p.170.

15. Cixous, preface to Sellers (ed.) *The Hélène Cixous Reader* (London: Routledge, 1994), pp.xvi–xvii.

16. Cixous, *Stigmata,* p.183.

17. 'Hélène Cixous in conversation with Sophia Phoca' , p.10.

18. Cavarero, *Relating Narratives* (London: Routledge, 2000).

19. In Parker, *The Self in Moral Space: Life Narrative and the Good* (Ithaca: Cornell University Press, 2007).

20. Cixous and Calle-Bruber, trans. E. Prenowitz, *Rootprints: memory and life writing* (London: Routledge, 1997).

21. Derrida, *Specters of Marx*, trans. Peggy Kamuf, (London: Routledge, 1994).

22. Cixous, *Stigmata,* p.170.

23. Derrida, *Monolingualism of the other, or, the prosthesis of origin,* trans. P. Mensah (Stanford: Stanford University Press, 1998).

24. Cixous and Calle-Bruber, trans. E. Prenowitz, *Rootprints: memory and life writing* (London: Routledge, 1997), pp.9–10.

25. Freud, *Moses and Monotheism,* (New York: Vintage, 1955).

26. Brennan, 'The Illusion of a Future: *Orientalism* as Travelling Theory', *Critical Inquiry* 26(3) (Spring 2000), p.577.

27. Said, 'Travelling Theory', in *The World, the Text, and the Critic* (London: Faber & Faber, 1984). Further refs. to WTC are in the text.

28. This difference in repetition might be one way of characterizing the postcolonial generally; see my 'Postcolonial piracy', *Critical Survey,* 16.2 (2004), pp.7–27.

29. Auerbach, *Mimesis: The Representation of Reality in Western Literature*, trans. W.R. Trask (Princeton: Princeton University Press, 1953).
30. For a robust defence of this notion's specificity, see Aamir R. Mufti 'Auerbach in Istanbul: Edward Said, Secular Criticism, & the Question of Minority Culture', *Critical Inquiry* 25 (Autumn 1998), pp.95–125.
31. Auerbach, *Mimesis.*, p.557.
32. 'He is perfect to whom the whole world is an exile'; quoted in Said, *The World, the Text and the Critic* (London: Faber & Faber, 1983), p.7, and in many other places.
33. See Foucault, *The History of Sexuality: Volume One*, (London: Penguin, 1978) esp. pp.92–96.
34. For a concise statement of these criticisms, see 'Foucault and the Imagination of Power' in D.C. Hoy (ed.) *Foucault: A Critical Reader* (Oxford: Blackwell, 1986).
35. Said, *Freud and the Non-European* (London: Verso, 2003), p.54.
36. Ibid., pp.54–55.
37. Rose, *The Question of Zion* (Princeton: Princeton University Press, 2005), p.155.
38. Kristeva, *Strangers to Ourselves*, translated by Leon S. Roudiez (New York: Columbia University Press, 1994) p.191.
39. Kristeva, *Powers of Horror: An Essay on Abjection*, trans. L. M. Roudiez (New York: Columbia University Press, 1982).
40. Douglas, *Purity and Danger* (London: Routledge, 1984), p.2.
41. Douglas, *Purity and Danger*, pps. 3, 4, 4.
42. In *Home Territories: Media, Mobility and Identity* (London: Routledge, 2000), David Morley summarizes Douglas's notion of home as 'bringing space under control' (p.16).
43. Kristeva, *Powers of Horror: An Essay on Abjection*, trans. L.M. Roudiez (New York: Columbia University Press, 1982), p.4.
44. Kristeva, *Powers of Horror: An Essay on Abjection*, p.67.
45. See Said, *On Late Style* (London: Bloomsbury, 2006).
46. Said, *Musical Elaborations* (London: Chatto and Windus, 1991).
47. On methodological similarity between Said and Adorno, see Thomas Pepper's *Singularities* (Cambridge: Cambridge University Press, 1997), which summarises one fragment from *Minima Moralia* in the following way: 'To speak, as Hegel did not cease to remind us, is to speak in the realm of the general. The particular is lost as soon as one begins to speak. There is only one option: love and be silent' (46).
48. Subotnik, *Deconstructive Variations: Music and Reason in Western Society* (Minnesota: Minneapolis University Press, 1996), p.218. Subotnik's comments highlight a point made by other commentators, especially Bruce Robbins, who notes that Said's reference to the full range of media is inconsistent.
49. Said, *Reflections on Exile and Other Essays* (Cambridge MA.: Harvard University Press, 2002), p.184.
50. Said, *Reflections on Exile and Other Essays*, p.185.
51. Said, *Reflections on Exile and Other Essays*, p.186. In 'Between Worlds', Said outlines what this means for his own academic voice in the time before *Orientalism*: 'Having allowed myself gradually to assume the professional voice of an American academic as a way of submerging my difficult and unassimilable past, I began to think and write contrapuntally, using the disparate halves of my experience, as an Arab and as an American, to work with and also against each other' (p.562).

52. Said, *Reflections on Exile and Other Essays*, p.177.
53. Confino, 'Remembering Talbiyah: On Edward Said's *Out of Place*', *Israel Studies* 3(2), p.188.
54. Said, *Reflections on Exile and Other Essays*, p.175.
55. Said, *Reflections on Exile and Other Essays*, p.176.
56. Said, *Reflections on Exile and Other Essays*, p.182.
57. *London Review of Books* 20 March 2003, p.5.
58. Said, *Reflections on Exile and Other Essays* (Cambridge MA.: Harvard University Press, 2002) p.567.
59. Weiner, 'My Beautiful old House' and Other Fabrications by Edward Said' *Commentary*, 1999.
60. But if we look at the ongoing discussion of the *Wikipedia* entry for Said, we can see that this is not over yet: see http://en.wikipedia.org/wiki/Talk:Edward_Said accessed on 22 September 2006.
61. Hitchens, *Commentary's scurrilous attack on Edward Said*, accessed at http://www.salon.com/news/feature/1999/09/07/said/index.html on July 2, 2007.
62. Said, *Power, Politics and Culture: Interviews with Edward W. Said*, (New York: Vintage, 2002).
63. 'Edward Said talks to Jacqueline Rose', *Critical Quarterly* 40(1), p.78.
64. I have already mentioned Justus Reid Weiner's notorious attack on Said in *Commentary*. It should be evident that there is invention *and* invention: Said's sense that, for his parents, 'There was always something wrong with how I was invented' (*Out of Place: a memoir* (London: Granta, 1999), p.3), is what I am concerned with here. Said considers how Palestinian self-invention is an always precarious magic that is perhaps 'wrong'.
65. Said & Jean Mohr, *After the Last Sky: Palestinian Lives* (London: Faber & Faber, 1986), p.67. Further refs. to *ALS* are in the text. Compare Said's *Beginnings: Intention and Method* (New York: Columbia University Press, 1975), p.378: 'The intellectual makes it his task to controvert the dynastic role thrust upon him by history or habit'. Further refs. to ALS are in the text.
66. Barthes, *Camera Lucida* trans. R. Howard (London: Jonathan Cape, 1982), p.97.
67. Derrida, *The Work of Mourning*, (Chicago: Chicago University Press, 2001), p.39.
68. Mustapha Marrouchi, writing on Edward Said, also draws on *The Work of Mourning*; see 'The Impossibility of Mourning the Deaths of Edward Said - a tribute by a friend and student', accessed at http://www.globalcomment.com/current_affairs/article_68.asp on 30 April 2004
69. Indeed, from one influential perspective this would apparently disqualify such a 'theory' from any role in politics; Peter Hallward, for example, writes the following: 'The criteria governing theoretical speculation must never be specified in advance, in terms of generic conformity or cultural authenticity. A theory's value depends solely on what it allows its *every* user to do.' (*Absolutely Postcolonial* (Manchester: Manchester University Press, 2001), p.335). I can happily agree with the first sentence while wondering about the sense of 'theory' implied by the second sentence; for Hallward, a worthwhile theory would never need translation. I will return to this question later.
70. Derrida, 'From Restricted to General Economy: A Hegelianism without Reserve' in *Writing and Difference*, (London: Routledge, 1978), pp.251–277.
71. Derrida, *The Work of Mourning*, pp.41–42.
72. Derrida, *The Work of Mourning*, p.53.

73. Said suggests that, 'Since our history is forbidden, narratives are rare; the story of origins, of home, of nation is underground' (*ALS,* 20).
74. See, for example, pp.100–101.
75. See *Out of Place* (London: Granta, 1999), p.4, on Said's self-objectification, which he directly relates to his mother's shifting between the homeliness of her Arabic and the objective tones of her English.
76. Compare *Peace and its discontents* (London: Vintage, 1995), p.126.
77. See, for example, the interview 'My right of return' in *Ha'aretz* August 18 2000; accessed at http://www3.haaretz.co.il/eng/scripts/print.asp?id=89666 on December 15 2000.
78. See also p.159: 'Too many details of our disparate and, it often seems, hopelessly scattered existence bombard me as I try to order my thoughts into sequential prose'.
79. Said, *Out of Place* (London: Granta, 1999), p.215. Further refs. to *OP* are in the text.
80. Derrida, *Monolingualism of the other, or, the prosthesis of origin,* trans. P. Mensah (Stanford: Stanford University Press, 1998) p.55.
81. Said, *Out of Place*, p.3.
82. See *After the Last Sky*, p.60.
83. Confino, 'Remembering Talbiyah', p.188.
84. Luca, 'Edward Said's *Lieux de Mémoire: Out of Place* and the Politics of Autobiography', *Social Text* 87, 24(2) (Summer 2006), p.140.
85. Luca, 'Edward Said's *Lieux de Mémoire: Out of Place* and the Politics of Autobiography', p.125.

3 Inventing the postcolonial author

Postcolonialism and dialectical thought

Much of what I have written so far can be described in terms of the way philosophies of difference have responded to dialectical thought. One very simple way of thinking about autobiography in theory is to see it as a residue that is both necessary to the formulation of the theory and necessarily something to be purged once the theory has been formulated. Autobiography, in this view, cannot be a proper part of any theory, and is sublated by any properly theoretical system. But if autobiography cannot be written off or out in this way, then it becomes an important element of any attempt to resist certain kinds of theoretical system. Autobiography can therefore usefully be brought together with postcolonial theory, given the latter's debt to the same philosophies of difference previously mentioned. Postcolonial theory is generally taken to exemplify a mode of thought hostile to dialectics as in some way a kind of primary colonialist philosophy, particularly for instance in its recourse to Frantz Fanon, whose more critical comments on the dialectic are seized upon and extended by Homi Bhabha in particular. Such a critical stance toward the dialectic also comes through in the postcolonial recourse to Foucault's work. Foucault does insist upon the endless mobility of the Hegelian dialectic in particular, and yet Foucault's work is generally taken to be a form of anti-dialectical thinking. So, writing about Gilles Deleuze, Foucault gives the following programmatic statement of an anti-dialectical thought:

> The freeing of difference requires thought without contradiction, without dialectics, without negation; thought that accepts divergence; affirmative thought whose instrument is disjunction; thought of the multiple – of the nomadic and dispersed multiplicity that is not limited or confined by the constraints of the same; thought that does not conform to a pedagogical model (the fakery of prepared answers) but attacks insoluble problems – that is, a thought which addresses a multiplicity of exceptional points, which is displaced as we distinguish their conditions and which insists upon and subsists in the play of repetitions.[1]

As I say, this is a programmatic expression of a non-dialectical thought's aims, but its programmatic nature usefully opens a series of questions that inform my reading of postcolonial theory and autobiography. The dialectic produces *constraint* and *fakery*: it must be countered by *nomadic* thought. Such a polarization can be found, in a similar form, in postcolonial theory, in which post-structuralist criticism is opposed by Marxist criticism. Discussing Bhabha's 'textual' approach to colonialism, in which she finds the influence of Foucault's anti-dialectical injunctions, Benita Parry recalls Frederic Jameson's comments on what he calls *the ideology of difference*: 'What is at stake [...] is the rolling back of Hegel and Marx by way of the conceptual discrediting of contradiction and dialectical opposition'.[2] In succinct response to Parry, Iain Chambers argues that such a 'rolling back' is precisely what is required, 'in order to listen to what that logic has silenced and ignored'.[3] From this perspective, the dialectic tends, despite its apparent neutrality, to operate through processes of massive and even predictable exclusion. Autobiographical theory would be one example of the kind of 'rolling back' practiced by postcolonial theory.

The most powerful example of the dialectical exclusion might be Hegel, discussed at length elsewhere. But there are other points in philosophical history that are blamed, like Kant and Descartes. Indeed, Descartes often seems to be a convenient target, with his separation of mind and body, and a kind of theoretical model that excises the specificity of any theory. However, it can of course be argued that this picture of Descartes is not only extremely simplistic, but also fits into a more general logic of difference that has no necessary political implications whatsoever, and therefore cannot be pressed into service against political logics of exclusion, as it always seems to be in postmodern theory. As an example of this objection, Anthony Easthope makes the following points in criticizing Homi Bhabha:

When Bhabha affirms that refusal of 'fixed identification' might allow us to entertain difference without an 'assumed or imposed hierarchy', that moving beyond the Cartesian ego might open up a subjectivity more able to tolerate difference, he is repeating a version of wishful thinking that is widespread among those concerned with post-structuralist theory. That it is utopian can be suggested in two ways. Theories of the ego and aggression imply that speaking subjects must have a coherent identity, that any identity is won at the expense of the other, and thus there can be no escape from an alterity which always represents a potential threat to the subject's stability ('entertaining difference' is as likely to lead to aggression as a world without hierarchy). Another is suggested by Ernesto Laclau (responding to Derrida's account of the spectre) when he points out that no single ethical or political consequence such as the end of hierarchy is *necessarily* imposed by openness to alterity. There was certainly no less hierarchy in the world before Descartes than there is now.[4]

Bhabha would surely not disagree with the first point, given his emphasis everywhere on the uncanny as explanatory category, and Derrida's work certainly makes the second point in many contexts. Nonetheless, Easthope's doubled reference to Descartes as easy scapegoat is very important as it connects the philosophy of difference with the autobiographical turn in post-colonial theory. The scapegoat version of Descartes has been very important in modern cultural theory generally, and it might as well be said that if he had not existed, someone would have had to invent him. Of course, in very familiar ways that is exactly what has happened, and there is nothing to stop us doing this again, for this context. As is well known, Descartes lacked a strong sense of home, and he was always physically on the move – yet another kind of exile. This is very fitting for someone who was intent on creating a universal philosophical method that anyone could use at any time and in any place. But of course Descartes' experience of movement is also one of disorder, and fits in with the famous visions he experienced in November 1619. From these most personal and irrational of experiences, Descartes somehow began to create a universal and rational system. Indeed, his universal method comes through so strongly that he begins to apply it before the end of his final vision, when he decides to interpret all of the events and symbols. Most of us do not try to understand our dreams until we have woken up, but Descartes was one step ahead. In his acceptance speech for the 2001 Theodor W. Adorno Prize, Derrida discusses dreaming, suggesting that the philosopher's response to the dream is always to wake, a negative response that 'links the responsibility of the philosopher to the rational imperative of wakefulness, the sovereign ego, and the vigilant consciousness'.[5] Adorno, he suggests, holds on to both the philosopher's response and the poet's hesitant response, but perhaps we can argue something similar for Descartes: Descartes's universal project begins with and is accompanied by a dream or what we could anachronistically call autobiography. Even though he seems to be the ultimate rationalist, and so opposed to many familiar tendencies in contemporary cultural theory, he shares this autobiographical emphasis in his writing. Philosophy in its modern form started from the question 'What can I know?' instead of questions like 'What is there?' Many versions of Descartes might register this as an irony, if it is registered at all, but it is more than that: clearly Descartes is not as straightforward as he has seemed to many people of varying theoretical persuasions, and this needs to be remembered. Contrary to the implications of Easthope's comments, when Derrida comes to discuss Descartes, he is careful to explore the complexity of this figure, particularly when it comes to the status of philosophy as speech act.

While I will argue that a thought of difference has been accompanied by transformation of critical personae and textual models, it is not quite the case that the autobiographical moment marks an absolute rejection of Cartesian certainty. The autobiographical turn in contemporary cultural theory accompanies the desire to hold on to multiplicity, and is instrumental in accomplishing this desire, particularly perhaps in postcolonial theory. But there are different and complex ways in which these autobiographical operations function, and some important ways in which the discussion of the truth of theory has already been discussed in a kind of post-structuralist pre-history of postcolonial theory. This pre-history can be very helpful in thinking about the kinds of debate that take place around postcolonial theory itself, and so it's worth going back to certain key theoretical texts from Barthes and Foucault. While Foucault's writing (and some early Barthes, but of course not the later) is apparently emptied of subjectivity, Said holds onto a situated subjectivity, associating it with agency in general.[6] However, this subjectivity sits uneasily with at least some of the conceptual apparatus borrowed from Foucault, and as this uneasy alliance spread through postcolonial theory, autobiography and post-structuralism have more and more clearly made for a problematic theoretical convergence. To explore this convergence, the following will look in particular at Derrida's constant stress on the complexity of any origin, whether textual, subjective, or epochal.

Constructing authorship: Barthes and Foucault

To get a sense of how Said comes to his ideas of subjectivity and beginning, it is helpful to return to some canonical theoretical texts concerning the institution of authorship. Much scholarship has explored the ways in which the idea of authorship has a history or histories. Our idea of authorship is not natural, of course. It is in some ways hardly worth stating that argument any more. However, certain misconceptions about the work of key theorists follow from the apparently simple dismissal of authorship associated with them, and these misconceptions can be followed through to certain perspectives in contemporary literary and cultural studies, and more specifically perspectives on autobiographical theory. And if we're going to look at canonical theory, we ought to look at what must be one of the most anthologized pieces of such writing, featuring such familiar passages as the following:

> The author is a modern figure, a product of our society insofar as, emerging from the Middle Ages with English empiricism, French rationalism and the personal faith of the Reformation, it discovered the prestige of the individual, of, as it is more nobly put, the 'human person'. It is thus logical that in literature it should be this positivism, the epitome and culmination of capitalist ideology, which has attached the greatest importance to the 'person' of the author.[7]

This undoubtedly familiar quotation comes from Barthes's 'The Death of the Author', in which he poses the questions, 'Who speaks? On what basis could we ever decide?' The famous answer, according to Barthes, is that, 'We shall never know, for the good reason that writing is the destruction of every voice, of every point of origin'(IMT,112). Knowing the speaker, being certain of the author of a meaning, this knowledge will have been a product of (Western) bourgeois individualism, as the above quotation invites us to infer. Further, despite the substitution of language in place of the author, there has been a continued hypostatization of the text quite in keeping with this capitalist ideology, the reign of the Author accompanied or succeeded by that of the Critic. So, as is well known, Barthes argues that, 'a text's unity lies not in its origin but in its destination'; (IMT,118) however, the reader who replaces the author is no 'who' as such, but rather an impersonal location of hosting, a subject coming after the text, or rather a subject constituted in an endless temporality of becoming *here and now*. A text's destination is constituted by the text, and so the destination (the reader) is not merely returning to him or herself via the detour of the text. Its addressees become through the text's performance, or rather always might not become: Barthes's reference to the language of speech-act theory recalls Derrida's reading of J.L. Austin in 'Signature Event Context',[8] in which Derrida finds the possibility of a performative's 'failure' necessarily haunting the possibility of its 'success'. Indeed, for Barthes there is apparently no certainty in the act of murdering the Western bourgeois author: 'to give writing its future' (IMT,118) is rather to give it a radically unpredictable and uncertain future.

It can be argued that this talk of authorial death is laughable, given the proliferation of sites for authorship we have seen created, perhaps most obviously right now in the so-called blogosphere. Yet of course the death in question is the death of only one conception of authorship, in particular that insisting upon the governing authority of an author, and it is hardly clear that blogs are that authoritative in the sense undermined by Barthes. But to listen to and answer such objections is to get drawn in to historicizing claims, and this is entirely understandable given the historical or historicist aspect of the thesis on which Barthes is apparently insistent. We need to ask, to what extent is the emphasis on the author or subject characterizable as 'Western', or 'capitalist'? The structures of intertextuality (the subject *as* intertext) he identifies have in fact come to dominate many contemporary understandings of literature, although that would have hardly constituted the limit of Barthes's ambition. It is clear, however, that although this *ought* to have been the case, or perhaps *really was* the case, previous to the kind of intervention Barthes makes, in fact things were rather different, for at least two hundred and fifty years, perhaps longer. So, Barthes is proposing something about the general structures of reading, but is also specifying a resistance or distortion of these structures within a specific historical period. The epistemological contexts are broadly specified as English empiricism and French rationalism: presumably Bacon and Descartes are somewhere behind these references, but at this point Barthes specifies no further. Elsewhere, however, Barthes does give detailed readings of examples, examples that reflect precisely on the role of intellectuals, but that also seem to justify criticisms of parochialism in his work. We can consider the example of Voltaire from 'The Last Happy Writer',[9] because Barthes makes an argument about an immobility and immobilism in

Voltaire's conception of history and philosophy, and this argument coincides with the emphases of 'The Death of the Author'.

Barthes suggests Voltaire was 'the last happy writer' because of his historical moment. However harsh that moment was, 'no period has helped a writer more, given him more assurance that he was fighting for a just and natural cause'(BR,152). The enemies of bourgeois culture were, Barthes suggests, uniformly condemnable by a swift pamphlet. By contrast, Barthes argues, in the twentieth century,

> [T]he very enormity of racist crimes, their organization by the State, the ideological justifications with which they are masked–all this involves today's writer in much more than a pamphlet, demands a philosophy rather than an irony, an explanation rather than an astonishment. (BR,151)

Here Barthes explicitly names the Second World War, and Auschwitz, asserting that no mere pamphlet can measure up to such events. The general structure of Barthes's argument presents an inordinate complication of political issues and intellectual engagement as we move further into the twentieth century. Barthes summarizes Voltaire's forgetting of history, his philosophy of immobility, in the following way: 'The writer was on history's side, all the happier in that he perceived history as a consummation, not as a transcendence which risked sweeping him along with it'(BR,153). Living at the glorious conclusion of history, Voltaire surveyed the globe with absolute confidence in his nation and class, and absolute confidence in the adequacy of his enunciatory position, which is an apparently enviable position, to the 'equivalent' figure in the middle of the twentieth century.

We might have our doubts about the picture given by Barthes in this essay, given that it grants such historical complexity to his own moment but naïvely denies it to Voltaire's context. This gesture seems to give Voltaire one kind of privilege, but one so cheaply bought: it's not so impressive to be that confident in one's importance, not when the world was that much simpler. However, Barthes is not nostalgic for a moment of bourgeois arrogance, and clearly wants to argue something more complex and complicitous than the mere and immediately apparent loss of Voltaire's context: Voltaire's immobility has doubled meaning, and comes at a price. Barthes considers Voltaire's exoticist rhetoric in the context of modern capitalism, and colonialism: '[F]or [Voltaire] the Oriental is not the object, the term of a genuine consideration, but simply a cipher, a convenient sign of communication'. Voltaire's space is surveyed rather than explored, the Voltairean journey, 'not even an operation of knowledge, but merely an affirmation'. Further, Voltaire's Orient is a series of, 'mobile signs without actual content, humanity at zero degrees (centigrade), which one nimbly grasps in order to signify [...] oneself'(BR,155). Presumably, this assertion refers to humanity under experimental conditions, as it were: humanity in the laboratory. Ultimately, although Barthes does not use these terms, for Voltaire, the 'exotic' world serves as *self-consolidating*

otherness: 'To aggrandize oneself in order to confirm, not in order to transform oneself–such is the meaning of the Voltairean voyage'(BR,156). If there
is the appearance of travel, this apparent mobility is accompanied by an arrogant immobility, a mobility that knows already what it will find, one that is
ceaselessly returning to itself, having arguably never ventured forth. Such a
presentation of arrogant self-confirming travel of course bears slightly mysteriously on Barthes's own *Empire of Signs*,[10] which is a kind of over-literal mimicry
of such exoticising attitudes, distinguishable only by its explicit naming of its
imaginary object as 'Japan', a very delicate gesture also demonstrated by his
suggestion (in *Roland Barthes by Roland Barthes*) that Japanese *represents*, 'the
organization of an altogether different subject'.[11] It would appear that Barthes
explicitly puts into play the violence of such naming, fixing, exoticising gestures; by contrast, Voltaire as exemplary of a bourgeois anti-intellectualism
was unable to think about such complicity.[12]

Some of the central polemical claims made in 'The Death of the Author'
are connected with the kinds of argument Barthes is making about Voltaire.
While the connections between 'The Last Happy Writer' and 'The Death of
the Author' remain implicit, Barthes's explanation of Voltaire's immobility,
and its identification as a privileged example in an understanding of the twentieth century intellectual's apparently insurmountable difficulties, strengthens
these implications. Barthes argues that, '[B]y identifying all system with stu-
pidity and all freedom of mind with intelligence, Voltaire grounded liberalism
on a contradiction'(BR,157). The bourgeois suspicion of organized philosophy translates itself straightforwardly, in Barthes's interpretation, into an
anti-intellectualism: '[Voltaire] ceaselessly dissociated intelligence and intel-
lectuality, asserting that the world is an order, if we do not try too much to
order it, that it is a system, if only we renounce systematizing it'(BR,156).
If Voltaire had a system at all, it was a systematic anti-systematicity: a system of the non-system. His simplicity (indeed, his *happiness*), argues Barthes,
was 'bought at the price of an ablation of history and an immobilization of
the world'(BR,157). This is a form of happiness, then, that can no longer be
desired with good conscience. It is the happiness of a writer who surveys the
world from a privileged perspective, never entertaining the idea that some
form of 'travel' might be necessary to make that happiness complete. It is, we
should say, the happiness of the author.

Near the end of the essay, Barthes briefly suggests that Rousseau worked
a parallel change on the afterlife of the modern intellectual, his insistence on
society's corruption of humanity conferring on that general figure, 'a responsibility he can never again completely honor or completely elude'(BR,157).
Rousseau, perhaps simplistically and predictably introduced here, undermines the happiness-in-immobility of the intellectual, putting in place a
responsibility to otherness that Voltaire simply cannot recognize. In this
way, it can be argued that Rousseau begins the critique of Enlightenment
self-image. In fact, this reading of Rousseau might appear to take his traditional understanding rather too much on faith. Bart Moore-Gilbert for one

has recently argued, in an essay on Rousseau's autobiographical writings, for his vacillating engagement with the non-Western:

> [I]f Rousseau is read as inaugurating the critique of the Enlightenment, one might suggest that opposition to Modernity, as much as its advocacy, has been from the outset at least partly inflected by issues of ethnicity – and not always in ways which do it credit.[13]

Moore-Gilbert makes the connection between Rousseau and Crusoe, and there is at least some sense in which Rousseau is rather more than less like Voltaire. And yet, as Moore-Gilbert points out, there are elements of a critique of the discourse of 'othering' present in Rousseau's texts. As I have been arguing, he reacts against a particular idea of intellectual responsibility, in which reading and writing subjects are always safely confined within their own bounds, prior to language. Yet I have insisted on Rousseau as working a *parallel* operation on what follows because it would seem that the urge to happiness of the Voltairean kind has persisted into the twentieth century. Rousseau, in Barthes's presentation, appears to inaugurate a tradition[14] counter to Western bourgeois individualism, or at least appears to provide the conceptual and textual resources for such a counter-tradition's retrospective construction. Yet, in one version of the argument, such oppositional resources will have already been accommodated by bourgeois individualism itself, reliant as those resources are on a certain model of subjectivity.

Barthes is not alone in calling for and constructing such a counter-tradition, which is really the kind of tradition that eludes commonplace ideas of being traditional. Foucault, whose work is an obvious point of comparison, will insist precisely that one cannot look to Rousseau for a serious alternative to the thinking of Man. Nor indeed, for Foucault, can one look to a supposed scourge of the bourgeois like Marx. He pursues this argument in *The Order of Things*, and this is yet another argument that is well known. By allusion Foucault references 'The Death of the Author' in his 'What is an Author?',[15] a text that announces itself as a re-evaluation of certain issues relating to authorship and subjectivity raised by *The Order of Things*. To recall its outlines, the essay examines our contemporary notion of authorship, identifying the so-called author function, a discrete discourse of specific socio-cultural significance. Foucault discerns a shift in attitudes towards the author occurring comparatively recently. Until the modern era, at least in European thought, the authorship of a piece of writing was relatively unimportant, with the exception of scientific thought, on which the signature was vital. Foucault identifies a shift in the conception of authorship, with scientific objectivity requiring the effacement of the author's signature, whilst other kinds of discourse (particularly philosophical and literary) become guaranteed only by the addition of the recognizable name. This reversal occurs in the seventeenth and eighteenth centuries. For Foucault it is a shift in power structures, helping to determine what is thinkable, and what can be said. Additionally, certain names acquire a kind of symbolic weight over time until they designate far more than writing by that specific author, but entire fields of study; these figures are 'founders of discourse', and Freud and Marx are examples. Basically, Foucault identifies the rise of the author in certain discourses as according with the rise of 'humanism' and the emphasis on the sovereign subject: in short, he identifies the rise of the author with *individualization.* This epistemological shift accompanies the emergence of the modern Western human sciences, something Foucault considers at length in *The Order of Things.*

As with Barthes, the argument of this essay is well known. Its relationship with 'The Death of the Author' is nonetheless important, and we need to examine the points of origin and rupture identified, and to think about the ascription of a concept of authorship to a supposedly specific class, geopolitical, or professional identity. What Foucault and Barthes have in common is the sense that indifference to authorship is an ethical principle of *écriture*:[16] this specific term is Foucault's, but Barthes undoubtedly seeks something with comparable resonance. Additionally, both writers assert that although the shift they are remarking on has been noted before, its significance has at best been minimized by emphases on different forms of unity: these forms are, for Foucault, *work,* and for Barthes, *text* traditionally understood. As Foucault suggests, 'The word *work* and the unity that it designates are probably as problematic as the status of the author's individuality'.[17] Foucault suggests (and Barthes's concern about the mere substitution of a relatively stable notion of *text* for the author is in accord with this) that theories of *écriture* elevate a kind of 'transcendental anonymity':

> To imagine writing as absence seems to be a simple repetition, in transcendental terms, of both the religious principle of inalterable and yet never fulfilled tradition, and the aesthetic principle of the work's survival, its perpetuation beyond the author's death, and its enigmatic *excess* in relation to him.[18]

The unity of a text or oeuvre amounts to the unity conferred by the elevation of an author, acting as a limit on signification, even if we invest the authorial figure with the supposedly proliferative quality of genius. In fact, the author-as-genius functions in a way opposite to its assumed role and is, for Foucault, therefore strictly ideological.

This conclusion about the ideology of authorship is implicit in Barthes also: a Marxian emphasis on a bourgeois ideology is compounded, and its scope is widened to include all that follows, including Marx himself. I have already alluded to the following assertion from *The Order of Things*: 'At the deepest level of Western knowledge, Marxism introduced no real discontinuity'.[19] Foucault suggests that for a time it appeared to be disruptive, but quickly found its place precisely because the fundamental discourses enabling Marxism also enabled what it opposed, bourgeois economics. In a familiar structure, the enabling discourses of Man condition both Ricardo and Marx. These figures become, whatever the qualification, equivalent: '*simultaneously, and according to the same mode*'. Marx's writing is seen as a mere continuation of the discourse on Man, and is in truth programmed by that discourse almost as a necessity. In the same way, we might speculate, the alternatives that Barthes puts forward (Voltaire and Rousseau) are written into the structure *The Order of Things* outlines: the immensity of a discourse soon perhaps to be effaced, 'like a face drawn in sand at the edge of the sea'.[20] In 'What Is an Author?' Foucault suggests that there are good reasons for returning to the problem of authorship, principally the 'return to the subject' with all it entails and all its functions. For a supposed revision of the earlier book, the essay makes few substantive changes, and this is not only because the notion of authorship was previously under developed. Foucault essentially follows through his diagnosis of the human sciences, perhaps finding the concept(s) of authorship to be the most developed expression of such discourses. And, not coincidentally, Foucault has a very specific point of origin in mind for this Western bourgeois ideological construction, one that '*any archaeology can situate with precision*'.

Western subjectivity from Descartes

Not unexpectedly, in terms of Foucault's own perspective, and a great many other and even opposed versions of this intellectual history, this precision situates the moment of Western subjectivity in the event of the Cartesian cogito: 'Before Descartes, one could not be impure, immoral, and know the truth. With Descartes, direct evidence is enough. After Descartes, we have a nonascetic subject of knowledge. This change makes possible the institutionalization of modern science'.[21] Foucault's ascription of centrality to Descartes is familiar from his other work: I will later consider Descartes's absolutely central, if brief, position in *Histoire de la folie à l'âge classique*, and the debate with Derrida this position occasioned.[22] In his later work on the care of the self, Foucault contrasts modern notions of the subject with those of Antiquity. He finds many continuities of practice between the Graeco-Romans and Christianity, for instance in writing of the self, but with variations in the value ascribed to these practices. Such techniques relate to a fundamental asceticism, meaning that ethics ultimately was the approach to truth: 'In Western culture up to the sixteenth century, asceticism and access to truth are always more or less obscurely linked'(EST,279). Descartes, Foucault maintains, puts forward *any* subject with access to *evidence.* Cartesian constructions, through an apparent scientific democratization, have led to Western philosophy's current impasse, according to Foucault's reading. Once Descartes has altered the state of practice and elevated rationalism, Kant inserts ethics into this modern rationality, making ethics a *procedure* of that rationality. In consequence it is no longer only the ethical subject who can know. Instead, after Descartes it is the knower who can be ethical.

Foucault's insertion of Kant into the Cartesian narrative is most fully expressed in 'What is Enlightenment?'. In that essay Foucault argues that Kant's brief text of the same name, with its focus on *du présent*, constitutes an opening onto what Foucault calls 'the attitude of modernity'(EST,309). Foucault's reading of Kant here emphasizes that this attitude of modernity is accompanied by a *counter*-modernity, which Foucault finds in Baudelaire's ironic heroisation of the present moment. Foucault suggests that this antagonistic set-up results in 'a permanent critique of our historical era'(EST,312). There is, then, a refusal to be either 'for' or 'against' the Enlightenment, and this is a refusal of this gesture of choice, rather than a feeling that either choice would be a simplification. This refusal of choice is in agreement with his assertion that he is not by any means recommending a return to the example of Antiquity. The emphasis is rather on precisely this aliveness to the present, the awareness of constant and ever-mutating danger. Foucault imagines a Kant who helps us to ask the following question: 'In what is given to us as universal, necessary, obligatory, what place is occupied by whatever is singular, contingent, and the product of arbitrary constraints?'(EST,315). This would be one construal of Foucault's philosophical history, with Kant providing a model of critique. But in a sense Kant would, for Foucault, be starting from an unfortunate universalizing stance. In his own 'What is Enlightenment?', Foucault recommends locality rather than globality, even if this local attentiveness would maintain a certain systematic quality. For Foucault, Kant inherits his unfortunate and universalizing or globalizing drive from Descartes. The point to which Foucault's archaeology most often returns (a point of relentless fascination and even perhaps contempt) is Descartes's substitution of the systematic and general sovereign subject of knowledge, a substitution that for Foucault puts in place the discourses of modern *subjectivation*. This position is, of course, familiar from an earlier Foucault text, his history of madness. Despite ruptures of various kinds quite in keeping with the perspectives associated with his work, Foucault's later writings repeat a great many of the themes from that history, and it is a history that helps us get a real sense of so-called post-structuralist subjectivity.

It is important to remember particular features of Foucault's narrative, a narrative that is a kind of history of recent Western philosophy. Foucault's emphasis on epistemological breaks or ruptures is one that entails a certain recourse to privileged textual moments (finally, authors), whatever the extent to which the notion of discourse would claim to concern matters definitively non-intentional, at least insofar as intention entails subjectivity. This recourse finds its usual expression in the elevation of certain literary texts to the status of privileged examples, marking frontiers between epistemes. In *Histoire de la folie à l'âge classique*, for example, Shakespeare and Cervantes become exemplary of constructions of madness in that moment of shift. But this recourse also tends to elevate certain examples to the status of being good-desirable rather than good-useful; however complex the play of associations and modifications,[23] figures like Nietzsche and Artaud are frequently invoked in series, announcing for Foucault the closing of the circle and the re-integration of madness, its being spoken-to once more in Western society. And, just as there are desirable examples, models that we might follow, there are bad examples, gestures that we might want to avoid, philosophies that tap right into the modern society of surveillance, or which in some complex way were (or now appear to have been) necessary to that society. Again, in *Histoire de la folie à l'âge classique*, there is the example of Descartes, who is not one example among many more or less equivalent others, but a centrally and essentially forceful example. In fact, Descartes apparently constitutes that event that any archaeology can situate with precision. Although this event would appear to change across Foucault's work, and would then be at least plausibly non-reductive, supple enough to account for various non-coincidental phenomena, the possibility of tying these disparate analyses into one derivation of the 'attitude of modernity' betrays itself through an immensity and consistency of reference. This reference appears to return to Descartes at specifiable moments in Foucault's text.

This repeated reference to Descartes has intrigued many commentators, and many have been rather sceptical about Foucault's claims, seeing a force of desire at work in his ascription of rupture to this moment. One point that can be made is proposed by Slavoj Žižek when he writes that, 'it seems as if the Cartesian Cogito itself has acquired the status of prescientific myth'.[24] He summarizes the familiar reading of Descartes in the following way: 'the elevation of the subject to the transcendental agent of the synthesis constitutive of reality is correlative to the abasement of its material bearer, to one among the worldly objects'.[25] Following this, however, Žižek argues that it is Descartes himself who constructs the standard by which we are able to judge his positivism, find it lacking, and further make a choice in favour of a post-Cartesian holism. Žižek thus presents the Cartesian revolution as the veiled condition of its judgment, a judgment that would then project back beyond Descartes, most often without realizing what it is doing, or the conditions that have allowed it to do this at all. This, for Žižek, is a particularly important example of a general structure and needs to mark our understanding of rupture:

> [T]he paradox to be fully accepted is that when a certain historical moment is (mis)perceived as the moment of loss of some quality, upon closer inspection it becomes clear that the lost quality emerged only at this very moment of its alleged loss.[26]

Whether or not this is really a general structure, it is certainly useful in understanding the significance of Descartes in Foucault's text, suggesting indeed that what is lost at that moment also comes into being at that moment, announced as a possibility hitherto unsuspected. Whenever we hear that Western reason divides mind and body, it will be worth remembering Žižek's argument, which can be rewritten to say that historical breaks shift the terms in which we conceive loss and gain. Of course, for Žižek what happens is that the apparent loss is produced: there is the production of a lack that can never be satisfied.

Lack might be described in the way Žižek suggests, but we still need to follow the specifics of this lack, this time. The general lesson learned here reminds us of the ever-present Hegel–Lacan, and that combination, particularly Hegel, is something to which we will return. But now we are reading Foucault, and so we need to return to the detail of his work. Already we have seen that for Foucault, Descartes refuses to make the ethical internal to the epistemological, a gesture that makes the reasonable entirely independent of practices of the self, and the philosophical life, one that is only reversed, or its reversal announced, by Nietzsche. The figure of Nietzsche is one of the central examples of Foucault's attempt to let madness speak itself. As he suggests: 'We must try to return, in history, to that zero point in the course of madness at which madness is an undifferentiated experience, a not yet divided experience of division itself'.[27] Foucault renounces what he calls terminal truths, putting forward a time of dialogue and coexistence. Indeed, he suggests that terminal truths originate at this moment he will identify: 'What is originative is the caesura that establishes the distance between reason and non-reason'(MC,xi). Foucault's basic argument is that the processes that made madness an illness led to a break in dialogue: there is a shift from the medieval confrontation of madness as mystery and secret power to modern containment via psychiatric knowledge. Moreover, Foucault makes this shift fundamental to 'the attitude of Modernity': 'the Reason–Madness nexus constitutes for Western culture one of the dimensions of its originality'(MC,xiii). Of course it's impossible to forget that those without reason are not only the mad, and Foucault's insistence from the beginning that his archaeology of silence will have more general significance is persuasive. Indeed, Foucault's scene enabling the break leaves many rather uncertainly literal and metaphorical factors implicitly offering structure. For instance, the end of leprosy so central to the Great Confinement comes, Foucault suggests, with the end of the Crusades and the break with 'Eastern sources of infection'(MC,6). Additionally, in writing about the Ship of Fools, Foucault uses the madman as a general figure of exile, which is suggestive for what is to come: '[The madman] has his truth and his homeland only in that fruitless expanse between two countries that cannot belong to him'(MC,11). He later suggests that, 'from the fifteenth century on, the face of madness has haunted the imagination of Western man'(MC,15). This language of 'haunting' is suggestive, and can of course be found throughout the work of Derrida, but also that of Julia Kristeva or Homi Bhabha, particularly perhaps the latter who conceives the postcolonial in general as the most privileged case of uncanny doubling, monstrosity, virtuality, and ghostliness.

Of course, the location of Foucault's most insistent marking of rupture is the Cartesian Cogito, conceived as inception of the moment of decisive, because *philosophical*, legislative action. Derrida is only the earliest commentator[28] to emphasize the specificity of Foucault's claim, and the particularity of the positioning of Descartes at the beginning of chapter two, given the minimal number of paragraphs dedicated to what appears to be a central ground of Foucault's most general argument, i.e. concerning what Foucault generally calls *subjectivation* [*asujettissement*]. And, given the seeming marginality of Descartes in the text, Derrida's focus on this aspect of *Histoire de la folie* also appears curious, a point he himself registers.[29] Clearly there are certain implications drawn from Foucault's treatment of philosophical discourse that Derrida finds problematic. Additionally, however (especially in the light of Derrida's suspicion about the nature of *epistemes*, epochs, and ages) Descartes appears a particularly powerful place to contest Foucault's production of regularity and definability, and this is true in relation to *geopolitical* and *geophilosophical* configurations also. In pursuit of an interruptive and disjunctive counter-tradition, Foucault sets up, against discursive regularity, equally regular and immense epochal structures. In *Archive Fever* Derrida's writes of a *sickness* constitutive of the archive;[30] for Foucault it seems we might construct a *healthy* alternative.

In this short section of the book, Foucault positions Descartes in a disrupted series, or rather proposes Descartes as the disruptive, deciding and dividing figure: 'A line of division is drawn that soon makes impossible the experience so familiar in the Renaissance, of unreasonable Reason, of reasonable Unreason. Between Montaigne and Descartes an event has come: something that concerns the advent of *ratio*'.[31] For Foucault, Descartes's exclusion of madness from the Cogito constitutes, as 'My Body, This Paper, This Fire' later makes clear, a juridical act: the dividing line in the passage above renders (*rendre*) that experience impossible, with judicial and administrative connotations, maximally including the returning of a verdict. The constitution of the Cartesian subject allows for no dialogue with madness. The division of Descartes from the specific figure of Montaigne is of course revealing, not only because of the specificity of Montaigne's own concerns about madness. There is additionally the question of the form of self-writing exemplified, not only as a mark of what has passed (has been excluded), but also (as in the case of Foucault's treatment of Graeco-Roman ethics and care of the self) implicitly as a suggestion of what is to come. Just as Nietzsche and Artaud herald the re-'integration' of madness, the renewal of dialogue,[32] we might suppose that there will be parallel accompanying or even perhaps dialogical re-workings of the sovereign scientific text. But that is all still (perhaps) to come, and here there is a general pessimism marking Foucault's argument: 'Since the end of the eighteenth century, the life of unreason no longer manifests itself except in the lightning-flash of works such as those of Hölderlin, of Nerval, of Nietzsche, or of Artaud'(MC,278).

The specificity of Foucault's reference here reminds us of his explicit argument, and warns us against an uncritical equation of the various narratives in Foucault's work. And yet, as Françoise Vergès has noted,[33] even here Foucault's suggestive argument feeds into the question of the Western-ness of these structures, reminding us of stories about Frantz Fanon 'breaking the chains', his supposed refusal to learn the language of his patients, and his later disillusionment with the geopolitical specificity and limitations of psychiatry, psychoanalysis, and phenomenology. And it is not only the suggestiveness of Foucault's argument and range of reference that insists upon this shadowy or even exotic context, but also his language:

> And this madness that links and divides time, that twists the world into the ring of a single night, this madness so foreign to the experience of its con-temporaries, does it not transmit—to those able to receive it, to Nietzsche and to Artaud—those barely audible voices of classical unreason, in which it was always a question of nothingness and night, but amplifying them now to shrieks and frenzy? But giving them for the first time an expres-sion, a *droit de cité*, and a hold on Western culture which makes possible all contestations, as well as *total* contestation? But restoring their primitive savagery? (MC,281)

In reading this passage we of course need to read *sauvage* as 'wild' or 'out-side civilization', 'good' rather than the 'bad' of 'savage';[34] be that as it may, here Foucault sets up a connection between 'madness' and the non-European 'Other', suggesting a certain intimacy between two nominally 'external' repositories of Unreason, which some might be tempted to con-vert into Foucault's terms of one 'internal' and one 'external'. And primitivist discourses, 'good' or 'bad', across a range of disparate names tend to make such names equivalent: the mad, children, animals, women, savages. So, Foucault's implicit equivalence of reference in the service of confirming a European society of surveillance has the immediate aspect of its own exclusionary action, an immobile self-confirming discourse of that Europe. Mentioning Mauss and Lévi-Strauss, Barthes's discussion of Foucault's text suggests that,

> Foucault might have found it advantageous to give some ethnographic references, to suggest the example of societies 'without madmen' (but not without 'excluded groups'); but also, no doubt, he would regard this additional distance, this serene purview of all humanity as a kind of reassuring alibi, a distraction from what is newest about his project: its bewilderment, its vertigo.[35]

As Barthes implies, the inclusion of such ethnographic examples might sim-ply lead to the kind of primitivisation found in Mauss's *The Gift*.[36] And yet Said, for one, structures an entire discussion around the formal equivalence of *L'Histoire de la folie* and Lévi-Strauss's *Tristes Tropiques*, a gesture that is uncritical; Said glosses Foucault in the following way: 'Madness is precisely that zero state that resists the encroachments of reason'.[37] It must be said that even without the ethnographic examples that Barthes seems to want,

Foucault's text broadly hints at such a perspective. Resistance to reason is not just something that is found in madness, but something that, scientific discourses notwithstanding, is also found in the non-West.

All of this argument can be connected with Barthes's mobilization of Rousseau as counter-example to Voltaire, and to Lévi-Strauss, particularly in the light of Derrida's analysis of forms of anti-ethnocentrism as mere reversals, but also in the light of the more obvious bracketed context of the 'noble savage'. What is implied and sometimes proposed as corollary of the dominance of the Western bourgeois ideological subject is the denial of that subjectivity to a host of equivalent others. Just as Derrida finds Lévi-Strauss (and Rousseau) merely confirming the immensity of ethnocentrism through a mere reversal of evaluation ascribed to qualities that remain in place (Europe remains scientific, its Others natural) so Foucault's positive grouping of various 'primitives' rather dangerously, in strategic terms, apparently makes the non-Western to some extent another name for *madness*, a madness that Western scientific subjectivity has excluded but that continues to haunt it, and may yet be revitalized through what appears to be completion going under the name of interruption. There is more than merely circumstantial evidence of such a perspective at work in Foucault's texts. Indeed, we might simply remember that despite the vagueness of Foucault's pronouncements on 'race' and colonialism, his work has been perhaps the most significant influence on postcolonial theory. The lacuna just mentioned might explain his work's occasional primitivism. Robert Young tentatively suggests that, 'Foucault's work appears to be so scrupulously Eurocentric that you begin to wonder whether there isn't a deliberate strategy involved'.[38] Paul Gilroy, on the other hand, suggests that Foucault's analysis of the emergence of Man, whilst being suggestive, remains incomplete in its exclusion of racial and colonial thinking: 'The human and the infrahuman emerged together, and "race" was the line between them'.[39] Rey Chow, in the context of an autobiographical text thematising autobiography, subjectivity and identity politics in postcolonial studies, writes that, 'If Man is a historical invention, it is because he is a Western invention, which relies for its inventiveness – its "originality" so to speak – on the debasement and exclusion of others'.[40] Homi Bhabha suggests a further development of this argument:

> The dehistoricized authority of man and his doubles produces, in the same historical period, those forces of naturalization that create a modern Western disciplinary society. The invisible power that is invested in this dehistoricized figure of Man is gained at the cost of those 'others' – women, natives, the colonized, the indentured and enslaved – who, at the same time but in other spaces, were becoming 'the peoples without a history'.[41]

Bhabha actually discusses this omission in terms of a *disavowal*. Foucault, in this reading, is insistent on identifying Descartes as originary, but simultaneously refuses to name subjectivation's material supplements: the long, brutal histories of colonial domination.[42] That Bhabha should choose to write in psychoanalytic terms about Foucault, who places such an emphasis on the psychoanalytic institution's constitutive role in disciplinary society, is not accidental. It is not that Bhabha simply ignores the status of psychoanalysis; in fact, Bhabha's emphasis implies a necessary impurity in Western subjectivity. It would appear that Foucault's account of the emergence of biopolitics places too great an emphasis on constructing a certain sovereign subjectivity, without perhaps recognizing the impurity of that subject, its originarily compromised nature. So, Foucault insists, for instance, on a transition from a *symbolics of blood* to an *analytics of sexuality* ...[43] Fundamentally for the argument, Descartes's text, conceived by Foucault as speech act, is assumed to be simply successful, to do what it describes, so to constitute an impermeably framed pure presence that can be resisted only from a nominal outside. Fundamentally, then, Foucault maintains an almost silent reliance on a narrative of Western philosophical performance, in which Descartes and Kant are positioned consistently. This narrative implies that the absolute otherness of madness, seemingly permeating reason in Foucault's works after the history of madness, has merely been displaced.[44]

Even on its own terms, however, Foucault's account of the emergence of biopolitics clearly is not so simple. Both thematically and formally, in Foucault's writing it is not simply the case that the importance of the Cartesian subject as a Western ideological construct (as specific to an epoch, age, space or even class) is displaced. And yet there is a gesture of this kind to be found in some of his texts, and many interviews.[45] By comparison, Nietzsche's writing produces its own staging of the genealogist, one that Foucault obscures in his ironic obliteration of the writing subject, a subject that seems to surface only to comment precisely on this obliteration. I want to consider the kind of reaction to Foucault that is exemplified by the articulatory position in Edward Said's *Orientalism*, how that position contests a facelessness of Foucault's archaeology, and also how it reproduces certain problems. I also want to consider the kind of choice that Said makes between Foucault and Derrida, a choice that seems to be a moral rather than theoretical choice. Of course there are specific consequences for his work (and the work of others) deriving from that choice.

Said on ideas of textuality

The specific nature of Said's choice is interesting in the context of this book's argument. In simple terms, taken directly from his work, Said sees Foucault moving in and out of the text, Derrida moves in but not out. This reading comes from a particular period of Derrida's English language reception, and has similarities with many other readings of that time. But this reading has also had lasting significance, because Derrida's influence on postcolonial studies remains a particular point of controversy. During a discussion of Derrida's influence on postcolonial studies, Bart Moore-Gilbert suggests that,

> It seems to me a grave misfortune that the attitude towards Derrida in a lot of postcolonial criticism [...] has been so influenced by Said's derivative account of him in *The World, the Text and the Critic* rather than by engagement with his actual writings.[46]

Although Said's account in *The World* is familiar, it is derivative to the extent only that it assumes the truth of Foucault's 'My Body, this Paper, this Fire',[47] which is cited but not discussed in the earliest form of the essay, and discussed only briefly in the revised and expanded book version. Moore-Gilbert does not specify the source of Said's derivations, although the works of Frederic Jameson and Terry Eagleton are possibilities. 'Criticism Between Culture and System' was originally published in a similar form as 'The Problem of Textuality',[48] representing a systematic response to both Foucault and Derrida, and one that is at times as critical of Foucault as it is of Derrida. Said has taken the time to read Derrida, and, importantly, to translate him for the 1978 version, so reading his interpretation may help explain how and why he rewrites genealogy, and why he denies himself resources found in Derrida's work, opting instead for a selective interpretation of Foucault.

One immediate response to Said's interpretation would be that it consistently misrepresents Derrida and, to some extent, Foucault. It might seem that, despite the force of the concept of 'worldliness', the very title *The World, the Text and the Critic* clearly states a spatial division inherent in the critic's role. 'The Problem of Textuality' was renamed 'Criticism Between Culture and System'. The spatial conceptualization is overburdened: the implication that to oppose one kind of system (the sovereign theoretical system) is necessarily to oppose the other (political system) is hardly self-evident, even on its own terms, a point with clear relevance to dismissals of dialectical thinking. Said's spatial language guides the essay, and as is well known he concludes his introduction by asserting that, 'Derrida's criticism therefore moves us *into* the text, Foucault's *in* and *out* of it'.[49] More importantly for my context, Said explicitly refers to a *de-definitional* action of Derrida's writing: 'Derrida's page become[s] the apparently self-sufficient site of a critical reading in which traditional texts, authors, problems, and themes are presented in order to be dedefined and dethematicized more or less permanently'.[50] This permanence seems to be, as Said himself implicitly concedes, rather less than permanent. It is possible to read, for example, Derrida's *Monolingualism of the Other* as an exemplary instance of the impermanence of this de-definition, at least when it comes to questions of identity. Of course, it might be objected that Derrida is reacting to a particular lack or inadequacy in his earlier writing. I want to undermine that particular developmental model by showing how de-definition and re-definition are presupposed by Derrida's works in general. It can be persuasively argued that all of the features of Derrida's later writings can be found in his earliest and most programmatic texts. While this may seem to institute a different developmental model, it can also be to see an uncanny presence in his thought. De-definition is not even really named in Derrida's writing; in fact I am locating its virtual presence as a way of understanding his reception and its importance for postcolonial theory.

This de-definition may be approached through Said's translation of Derrida. The essay was published at a certain point in Derrida's Anglophone reception, with many of the major early texts at that time being un-translated. Said, as professor of comparative literature, gives his own translations in foot-notes. Following his introduction, he quotes from 'La Pharmacie de Platon', identifying 'jamais' as the problematic word structuring his reading of Derrida: 'La loi et la règle ne s'abritent pas dans l'inaccessible d'un secret, simple-ment elles ne se livrent jamais, au *présent*, à rien qu'on puisse rigoureusement nommer une perception.' Said translates as follows: 'Its law and its rule do not merely shelter themselves inside something so inaccessible as a secret, because they quite simply do not ever give themselves up, at present at least, to anything that we might rigorously call a perception'.[51] Said's understand-ing of Derrida is not reducible to mis-translation, and it is impossible to make of this moment an origin; however, 'au *présent*' is not 'at present' but 'in the present', and so 'into a moment of presence' or 'into presence'. This moment suggests a complex of metaphors that return to destabilize Said's arguments here and elsewhere. The sense of 'jamais' is obviously signifi-cantly different in relation to these two translations. Law and rule are never delivered into presence. Barbara Johnson's translation as 'Plato's Pharmacy', in *Dissemination*, offers the following translation: 'Its law and its rules are not, however, harbored in the inaccessibility of a secret; it is simply that they can never be booked, in the *present*, into anything that could rigorously be called a perception'.[52] Aside from the translation of 'livrent' as 'booked', offering almost a mocking reference to the misconception that, for Derrida, everything happens in books, this rendering places the due emphasis on the status of that present. Said's translation unintentionally brackets the ques-tion of temporality, leading to certain effects on his work as a whole, and these effects may be found in postcolonial theory generally. It's not that law and rule do not exist, are never present, not if that means we are free to make it up as we go along, with reference only to desire and contingency: again, this point is crucial to any understanding of autobiographical theory. It is that the points of reference are not absolutely justifiable, but there are nonetheless points of reference, and as any autobiographical theory insists upon, we do not parachute into a critical context from some strictly utopian location.

We can read Said's translation for its continuing relevance, despite the fact that it is replaced by Johnson's in 'Criticism Between Culture and System'. Presumably Said approves of Johnson's translation, and is not quoting it solely because it is widely available by this point, as he makes neither modification nor comment; additionally, his commentary is effectively unchanged. Again Said notes the qualifications to 'jamais', and again he asserts that, 'I shall ignore the qualifiers and retain the obvious assertiveness of the statement'.[53] These qualifiers are, however, important. In the first version of his essay, 'jamais' is 'rather' troublesome, in the second it is only 'probably': the difference this change makes is difficult to pinpoint. More clearly, in the first version Said has Derrida qualifying 'jamais' 'so subtly', and in the second Derrida 'so trickily': these are not innocent terms, and the change has clear evaluative implications. In either version of the essay it is difficult to understand why these qualifiers only 'partly' lessen the 'interdictory force' of the paragraph. Cautiously following Said we could assume that we know what is being proscribed, despite the many indications that Said has chosen to ignore central aspects of the argument. In Said's own terms, the following from Derrida undermines his argument: 'And hence, perpetually and essentially, they run the risk of being definitively lost. Who will ever know of such disappearances?'[54] Risks are being run, a call is sent out: the rhetoric stages a situation to which we need to be attentive. Said's criticism is derived from moral dissatisfaction with an inferred model of intellectual responsibility. In maintaining the supposed interdictory force of the first paragraph Said implies a certain resignation in Derrida's text. He might even be detecting a joy, for such resignation appears to always be on the verge of celebration: there might seem to be a joy at the loss of the law and rules of the text, a joy at being able to impose reading on the text.

The essay continues to read a certain attempted, although still apparently inadequate, reconstruction of these rules in Foucault. It is arguable that Said has misread both Derrida and Foucault, but clearly a choice has been made, specific reductions have occurred, and both choice and reductions are explicit. It may be tempting to trace certain anti-theoretical aspects of postcolonial studies to Said's choice, but this would emphasize many problems. Obviously Foucault is not anti-theoretical, despite the implications of certain extrapolations of his thought.[55] To suggest otherwise ignores not only the general tenor of his reception, but also the specific debates with which his work engages. Accordingly, criticism of Said's work, especially *Orientalism*, has often focused on the various epistemological problems associated, rightly or wrongly, with post-structuralism. It is not that Foucault has been appropriated uncritically in postcolonial studies. What might be identified in Said's discussion of Foucault and Derrida is a certain misrecognition of the debate, leading to a misreading of both. It is this misreading which is woven into the most minute textures of postcolonial studies, and which needs to be very carefully considered if we are to get anywhere thinking about autobiography in postcolonial theory.

Accordingly, further close theoretical reading is necessary. Approaching the debate on *Histoire de la folie* from the perspective of postcolonial criticism, it initially appears that the most telling criticisms of *Orientalism* repeat those made by Derrida of Foucault. These criticisms, which are the more important aspects of 'Cogito and the History of Madness', concern the generality of reason. Really, Foucault short-circuits the debate through his appeal to supposedly decisive empirical detail. It might even be argued that because Foucault chooses to reply to Derrida concerning the minutiae of Descartes's text, he is in a sense conceding the force of Derrida's argument: it is as if the letter of the philosophical text does indeed have a certain privilege, at least in this context. This is arguable, and clearly part of the force of Foucault's response derives from its over-literal mimicry of philosophical argument, its assertion that it not only masters Derrida philosophically, but also then diminishes just that philosophy. Concerning the other aspects of Derrida's paper, Foucault implicitly (and significantly) brackets the question of the generality of reason. In addition, it is not clear that Foucault justifies or even makes explicit the criteria that allow the appropriation of Descartes's text in this way. Similarly, it has been asserted that the choice of examples in *Orientalism* is governed by the common-sense force of the structures of orientalist discourse, rather than by any theoretical principles. It can therefore be argued that Derrida is asking the questions about history which Foucault and Said need to answer. This returns us to the argument about the projection of otherness operating in Foucault's text.

Of course questions about history are precisely the ones that Said criticizes Derrida for avoiding:

> What [Derrida's] readings of a text are meant to uncover is silent complicity between the superstructural pressures of metaphysics and an ambiguous innocence about a detail at the level of base. [...] Yet the mediating agency between the level of detail and the superstructural level is neither referred to nor taken into account.[56]

Said's question is simple: why does Derrida choose *these* texts? The logic of exemplarity is called into question. He argues that Derrida cannot do without a certain notion of intention. He must believe that these texts were significant for their authors. This is not saying much, but because Said leaves these concepts unexamined (or rather brackets the result of such examination) he assumes that their implicit presence compromises Derrida's argument. It is necessary to return to the specifics of Derrida's discussion of Rousseau, where we can say that he does not ask exactly the questions suggested by Said's gloss. Derrida argues the following:

> 3. In Rousseau's text, after having indicated—by anticipation and as a prelude—the function of the sign 'supplement,' I now prepare myself to give special privilege, in a manner that some might consider exorbitant, to certain texts like the *Essay on the Origin of Languages* and other fragments on the theory of language and writing. By what right? And why these short texts, published for the most part after the author's death, difficult to classify, of uncertain date and inspiration?

> To all these questions and within the logic of their system, there is no satisfying response. In a certain measure and in spite of the theoretical precautions that I formulate, my choice is in fact *exorbitant.*[57]

Said quotes Spivak's translation, as given above. An important focus has to be on Said's understanding of Derrida's use of 'exorbitant'. Spivak leaves this as 'exorbitant'. The rhetorical force of the passage requires a nuanced reading, as Derrida seems to declare his choice 'exorbitant' *in opposition* to 'que certains' who also find it 'exorbitant'. This is more than a doubling, repetition with variation. Said reads it as repetition, and so neglects the consequent argument. Derrida initially uses 'exorbitant' in something like an everyday sense of 'outrageous'; otherwise the argument is confusing, in precisely the way Said suggests. The second 'exorbitant' might be glossed as 'deviating' (or 'leaving', to minimize evaluative connotations) from the norm ('traditional' paths, so giving the sense of *pioneering*). To an extent there must be interplay between these meanings in both uses, and the sense of 'excessive' inflects both, with both positive and negative charge implications. To leave these two uses of 'exorbitant' unexamined is to allow a reading in which Derrida *escapes* into the outrageous.

Escape in this context is clearly from responsibility. Said criticizes Derrida's sense of 'privilégier' as 'his escape'. He continues: 'What Derrida is really asking himself is whether what he does and whether the texts he has chosen for his analysis of Rousseau have anything to do with Rousseau, what Rousseau did or intended to do, or not'.[58] The statement is intended as provocation: Derrida's meditations are dismissed, in favour of what he *really* thought, which is of course what Said claims Derrida is doing with Rousseau. It might be argued that Derrida's 'exorbitance' of method is both an 'excess' and a 'deviation' in which the marginal is given attention hitherto denied it. This is a standard comment on Derrida's method, allowed for by Derrida: 'there is no satisfying response'. Yet Said should recognize that the exorbitance – the excess – that Derrida brings to these texts belies the notion of the 'réponse satisfaisante', at least in the loosely humanist sense which informs *The World*. Said's analysis breaks off at this point, and he does not explicitly discuss Derrida's continuing meditation in the very next paragraph. Said's analysis therefore becomes detached from its object, because Derrida's very next sentence is, '*But what is the exorbitant?*'

A further possible meaning of 'exorbitant' that Said considers but finds problematic is 'from exteriority'. Said wonders how Derrida could be exterior to logocentrism. There is no discussion of the essay 'Structure, Sign, and Play' in 'The Problem of Textuality', which might explain Said's misunderstanding. Even so, the reach of metaphysics is clearly signalled throughout *Of Grammatology* itself. Said cannot allow the persistence of logocentrism to coexist with Derrida's claims for his method, and assumes that Derrida is covertly and simplistically ascribing intention to Rousseau. Because of this assumption, Said retains the assumption that to deconstruct a pervasive historicism is to deny history altogether. Said makes some reference to 'My Body, This Paper, This Fire', where he hastily assumes that Foucault has answered all questions regarding *his* method. This reading is rather cursory compared with Said's reading of Derrida, whose reflections on method are understood to be superficial. But this cannot be accepted, if we continue with Derrida:

> I wished to reach the point of a certain exteriority in relation to the totality of the age of logocentrism. Starting from this point of exteriority, a certain deconstruction of that totality which is also a traced path, of that orb (*orbis*) which is also orbitary (*orbita*), might be broached. The first gesture of this departure and this deconstruction, although subject to a certain historical necessity, cannot be given methodological or logical intra-orbitary assurances. Within the closure, one can only judge its style in terms of the accepted oppositions (OG,161,231)

There is clear reference to 'une *certaine* extériorité' [italic added]; although the following sentence refers without qualification to 'ce point d'extériorité', this point is clearly the same point. The passage progresses to some form of answer to its initial question, and attention must again be given to the play on *orbis/orbita*. It is clear that Derrida's method derives no authority from 'des assurances méthodologiques ou logiques intraorbitaires'. This position is a singular form of exteriority that Derrida demands of himself (rather, demands that he honour) as his point of departure. The lengthy theorization of this departure point marks a difference between Foucault and Derrida (at least the texts in question), for it could be argued that Foucault's understanding of Derrida's term 'writing' is inadequate, and that Said inherits this understanding, converting it into the spatial language mentioned earlier. When Derrida continues, suggesting that, 'It may be said that this style is empiricist and in a certain way that would be correct', the qualification is again, for Said, sufficiently weak to be overridden. But it is an important qualification. The manner in which this method is empiricist is important, because it is not empiricist in any straightforward sense. It is explicitly stated that, 'The departure is radically empiricist'; more fully, and famously, Derrida writes that,

> We must begin *wherever we are* and the thought of the trace, which cannot not take the scent into account, has already taught us that it was impossible to justify a point of departure absolutely. *Wherever we are*: in a text where we already believe ourselves to be. (OG,162)

> [Il faut commencer *quelque part où nous sommes* et la pensée de la trace, qui ne peut pas ne pas tenir compte du flair, nous a déjà enseigné, qu'il était impossible de justifier absolument un point de départ. *Quelque part où nous sommes*: en un texte déjà où nous croyons être. (OG,233)]

This appears to be an almost impossible thought, beyond the sense Derrida has already suggested, and perhaps not one we could comfortably or easily call a thought of autobiography. It is, in a sense, the denial of specificity, while being simultaneously the affirmation that all we can ever hope for is the more or less persuasively presented instance or example, all of which will be autobiographical.[59] Said finds these quasi-justifications, on the impossibility of final justification, to be unpersuasive. His position is that Derrida needs to outline a system despite the careful meditation on system and method (despite Said's own opposition to sovereign thought), and further suggests that Derrida is somehow *lapsing* into reliance on intention. According to this argument, Derrida a-historically inserts examples into an already complete generalization. From such a perspective, Derrida has a system just as powerful and all consuming as Hegel, for only the most obvious example. His reading is directed toward certain goals, with the consequence that historical dimensions of the texts in question are lost. This of course was a very familiar response to Derrida's writing for a long time. But as Julian Wolfreys has recently reminded us, Derrida's reading method is a most peculiar one, by many common sense standards. While cautioning us about the specificity of his example, Wolfreys reminds us of the moment in *Glas* when Derrida puts forward the idea of the dredging machine as figure for reading, about which we must remember the following: 'we do not have complete control over what is being dredged/read [and] the machine grasps what it will, leaving other matter behind, despite our place behind the controls'.[60] Accordingly, we will never be done with reading, and our points of departure are never quite as subjective and partial as we might think, whether we think that this subjective or partial quality is positive or negative.

In any case, *Of Grammatology* consistently implies, and in this section explicitly argues, that the point of departure just is where it is; it is therefore no surprise that it has seemed a most dangerous method. 'This avowal of empiricism can sustain itself only by the strength of the question', and it is the unavoidability (for philosophers) of the question which is suggested by the fact that, 'No other trace is available' (OG,162). In the instance of *Of Grammatology* the question is, it might be argued, the question of questions, and Derrida explicitly proceeds to focus the argument in the following paragraph. However, in the context of the meditation on empiricism that has immediately preceded this, it ought not to be surprising when the 'themes of themes' explanation is conflated with a form of intentionality: 'Thus Rousseau inscribes textuality in the text'. Although Said acknowledges that these questions of method are echoed in 'Cogito and the History of Madness', he is too quick to gloss these passages from '... That Dangerous Supplement ...' as confused rather than cautious. Said prefigures the tendency[61] to imply that these early Derrida texts are encumbered by pseudo-Nietzschean posturing. Despite Said's reading, we can see that Derrida makes careful distinctions in these passages, and again it must be stressed that the repetition of 'exorbitant' through this chapter needs to be closely read if we are not to misunderstand, 'The supplement itself is quite exorbitant, in every sense of the word' ['Le supplément lui-même est bien, à tous les sens de ce mot, exorbitant']. This last formulation demands that we at least re-read earlier passages.

Said's readings of these passages lead him to describe deconstruction in particular ways. A key literal meaning of 'exorbitant' is 'out of orbit'. The exorbitant is only something that is no longer (or was not ever) in thrall to a centre of gravity. The spatial aspects of this language cannot be used against Derrida, as if he is blind to the question of his own metaphors. Indeed, there is a knowing exorbitation of exorbitance throughout not only this sequence, but the text as a whole. In contrast, Said's characterization of deconstruction seems rather carelessly metaphorical: it is a, 'military operation. ...[An] attack on a party of colonialists'.[62] Robert Young, for one, has characterized post-structuralism as the 'decolonization of western thought', but the emphasis is rather different. Said's rhetoric conjures a peculiarly out-of-place anti-imperialism, and a rather clear-cut space for the worldly critic. For Said, it is in this sharply defined space of opposition that Derrida is lacking; however, that space cannot be so sharply defined, and Young, following Derrida, acknowledges the banality that conceptual decolonization is a process of self-knowing.

It is not that Said ever argues simply for the occupation of a pure oppositional space, but it is evident that the problems for Said's oppositional critic cannot be circumvented by straightforward spatial concepts. As already mentioned, Said does not discuss 'Structure, Sign, and Play', and perhaps that essay might clarify some of the questions being posed. Said does consider this paper elsewhere, briefly but revealingly in *Beginnings*.[63] There is lengthy consideration of the literary-critical sense of its own justificatory moment or space. It is an intricately argued text, but the passages on Derrida must complicate Said's sense of his own beginnings. The following passage is exemplary of Said's argument, and the later essay on Foucault and Derrida confirms this exemplarity. Said is giving a programmatic summary at this point in the text:

> Two kinds of beginning emerge, really two sides of the same coin. One, which I will call temporal and transitive, foresees a continuity that flows from it. This kind of beginning is suited for work, for polemic, for discovery [...] There is always a danger of too much reflection on beginnings. [...] In attempting to push oneself further and further back to what it only a beginning, one is caught in a tautological circuit of beginnings about to begin. This is the other kind of beginning, the one I call intransitive and conceptual. It is very much a creature of the mind, very much a bristling paradox, yet also very much a figure of thought that draws special attention to itself. Its existence cannot be doubted, yet its pertinence is wholly to itself. Because it truly cannot be known, because it belongs more to silence than it does to language, because it is what has always been left behind, and because it challenges continuities that go cheerfully forward with *their* beginnings obediently affixed – it is therefore

something of a necessary fiction. It is perhaps our permanent concession to an ungraspable absolute. (B,76–7)

Despite my ellipses, the form of this passage remains intact in a way that will elucidate Said's reading of 'Structure, Sign, and Play'. The rhetoric implies a criticism of this second position that works against the passage's even-handed approach. The text performs a certain intoxication that seems to be intrinsic to the 'intransitive' beginning. Despite warning of a *danger* in this second form (which implicitly is the first turned in on itself), the rhetoric builds this intoxication through a seductive rhythm to the melodramatic climactic suggestion. If we return to the start of the second paragraph, however, our attention is directed towards 'what is *only* a beginning' [italics added], a notable emphasis for a book entitled *Beginnings*. This is part of Said's rhetoric that argues that the second form of beginning is a kind of unfortunate circle that must be broken to achieve the first form (in order to perform, as is stated, useful tasks). The intransitive beginning is no beginning at all, as nothing is begun. Rather, all that is begun is itself: it is 'a bristling paradox', and because intransitive it of course begins no action upon anything. In the present context, the implications of this thought of beginnings are far-reaching for Said's reading of Derrida. The performative intoxications of this description have a precise relation to the later reading of 'Structure, Sign, and Play'. Said argues that *jeu* forms no basis for a beginning, but the form of this argument is no straightforward dismissal.

Said's reading of 'Structure, Sign, and Play' builds to a conviction that a choice must be made. This conviction builds throughout the 'Abecedarium Culturae' sequence, which discusses structuralism. Said writes that, 'like Nietzsche's outpouring of philosophy that is already in the throes of self-destruction, Derrida's writing converts the principles of structuralism into surreal, large objects, whose overaccurate relationship to the original versions mocks them, overwhelms them, plays havoc with them'(B,340). What is interesting here is Said's appropriation of Derrida *against* structuralism. Said elaborates Foucault's position at length before detouring via Derrida to emerge with the distinct possibility of choosing between the two interpretations of interpretation. It is well known that Derrida argues the following:

> For my part, although these two interpretations must acknowledge and accentuate their difference and define their irreducibility, I do not believe that today there is any question of *choosing*—in the first place because here we are in a region (let us say, provisionally, historicity) where the category of choice seems particularly trivial; and in the second, because we must first try to conceive of the common ground, and the *différance* of this irreducible difference.[64]

Despite his earlier caveats regarding 'two sides of the same coin', Said ignores Derrida's stress in this passage on common ground. Said explicitly argues that

Derrida's conclusions are incorrect, and the impossibility of finally distinguishing these two phenomena is lost. Said's conclusion about Derrida serves to confirm a supposedly Foucauldian perspective. It's possible to understand the moves Said is making by looking at other readings from this same section of *Beginnings*. In particular, if we look at the discussion of Lévi-Strauss, particularly on pp.336–337, we find a standard account of the structuralist anthropologist that illuminates Said's position: 'Outside the society stands an observer who notes constants ...' A straightforward statement of Said's reading of Derrida would say that Derrida denies himself criteria for judgment by refusing this model, and this is Said's basic conclusion regarding Derrida's work. By contrast, for Said, Foucault makes the choice that Derrida refuses: if we follow Foucault, we move in and then out of the text, and are able to take exterior positions of critical distance. But we've already seen that such a choice can never be absolutely justified, once and for all, and this is what we need to recall, particularly in the context of thinking about autobiographical theory, which continually poses the question of the interior and exterior of any text or even situation as such.

To get a clearer sense of how autobiographical theory is inflected by the supposed choice between Derrida and Foucault of course requires a closer look at Foucault's work, especially when so many aspects of that work are resistant to the kind of reading put forward by Said. Said's is a difficult argument to pursue when faced with Foucault's work pre-1975, or many elements of its reception. To get a clear sense of the issues, we ought to explore Foucault's explicitly theoretical texts, and the function that these texts assign themselves in relation to Foucault's other work, particularly his early studies in psychiatry and the clinic. I will focus the following reading around the following assertion from the introduction to *The Archaeology of Knowledge*: 'I am no doubt not the only one who writes in order to have no face'.[65] We should not literalize Foucault's statement, at least not immediately,[66] but at the same time it is a potent formulation set against Said's own position, which tends to preserve the individual genius, whether that of the artist or poet, and the genealogist.[67] If Said, as many critics have suggested, attempts to marry incompatible discourses, then those critics repeat his mistake. For example, Aijaz Ahmad argues in detail that Foucault's strict observance of discursive boundaries is jettisoned in *Orientalism*, which contains inevitable recourse to certain 'Western' conceptions of subjectivity. Without directly engaging Foucault, Ahmad proceeds to assume that Said is in effect a lapsed Marxist. Ahmad has two questions: first, is Said, as he claims (although it is clear that this representation of Said is unsympathetic), in any meaningful sense the 'Oriental subject'? and second, is anyone solely constituted by the facts of orientalism, colonialism or postcolonialism? These are pertinent questions, but they do not and cannot engage with Foucault's text, because the order of discourse is in a different space and a different time, its specificity to be respected.

The question of this order's specificity is the focus of *The Archaeology of Knowledge*, raised in the introduction and constantly addressed throughout.

That the introduction details a new history of discontinuity and irruption, which might casually be associated with Foucault, should not elide the differences that Foucault will elaborate. Although Foucault asserts that this new history has freed itself from traditional history, and that its problems intersect with those of structuralism, his own warnings about generalization should remind us of his plentiful assertions of distance between his work and structuralism. The relationship between this history of irruptions and archaeology is carefully nuanced, and signs of distance are evident in the introduction. Tracing the new history back at least as far as Marx, Foucault asserts that its effects have been delayed: 'As if we were afraid to conceive of the *Other* in the time of our own thought'(AK,12). Importantly, continuous history would form a shelter for the unified subject. He continues by asserting that, upon writing discontinuous history,

> One will be denounced for attacking the inalienable rights of history and the very foundations of any possible historicity. But one must not be deceived: what is being bewailed with such vehemence is not the disappearance of history, but the eclipse of that form of history that was secretly, but entirely related to the synthetic activity of the subject. (AK,14)

To fully eliminate the unified subject, it will be necessary to move beyond not only continuous history, but also beyond a sense that the *synthetic* subject could be incorporated within discontinuous history. Said's *Orientalism*, in its recourse to notions of genius and the power of the individual, accordingly seems to fall into certain traditional forms of narrative. The important point is that Foucault's order of discourse is of a different order to such notions. This is not to say that it is hermetic, but that mapping of one level on to the other, transition between discourse and historical acts, is complex and needs careful consideration each time. For example, it is worth stating that discourse is itself material, as seen for example when philosophy is interpreted as speech act. However, a speech act's announced or apparent intention is not guaranteed merely by announcement, and indeed the mapping will often have been incomplete, the act ineffective or productive of something unpredictable and unexpected. This caveat about the mapping of discourse onto history means that the subject who announces the intention of a speech act ought to be put to one side. That Foucault is bracketing the subject is stated throughout *The Archaeology*, even if it is still clear that the delineation of discourse will ideally transform what he defines as 'humanist' notions:

> These pre-existing forms of continuity [the book, the œuvre, etc.], all these syntheses that are accepted without question, must remain in suspense. They must not be rejected definitively of course, but the tranquility with which they are accepted must be disturbed... (AK,25)

Of course this leaves open the question of just how long these ideas will remain in suspension, or how much the tranquility of their acceptance should be disturbed, and there have been varied answers from those who have written after Foucault: for example, we can sense that postcolonial criticism is one form of theory that has re-energized these forms of continuity, particularly the anti-colonial agent or subject.

Foucault continues by suggesting that he wants to free the questions these forms pose, to ask why they should appear self-evident, and whether or not they should they be maintained or replaced. Such a suggested questioning is perhaps rather modest in scope, and when reading *The Archaeology of Knowledge* it is difficult to ignore its persistent rhetoric of modesty. There is the sense that it was a difficult text to compose, and Foucault refers to, 'the cautious, stumbling manner of this text'(AK,17). However, it is not long before the objections to his work, which are initially made to seem insurmountable, are overcome by Foucault's arguments, as Foucault's staged presence in the text always 'knew' they would be: it is of course a *rhetoric* of modesty. Foucault's dismissal of what comes 'before', of what must already be there, is at the least problematic. For Derrida, the beyond of metaphysics is not an absolute beyond, and certainly not a temporal beyond in a simplistic way. According to Derrida, we must continue to ask questions *of* presence, but we must ask in a different way: 'In the openness of this question *we no longer know*. This does not mean that we know nothing but that we are beyond absolute knowledge'.[68] Conversely, Foucault's drive to create new terminology at the close of 'the age of Man' apparently strives to take us into a time without time, external to that of Western philosophical discourse.[69] This perspective comes through in Said's most Foucauldian writing, in which several questions remain unanswered. There is an absolute spatial and temporal non-superposability of discursivity and the traditionally historical subject: 'The time of discourse is not the translation, in a visible chronology, of the obscure time of thought'(AK,122). Later Foucault would probably give a very different emphasis to 'thought'. In *The Archaeology*, the quoted assertion could be understood to mean that the order of discourse is not simply a new way of thinking about thought. This loses the temporal stress, which suggests an absolute disruption of perceived orders of continuity. When in section 5 of the 'Archaeological Description' chapter, Foucault answers questions about archaeology and the temporal, there is a weary tone: to ask 'does archaeology freeze change?' is fundamentally to misrecognise his enterprise. The conclusion to *The Archaeology* clarifies the situation, helping us to understand his asserted *will-to-lose-face*. He once again identifies the question of the subject as the barely hidden cause of any controversy surrounding his methods: 'for the moment, and as far ahead as I can see, my discourse, far from determining the locus in which it speaks, is avoiding the ground on which it could find support'(AK,205). Of course Foucault writes from his own constrained position, but he counters that positivities just are what enable any expression whatsoever. Homi Bhabha understands Foucault's recognition in this passage as enabling a transformed historical postcolonial agency.[70] He asks, 'What is that fear which makes you seek, beyond all boundaries, ruptures, shifts, and divisions, the great historico-transcendental destiny of the Occident?'(AK,210). Concluding that there must be a political reason for this fear, Foucault breaks off. However, it's possible to see the politics motivating this fear in many responses to postcolonial criticism, including responses to the autobiographical tendencies animating its theoretical development. Once again Aijaz Ahmad's writing will be an invaluable example.

Postcolonial personalism

Ahmad's criticisms of Said are provoked by the theoretical problems of *Orientalism*, but Ahmad's arguments do not really engage with Foucault. Ahmad discusses Said's later work, which moves away from Foucault, with greater interest and facility than the earlier work. This emphasis is unsurprising, and so Ahmad does not examine Foucault's position on Marxism, particularly Marxism's continuity with bourgeois economics. There is a much clearer grasp of the stakes involved in the confrontation between Marxism and humanism than between Marxism and post-structuralism. The notorious *ad hominem* attacks in his writing accompany his dismissal of postmodern or post-structuralist theory. Within the schema of Young's *White Mythologies*, Ahmad's arguments place him alongside Frederic Jameson. Ahmad of course responded to Jameson's 'Third World Literature in the Era of Multinational Capitalism' by writing that, '[T]he man whom I had for so long, so affectionately, albeit from a physical distance, taken as a comrade was, in his own opinion, my civilizational Other. It was not a good feeling'.[71] The relationship between Ahmad and Jameson is complex, with their work predictably converging. More than that, Ahmad's curiously touching response to Jameson is where my investigation of postcolonial space and time again encounters the strange, non-theoretical theoretical moment that is the autobiographical moment. This particular instance of the autobiographical moment has its own context. Jameson's essay is a polemical piece written for an implicitly North American audience, while Ahmad's response is a critique of one form of what he calls the 'Three Worlds Theory'. Their views on history are essentially the same, but they clash over how to imagine the geospatial point of the intellectual's departure; we can use Foucault's work to get a clearer sense of this clash.

I have already argued that, for Foucault, the space and time of discourse are radically incommensurable with what Said, in *Orientalism*, calls geography and history. Foucault's discoveries are designed to transform traditional categories, to the point when history would occur within the space and time of archaeology, or what throughout *The Archaeology* becomes 'cartography': 'I accept that my discourse may disappear with the figure that has borne it so far'(AK,208). The transformation of traditional categories would collapse the authority of that figure, Foucault's discourse being borne by the discursive flux rather than the distant but distinct figure of the name. Again there is a feeling that Foucault desires the absolute break, a feeling that many critics have expressed, pointing to his emphasis on discontinuity and the epistemological rupture. If we re-approach the question via Foucault's other major theoretical statement from the beginning of the 1970s, 'The Order of Discourse', it is possible to situate this drive toward rupture more completely. Much of this paper is familiar from the longer work but there is an important concluding sequence on Jean Hyppolite and Hegel. This sequence – part of Foucault's inaugural address to the Collège de France – is a personal testament to one of his teachers. Foucault asserts that the order of discourse, 'is very unfaithful to the Hegelian logos'.[72] To whatever extent we limit Hegel to being a teleological philosopher, Foucault seems to be describing a radically different order to that of the dialectic, however mobile that is considered to be. However, Foucault continues:

> [T]o make a real escape from Hegel presupposes an exact appreciation of what it costs to detach ourselves from him. It presupposes a knowledge of how close Hegel has come to us, perhaps insidiously. It presupposes a knowledge of what is still Hegelian in that which allows us to think against Hegel; and an ability to gauge how much our resources against him are perhaps still a ruse which he is using against us, and at the end of which he is waiting for us, immobile and elsewhere.

While Foucault suggests that it may be impossible to be strictly Hegelian by now, he concedes that there remains a certain mobile percipience to the Hegelian text. Foucault's conclusion is a condensed and elliptical consideration of the nature and role of philosophy, which inevitably closes by thinking about the conjunction of history and the individual: '[I]f philosophy must begin as an absolute discourse, what about history? And what is this beginning which begins with a single individual, in a society, in a social class, and in the midst of struggles?' This is an intriguing end to the essay, and also raises again the question of mobility, both conceptual and by extension class, which of course is so often the real focus of discussion in the context of postcolonial critics. These forms of mobility perhaps too easily direct us toward Aijaz Ahmad once again. Ahmad objects to a certain privileging of the metropolitan intellectual, as we can see in the section of *Culture and Imperialism* called 'The voyage in and the emergence of opposition'. Ahmad finds a privilege associated with the exiled intellectual, a position he thinks is repeated in Salman Rushdie and Bhabha. Ahmad's indignation at Said, and to some extent Jameson, is presented as being provoked by metropolitan attempts to limit his own intellectual production. His own academic travels could be dismissed as marginal to his argument, but then he has insisted on the importance of such facts, and he is right to suggest that postcolonial theory must resisted identifying itself with the subaltern, a gesture about which Spivak is so indignant of course. Yet perhaps there is something in Said's conception of the intellectual that moves this argument into a more interesting and productive realm than the contestation of margins and centres. Earlier I suggested that some of Said's non-theoretical works provide searching perspectives on his theoretical texts, but of course the opposition between theory and non-theory is not easily maintained. The non-theoretical, like the autobiographical that this book considers, 'ruins' the theoretical, as Derrida might say. In the stirring conclusion to one of his 1993 Reith lectures, Said argues the following:

> For the intellectual an exilic displacement means being liberated from the usual career, in which 'doing well' and following in time-honored footsteps are the main milestones. Exile means that you are always going to be marginal, and that what you do as an intellectual has to be made up because you cannot follow a prescribed path. If you can experience that fate not as deprivation and as something to be bewailed, but as a sort of freedom, a process of discovery in which you do things according to your own pattern, as various interests seize your attention, and as the particular goal you set yourself dictates: that is a unique pleasure.[73]

Foucault empties genealogy of subjectivity to break from reason, and to refuse the stately progress or even onward rush of the dialectic. Here Said reinstates a particular kind of subjectivity toward roughly the same end, elevating the exile as a general category. His conception of a certain mobility of the intellectual is not a novel one, and cannot make up a system. It functions in Said's work by insinuating itself into the epistemological difficulties of *Orientalism*, providing a reckless mobility which matches that of literature. This mobility is both elusively enigmatic and, as is dictated by the general nature of the field, a material fact.[74] Foucault, finds a certain mobility in the Hegelian dialectic, and so obliterates all 'movement' in his writing. It is interesting, indeed, that Said finds such an obliteration operating in both Foucault's work and his perhaps most written about novelist, Joseph Conrad; in *Beginnings*, for example, Said compares Foucault's prose and *Heart of Darkness*, and suggests that both produce a 'dissolution of man in discourse'.[75] Nonetheless, whatever seems to be happening in theory or literature, there is we might say a world of difference between 'man' and 'author'. Accordingly, there is an everyday sense of the author that continues, and that Said wants to retain. In 'What was an author?', Molly Nesbit makes the following comment in response to Foucault: 'Authors function, whether the state of knowledge recognises their existence or not'.[76] This everyday functioning operates just as much in a theoretical context, and might well be that which Foucault requires for an un-deluded response to Hegel and Descartes. Against his response, Said insists on something like the everyday functioning of the author and the subject. Asha Varadharajan makes this point very clearly when she writes the following: 'Far from being empty, the place of the subject in Said's discourse is that of the postcolonial intellectual, one in which this intellectual can be at home with homelessness'.[77] However, this seeming paradox of postcolonial intellectual subjectivity requires careful philosophical positioning, and Said rejects arguably the most important theoretical resources to understand the persistence of subjectivity on which he insists. De-defining the theorizing subject will take us further into Derrida's work, which can help develop a thought of the subject as more than just empirical shell to be discarded once the theory is up and running, and a thought of thought as more than self-thinking and self-sustaining.

References

1. Foucault, 'Theatrum Philosophicum', in *Aesthetics, Method, & Epistemology* (London: Allen Lane, 1998), pp.358–359. Foucault argues that, 'In actuality, dialectics does not liberate differences; it guarantees, on the contrary, that they can always be recaptured. The dialectical sovereignty of the same consists in permitting differences to exist but always under the rule of the negative, as an instance of nonbeing. They may appear to be the successful subversion of the Other, but contradiction secretly consists in the salvation of identities' (p.358). Said discusses Deleuze in *Beginnings*, New York, Columbia University Press, 1975, p.378.
2. Parry, 'Signs of the Times', *Third Text* 28/29, p.6; Jameson, *Postmodernism or, the Cultural Logic of Late Capitalism* (London: Verso, 1991), p.344.
3. Chambers, 'Exposure, abeyance and dislocation', *Third Text* 31, 1994, p.109.
4. Easthope, 'Bhabha, hybridity and identity', *Textual Practice* 12(2), pp.341–348.
5. Derrida, *Paper Machine* (Stanford: Stanford University Press, 2005), p.165. See also the comments on dreams and responsibility, from the beginning of the next chapter.
6. Said's *Beginnings* (New York: Columbia University Press, 1975), constantly attends to Foucault's performance, the way his, 'prose, and concurrently his argument, makes us lose our grip on man' (287). Referring to the 'impersonal modesty' (294) of Foucault's prose, Said contends that, 'an intellectual event takes place, with a directness we normally associate not with words *meaning* something, but with words *saying* something' (314), which might well be read in terms of the performative.
7. Barthes, 'The Death of the Author', from *Image-Music-Text*, essays selected and translated by Steven Heath (London: Fontana, 1977), p.112. Refs. to IMT in the text.
8. In *Margins: Of Philosophy*, trans. A. Bass (London: Harvester Wheatsheaf, 1982).
9. In S. Sontag (ed.) *A Barthes Reader* (London: Cape, 1982). Further refs. to BR in the text.
10. Barthes, *Empire of Signs* trans. R. Howard (New York: Hill & Wang, 1982).
11. Barthes, *Roland Barthes by Roland Barthes,* trans. R. Howard (London: Macmillan, 1977), p.116.
12. In *A Critique of Postcolonial Reason* (Cambridge, MA: Harvard University Press, 1999), Spivak suggests that 'later' Barthes, 'in the name of going beyond semiotics, reinstates the geo-politically differentiated confessional subject' (341).
13. Moore-Gilbert, 'Western Autobiography and Colonial Discourse: the case of Rousseau's "Orientalism"', *Social Identities* 11(4) (July 2005), p.313.
14. I am thinking of T. S. Eliot's 'Tradition and the Individual Talent', from his *Critical Essays* (London: Faber & Faber, 1932), which puts forward an immensity of

tradition *simultaneously* quite able to incorporate the new, a thought comparable to the immobility of Barthes' Voltaire.

15. In P. Rabinow (ed.) *The Foucault Reader* (London: Penguin, 1984).

16. Foucault quotes Beckett's 'Texts for Nothing'; in *The Complete Short Prose 1929–1989* (New York: Grove Press, 1995): 'LEAVE, I was going to say leave all that. What matter who's speaking, someone said what matter who's speaking' (109).

17. *The Foucault Reader*, p.104.

18. *The Foucault Reader*, p.105.

19. Foucault, *The Order of Things*, trans. A.S. Smith (London: Tavistock, 1970), p.261.

20. Being, of course, the final words of *The Order of Things*, p.387.

21. Foucault, 'On the Genealogy of Ethics', in Paul Rabinow (ed.) *Ethics, Subjectivity and Truth* (London: Allen Lane, 1998), p.279. Further refs. to EST in the text.

22. Despite quoting Derrida's 'Cogito and the History of Madness', Sean Burke in *The Death and Return of the Author* (Edinburgh: Edinburgh University Press, 1998 [2nd Ed.]) mysteriously suggests that no-one has seriously taken Foucault up on his 'contemptuous' treatment of Descartes; this perhaps relates to Burke's argument that Derrida has not 'found a voice' (pp.170–171), an argument from an earlier phase of Anglophone reception of Derrida.

23. Derrida, for instance, finds Freud marking what Foucault explicitly calls a *pivotal* role in *Histoire de la folie*, operating as hinge, or pendulum; Derrida is, then, not exactly criticising any simplicity or contradiction in Foucault's treatment of such thinkers. See "'To Do Justice to Freud': The History of Madness in the Age of Psychoanalysis", *Critical Inquiry* 20 (Winter 1994), 227–266.

24. Žižek, 'Cogito as a Shibboleth' in Žižek (ed.) *Cogito and the Unconscious* (Durham: Duke University Press, 1998), p.6.

25. Žižek, *The Plague of Fantasies* (London: Verso, 1997), p.12.

26. Žižek, *The Plague of Fantasies*, pp.12–13.

27. Foucault, *Madness and Civilization*, trans. R. Howard (London: Tavistock, 1967), p.xi. Further refs. to MC in the text.

28. Derrida, 'Cogito and the History of Madness', in *Writing & Difference*, trans. A. Bass (Chicago: Chicago University Press, 1978).

29. Both in the above essay and in 'To Do Justice to Freud', in which he considers Foucault's insertion of Freud into various series.

30. Derrida, *Archive Fever: A Freudian Impression*, trans. E. Prenowitz (Chicago: Chicago University Press, 1996).

31. 'Une ligne de partage est tracée qui va bientôt rendre impossible l'expérience si familière à la Renaissance d'une Raison déraisonnable, d'une raisonnable Déraison. Entre Montaigne et Descartes un événement s'est passé: quelque chose qui concerne l'avènement d'une *ratio*.' (*Histoire de la folie* (Paris: Gallimard, 1972), p.58).

32. Derrida considers Freud's complex association and dissociation from this 'good' series in 'To Do Justice to Freud'.

33. Vergès, 'Creole Skin, Black Mask: Fanon and Disavowal', *Critical Inquiry* 23(3) (Spring 1997), pp.578–595.

34. See Lévi-Strauss, *The Savage Mind* [*La Pensée sauvage*] (London: Weidenfeld & Nicholson, 1966), with its misleading translated title.

35. Barthes, *Critical Essays* trans. R. Howard (Evanston: Northwestern University Press, 1972), p.165.

36. See *The Gift: The Form & Reason for Exchange in Archaic Societies* trans. W.D. Halls (London: Routledge, 1990), particularly the conclusion, where he suggests that, 'we can and must return to archaic society' (69).
37. Said, *Beginnings: Intention and Method* (New York: Columbia University Press, 1975), p.320.
38. Young, 'Foucault on Race and Colonialism', *New Formations* 25, 1995, pp.57–65.
39. Gilroy, *Between Camps: Race, Identity & Nationalism at the End of the Colour Line* (London: Allen Lane, 2000), p.44.
40. Chow, 'The postcolonial difference: lessons in cultural legitimation', *Postcolonial Studies* 1(2) pp.161–70.
41. 'In a Spirit of Calm Violence', in G. Prakash (ed.) *After Colonialism* (Princeton: Princeton University Press, 1995), p.328.
42. Bhabha focuses on the following from *The Order of Things*: 'There is a certain position in the Western *ratio* that was constituted in its history and provides a foundation for the relation it can have with all other societies, *even with the society in which it appeared*' (52; Bhabha's italics).
43. See Foucault, *The History of Sexuality: Volume One* trans. R. Hurley (London: Penguin, 1978), pp.148–49.
44. Robert Young's *White Mythologies* (London: Routledge, 1990), contends that after Derrida's critique, '[Foucault] could no longer postulate madness or the other as outside' (p.86); perhaps such a postulation is rather displaced or transformed.
45. See, for example, 'An Aesthetics of Existence' in L. Kritzman (ed.) *Politics Philosophy Culture* (New York and London: Routledge, 1988), pp.50–55.
46. Moore-Gilbert, *Postcolonial Theory* (London: Verso, 1997), p.163. For a concise example of such influence, see Bill Ashcroft and Pal Ahluwalia, *Edward Said* (London: Routledge, 2001), pp.22–23.
47. Foucault 'My Body, this Paper, this Fire', trans. G. Bennington, *Oxford Literary Review* 4(1), pp.9–28.
48. Said, 'The Problem of Textuality: Two Exemplary Positions', *Critical Inquiry* 4(4)(Summer 1978), 673–714.
49. Said, 'The Problem of Textuality: Two Exemplary Positions', p.674.
50. Said, 'The Problem of Textuality: Two Exemplary Positions', p.691.
51. Said, 'The Problem of Textuality: Two Exemplary Positions', p.674.
52. Derrida, *Dissemination* trans. B. Johnson (London: Athlone Press, 1981) p.63.
53. Said, 'The Problem of Textuality: Two Exemplary Positions', p.675.
54. Derrida, *Dissemination,* p.63.
55. These implications derive not only from what might seem the narrow case of Foucault's engagement with Derrida and their mutually contested sense of the significance and privilege of philosophy; they can also be derived from the implicit criticism of various aspects of the sciences Foucault analyses. This relates directly to the larger question of Foucault's attitude to the rational, which we might begin to answer through 'What Is Enlightenment?', reprinted in P. Rabinow (ed.) *The Foucault Reader* (London: Penguin, 1984). This question would return us to Derrida's 'Cogito and the History of Madness', and the debate on the *scope* and *other* of reason.
56. Said, 'The Problem of Textuality: Two Exemplary Positions', pp.678–679.
57. Derrida, *Of Grammatology*, trans. G. C. Spivak, (Baltimore: John Hopkins University Press, 1976). Further refs. to OG in the text.
58. Said, 'The Problem of Textuality: Two Exemplary Positions', p.679.

59. See also Robert Smith's *Derrida and Autobiography* (Cambridge: Cambridge University Press, 1995), discussed elsewhere; Smith writes that, 'To come (to say "I") is always to come from generality and to limit thereby, in a manner lacking method and application, lacking genealogical orientation, generality's functioning' (p.143).

60. Wolfreys, *Occasional Deconstructions* (New York: SUNY Press, 2004), p.29.

61. In, for example, Richard Rorty, *Essays on Heidegger and Others* (Cambridge: Cambridge University Press, 1991), pp.107–118.

62. Said, 'The Problem of Textuality: Two Exemplary Positions', p.683.

63. Said, *Beginnings: Intention and Method* (New York: Columbia University Press, 1975). Further refs. to B in the text.

64. Derrida, *Writing and Difference* trans. A. Bass (Chicago: Chicago University Press, 1978), p.293.

65. Foucault, *The Archaeology of Knowledge*, trans. A. Sheridan Smith (London: Tavistock, 1972) p.17. Further refs. to AK in the text.

66. See James Miller's *The Passion of Michel Foucault* (London: Flamingo, 1993). Miller approaches Foucault's work with the view that if there might be a single truth of Foucault then it can be found in a 'writing to efface'. The conclusion to *The Archaeology*'s introduction becomes, alongside the conclusion to *The Order of Things*, a statement of a directly personal nature. Miller quotes the following: 'One makes to oneself, in pleasure and in pain, confessions impossible to make to anyone else, and one writes books about them.' (cited, p.372).

67. In her *Critique of Postcolonial Reason* (1999), Spivak transforms Foucault's notion of subject-position into the (poetic) invention of the Postcolonial: 'If a figure makes visible the impossible, it also invites the imagination to transform the impossible into an experience, a rôle' (p.394).

68. Derrida, *Speech & Phenomena*, trans. D.B. Allison (Evanston: Northwestern University Press, 1973), p.103.

69. Elsewhere I discuss Spivak's criticism of Foucault and Deleuze, who to her lack a concept of ideology. To summarize: for Spivak, the straightforward supposed transcendence of the concept of ideology is a serious weakness that leads to a false transparency of the intellectual (Foucault's discussion of ideology in *The Archaeology* is evasive; also, see p.185 on political economy).

70. As indicated elsewhere, Bhabha finds this recognition tracing enabling a trans-formed historical postcolonial agency. See 'In a Spirit of Calm Violence', in G. Prakash (ed.) *After Colonialism* (Princeton: Princeton University Press, 1995), p.327.

71. 'Jameson's Rhetoric of Otherness and "National Allegory"', *In Theory* (London: Verso, 1992).

72. Foucault, 'The Order of Discourse', in Robert Young (ed.) *Untying the Text: A Post-Structuralist Reader*, (London: Routledge, 1981), p.74.

73. Said, *Representations of the Intellectual* (London: Vintage, 1994), p.46.

74. See Bruce Robbins, 'Secularism, Elitism, Progress and Other Transgressions: On Edward Said's "Voyage In", in *Cultural Readings of Imperialism: Edward Said and the gravity of history* (London: Lawrence & Wishart, 1997): '[T]he story of Third World intellectual migration has conferred a certain authority upon oppositional intellectuals in and from the First World, including many for whom the work of representing colonial and postcolonial experience must unequivocally *be* work, that is, cannot even be misperceived as a matter of simple identity. And all this

has been possible – this is the key point – because of the risky and unstable fusion of personal mobility and impersonal representativeness' (80). Robbins returns to similar themes when he links Spivak's reading of *Jane Eyre* with her criticism of 'chromatism'; see 'Soul Making: Gayatri Spivak on Upward Mobility', *Cultural Studies* (Jan 2003) 17(1), pp.1–26

75. *Beginnings* (New York: Columbia University Press, 1975), p.287. Said's first book was *Joseph Conrad and the Fiction of Autobiography* (Cambridge, MA: Harvard University Press, 1966), and he frequently returns to questions of narrative, framing, and subjectivity in Conrad: see, for example, 'Conrad: The Presentation of Narrative', in *The World, the Text and the Critic* (London: Faber & Faber, 1984).

76. Nesbit, 'What was an author?' in Seán Burke (ed.) *Authorship: From Plato to the Postmodern* (Edinburgh: Edinburgh University Press, 1995), p.256.

77. Varadharajan, *Exotic Parodies: Subjectivity in Adorno, Said, and Spivak* (Minneapolis: University of Minnesota Press, 1995), p.114.

4 Writing spirits autobiography

Preface

Writing about the place of the preface in the Hegelian philosophical system, Derrida wonders what it would be like if Hegel had only written prefaces, or if all his prefaces had been published in a single volume like Henry James's *The Art of the Novel.* In a moment of explicit Shandyism, Derrida further daydreams[1] that the preface to the *Greater Logic* somehow appears *in media res*, complicating our sense of the logic's beginnings, and disrupting its apparently serene progress. Prefaces signal the contingency and written-ness of the philosophical system, but the Hegelian system apparently dismisses these facts in favour of a sense of what Derrida calls a logic of *autoinsemination.* Such a system is what it is, prior to its setting down: it engenders itself. According to this understanding of philosophy, the writing of this system is merely an accident, and the need for its writing (with all such a need would imply, i.e. the incompleteness of any 'autoinsemination', requiring as it does supplementation) is explained away, writing imagined to be just empirical *husk*, as Derrida puts it. So, Derrida continues, 'Hegel never investigates in terms of writing the living circulation of discourse. He never interrogates the *exteriority*, or the repetitive autonomy, of that textual *remainder* constituted for example by a preface, even while it is semantically sublated within the encyclopedic logic.'[2] The preface is strictly supplementary, but as is well known any supplement has a dual quality in Derrida's work, being both an unnecessary addition and something that is necessary to fill a gaping hole in that which wants to be whole and fully present. According to the Hegelian system, a preface is an unnecessary remainder once the necessary philosophical work is gathered up by the dialectic. It is, however, also that which will always remain, a spectrality always there to be read, and something that guarantees readability. That is to say that contingency, surprise, and a certain kind of embeddedness are what enable any form of system that might wish to disclaim them, and they remain obscurely present within any such system. To argue this is to say more than that autobiography is always present in theory. It is also not quite to argue that theories are autobiographical, whatever their pretensions to universality: that would be too simple, misleading, and rather *irresponsible* in important ways.

Indeed, the very qualities of writing that so trouble philosophy have similar effects on autobiography, and it is this similarity that is so important to a consideration of the connections between autobiography and theory, especially perhaps postcolonial theory.

In the context of this similarity, it must also be remembered that Derrida's comments on Hegel are hardly a straightforward criticism of his system, even though many of his readings do appear to define a position contrary to Hegel's. When we read *Hegel After Derrida* we are immediately reminded that according to Derrida we will never be done with reading Hegel.[3] Indeed, for a long time, many thinkers have warned against any kind of facile anti-Hegelianism, and we should take these warnings very seriously, echoing as they do many important points that can be made about an autobiographical disruption of theory. A very important example is Foucault, who as we have seen warns those who believe that some form of philosophy of difference can elude the systematic or scientific drives commonly associated with philosophy as such. According to Foucault, our attempts to elude Hegel lead to the recognition that, after all, 'he is waiting for us, immobile and elsewhere'.[4] This recognition influences Foucault's own rhetoric of apparent facelessness. From this perspective, Hegel allows us to think against Hegel, and even demands it. Hegelian philosophy is the most systematic instance of philosophy, and the Hegelian dialectic a powerful logical structure. Yet, from Hegel himself onwards, these structures have blurred into semi-mythical narratives of European exemplarity. Accordingly, many writers have felt urgency in resisting the system, and have tried to be unfaithful to the Hegelian logos. This infidelity enables a hard-won escape from the determination of all difference as being on its way to sameness. For some writers, one strategy that might expedite this escape is the writing of autobiographical texts that persistently undermine claims to their own objectivity: it is better to speak from an honest if circumscribed space than to pretend disingenuously to speak from no space at all. The names of certain philosophers have become closely identified with the thinking of difference entailed by this autobiography: Deleuze, Derrida, and Foucault himself. However, Foucault for one is aware of potential objections, objections equally applicable to autobiographical thinking: it might be argued that difference is always *en route* to totalization, autobiography always about to become a theory.

This chapter will consider how Derrida's reading of Hegel proposes a thought of autobiography that accounts for these various objections without ever becoming simply that which Hegel has always already accounted for. It will initially discuss Hegel's philosophy of history, before considering his logic; it will then bring together these two realms of Hegel's thought, a conjunction that the thought insists upon itself. Bringing these two realms together does not imply the logic of history, or history's demonstration of the logic. The aim, simply stated, is to suggest that the racist incoherence of the philosophy of history is not merely accidental, but also to suggest that the flexibility of the logic evades simple determination and dismissal. Considering this question in the context of autobiography implies a formal thought of resistance to colonizing sovereign systems, but one that resists simply romanticizing the local or chaotic.

Philosophy and history

When reading Hegel's philosophy of history and his history of philosophy it is possible to conflate the two, because their structures and chronologies are essentially the same. This is not fortuitous, nor merely the result of Hegel's need to map the conceptual onto the chronological, but it is the result of the particular kind of history that the history of philosophy constitutes: this history is essentially philosophical. Hegel considers at length the objections to his conception of a history of Philosophy, the principal objection being: Philosophy is necessary and therefore should not have a history. This injunction operates in two senses. First, the history of Philosophy cannot be the history of its instances, the history of its 'heroes'. Second, this history also cannot be the tracing of the grammatical meaning of its individual instances for, as Hegel notes, so many of these instances seem to be instances of different things. Yet these phenomena do relate to Philosophy, that which is necessary, in for instance the progress of *World-Historical Individuals,* whose aims collide the existing law with that which threatens to destroy it. But this would in a familiar way seem to make such individuals the agents of the production of Philosophy, which for Hegel is just not an adequate understanding of the history of the Idea. The Idea is necessary, and is self-producing, working itself out and making itself manifest. It follows that,

> In Philosophy, the less desserts and merits are accorded to the particular individual, the better is the history; and the more it deals with thought as free, with the universal character of man as man, the more this thought, which is devoid of special characteristic, is itself shown to be the producing subject.[5]

One way of thinking about this is to take Hegel's assertion that the world spirit cannot be static, although an individual nation like China is more than likely to reach stasis. This notion of movement cannot be taken literally, or at the level of agency, but must be understood at the level of the Idea. Even Hegel could not maintain that nothing had happened in China for two millennia, and his descriptions of Africa, that mass apparently not yet (and perhaps not ever) to enter history, are full of details of 'slaughter'. So, although the mapping of the national and the philosophical is consistent, and more than adequate to Hegel's purpose of tracing the progress of *Geist,* at the same time this parallel is not absolute, as is seen in the discussion of philosophical tradition. For Hegel each generation and nation gladly adds to the philosophical tradition, but this addition follows the logic of supplementarity whereby the seemingly optional or superfluous also fills a lack in the nominally complete object. In the Hegelian system, tradition receives not only addition but also alteration, and ultimately improvement. The movement of philosophical tradition is therefore one of sublation. If Hegel extended the convergence of national and philosophical narratives, there would be an easily imaginable problem awaiting him: sublation is the preservation, the elevation, *and* the annihilation of the sublated. I have already discussed this in the context of Said and Palestinian identity. At a philosophical level this annihilation is 'neutral', but at the level of nation, or 'culture', this presents a problem surely irresolvable even in the terms of a Eurocentric narrative of beneficial colonial expansionism. Hegel was rather more aware of the historical status of, for instance, 'Africa', than his apparently merely ignorant pronouncements suggest. His history of Philosophy sidesteps the question of any projected future judgment on philosophical implication in the supposed contingencies of Eurocentrism (although this could not be its aim, in any meaningful sense). As he suggests:

> The thought which may first occur to us in the history of Philosophy, is that the subject itself contains an inner contradiction. For Philosophy aims at understanding what is unchangeable, eternal, in and for itself: its end is Truth. But history tells us of that which has at one time existed, at another time has vanished, having been expelled by something else. Truth is eternal; it does not fall within the sphere of the transient and has no history. But if it has a history, and as this history is only the representation of a succession of past forms of knowledge, the truth is not to be found in it, for the truth cannot be what has passed away. (LHP,7–8)

The transient is not the philosophical, cannot be the philosophical, and has no necessary connection to the philosophical. There is a movement of history, one of expulsion and marginalization, but this is not the movement of the Idea. There is also a movement of 'contingent thoughts', which for Hegel would be the most abstract and the least concrete, which again has no necessary connection to the philosophical. Contingent thought is opinion, and there are no philosophical opinions; likewise there are no philosophical theories to be tested. But Hegel is not dismissing such phenomena completely; he is, after all, delineating an object for his lecture course. He suggests the following:

> Philosophy has a history of its origin, diffusion, maturity, decay, revival; a history of its teachers, promoters, and of its opponents – often, too, of an outward relation to religion and occasionally to the State. This side of its history likewise gives occasion to interesting questions. Amongst other such, it is asked why Philosophy, the doctrine of absolute Truth, seems to have revealed itself on the whole to a small number of individuals, to special nations, and how it has limited itself to particular periods of time. (LHP,9)

It is difficult to see how the itinerary of the Idea could begin to explain this chanciness of geography, nation, language, and 'race', which is at the heart of Philosophy. So historical narrative would have to be invoked, and this is something that Hegel conspicuously does not do. The progress of the concept is continually distinguished from the progress of history, imagined as linear Eurocentric history. This distinction is not absolute, and is mainly invoked at points where the correspondence becomes stretched. Hegel has already allowed for these difficulties: 'The way shown by mind is indirect, and accommodates itself to circumstances'(LHP,36). Further, that which causes difficulties in the explanation – contingency – is also that which is banished by the triumph of Philosophy: 'Contingency must vanish on the appearance of philosophy'(LHP,36–7). This is not to say that Philosophy escapes contingency, only that what makes it philosophical is what links it to previous philosophies: whatever its historical marking, no philosophy can be a philosophy without being in principle an example of Philosophy. The newest philosophy, having sublated all the previous philosophies, is both the richest and deepest available philosophy: it contains most of what is (rather, in principle, will be) Philosophy. This is not to praise the new philosophy in isolation, or to blame earlier philosophies. 'Every philosophy is the philosophy of its own day' (LHP,45), Hegel asserts, an acknowledgement of finitude that makes Hegel in one sense a philosopher immersed in history, and eventually even the (auto)biographical. At the same time, however, it is impossible to dissociate this Hegel from the thinker of totality and necessity. Each philosophy is contingent but Philosophy is necessary.

The development of the Idea can only be seen in its totality from the vantage point of the fulfilment of the Absolute, and as Hegel argues at length, this Absolute is an indeterminate concept which is by definition infinitely open. So, there would be no achievable finite instance of that vantage point: it could not occur in the history of humanity, for that would make it determinable. At the same time, the fact that Hegel's philosophy can begin to pose this problem suggests that *this* philosophy can reflect on Philosophy, and can see the totality of history. Hegel apparently installs himself at the end of history. This is one denuded way in which Hegel is everywhere we turn: his philosophical history becomes a philosophical geography too, claiming space as its province. In this way Hegel is more ethnocentric, more bound to his period, its institutions, and its prejudices, than is necessary within the terms of his own philosophy. In principle, Hegel sets up the need for flexible and illimitable effort, so that even his philosophy is contingent to capitalized Philosophy. In fact, very often it appears that Hegel's philosophy presents itself as Philosophy.

It appears that we can read Hegel at two levels of consequence, only one of which has entered into widespread currency, for predictable and important reasons: that is Marx's critique, supposedly turning Hegel 'downside up'. Marx argues that Hegel's account of the modern, nominally 'rational' state is true to its object in its illogicality and inconsistency. This truth is necessary in that this state is characterized by illogic and inconsistency, both symptomatic of an alienated society. Marx's reading ties the logic very closely to its tracing as an empirical example: the history of philosophy at the level of philosophy of history. In Marx's interpretation, the assumption appears to be that the uncovering of contradiction in Hegel's derivation of State from Reason is the necessary uncovering of contradiction in the concept and actuality of that State. Similarly, one might assume that to uncover contradiction in Hegel's reading of, for instance, the Oriental World and its philosophy must necessarily be to undermine his entire derivation of Oriental Spirit from its empirical instances. Such contradiction might be at the level of either factual inaccuracy or logical difficulty, but in either case it would cast doubt on the validity of the philosophical narrative that Hegel outlines.

The careful distinction made between the progress of the concept and historical progress is often cancelled, and Hegel's flexibility begins to look more like mere self-justification. The expectation must be that the flexibility of the dialectic has a ready answer for such an argument, i.e. that the (philosophically) contingent failings of Hegel the individual do not compromise the philosophy. In this interpretation, the dialectic does not envisage a strict connection between the logi and empirical content, and its weakness is its strength. For instance, against Marx's reading of the *Philosophy of Right*, it might be argued that Marx destroys one historical narrative without touching the logical narrative. In this presentation, Hegel pushes the logical-empirical connection far beyond its limits of plausibility. Hegel defends the actually existing institutions of his time as if they constituted the necessary institutions of the rational state. However, this does not disallow the logic of the rational state, nor does it necessarily push the argument into the abstraction Hegel always dismisses. One can back this argument by reflecting on Hegel's dislike of the French Revolution, seemingly representing a political equivalent of the desire to 'leap over Rhodes', to jump into the a-historical realm of finality. The flexibility and pragmatism of Hegel's logic eludes Marx's attempt to reduce it to a narrative full of merely contradictory moments.

The gesture is basically to outline two Hegels: one is 'bad', lulled into nationalistic and ethnocentric banality, the other 'good', committed to an infinite effort of perfectibility. Furthermore, the 'good' Hegel predicts the 'bad', to the extent that the good is always what the bad will have meant to say. Additionally, this prediction is not the prediction of necessity, but of the kind of possibility that we might one day eradicate. No philosophy is a philosophy of all time ('Philosophy') but some (this) philosophy at least acknowledges finitude and is therefore vigilant against the risks of dangerously a-historical assertion. Against Marx, this argument proposes that there is no necessary connection between the individual error and the philosophical position. Further, Hegel in this mode of ethical infinite flexibility is arguably closer to much of Marx than Marx himself in his critique of Hegel. One way of phrasing this is to suggest that Hegel proposes a fluid interconnection of philosophy and materiality, just the fluidity that Marx proposes but then appears to undermine. Gillian Rose makes this argument in her reading of the first thesis on Feuerbach, in which, she argues, 'Marx reinforces the abstract oppositions between idealism and materialism, theory and praxis, which he claims to be transcending'.[6] For Rose, Marx's understanding of 'sensuousness' is abstract, putting his thesis firmly on the side of common sense. There is nothing fortuitous about this, according to Rose, because Marx has recourse to received oppositions when he is positioning himself in relation to Hegel. Hegel would avoid this abstraction through a flexible attention to the hesitations, anticipations, and particularities of the dialectic. Without this recognition it would be very easy to dismiss Hegel's logic in the following terms. Flexibility is construed as simply vagueness or abstraction. The counter to this objection is the constantly restated connection to the concrete. This returns us to the distinction, so seemingly vital – in that the contingent cannot be allowed to compromise necessity – between the contingent and the concrete. The flexibility that allows Hegel to elude the terms of Marx's critique implies the complication or even dissolution of received oppositions, like theory/praxis; however, this very flexibility can be pushed through to blur the distinction between contingent and concrete, implying that the contingent compromises the necessary. Rather, the moment at which such distinction is decided at times has the appearance of arbitrariness.

This argument requires specific examples, perhaps those given by Hegel himself. Every philosophy is a philosophy of its own day. We might, however, ask the question proposed by Robert Bernasconi:[7] does Hegel fulfil the requirements of good interpretative practice in tracing the movement of *Geist*? Bernasconi's answer, after careful consideration of the evidence of Hegel's treatment of sub-Saharan Africa, is that Hegel fails to interpret the evidence in an adequate and fair manner. So, Bernasconi suggests that Hegel has often been excused as not only a product of his time, but also a product of generalized European ignorance about Africa. This defence implies that if Hegel had been able to read more accurate sources, things might have been different. Bernasconi argues, against this defence, that Hegel's sources, Eurocentric or racist as they may have been, were significantly more accurate than Hegel himself. He makes the case that Hegel selectively appropriated, and in some cases inaccurately re-wrote, these sources (T. E. Bowdich, Antonio Cavazzi, Archibald Dalzel, Karl Ritter) in order to reinforce his East-West narrative of *Geist*'s progress. Noting Hegel's continued significance to our thinking, Bernasconi suggests that, 'Questions remain about the extent to which contemporary ideas, for example of social development, remain tied to a model that can best be described as colonialist'.[8] These questions do remain, but perhaps demonstrating that Hegel was racist does not begin to address the significant questions, which in a sense are already posed for us in Hegel's work. Bernasconi suggests in a footnote that he is not really interested in arguing that Hegel was racist, but it sometimes seems that his discussion does not move beyond the demonstration of empirical taint. Against Bernasconi, it is possible to say that Hegel, unlike Kant (unsympathetically read), sidesteps the problem of leaping into infinity. Hegel's criticism of Kant emphasizes the problems of founding universalist ethical programmes on Kantian terms. At least that is the presentation of a certain Hegel common to Foucault and Derrida, one that both writers acknowledge as well as work against. To think about the extent to which 'our' thinking is Hegelian, and whether or not the kind of problems identified by Bernasconi can help us think through this question, we can consider Hegel's treatment of the Orient, perched uneasily on the cusp of non-history/history.

In both the history of philosophy and the philosophy of history, Hegel suggests that he considers the Orient only to demonstrate why he need not consider it. In the various versions of the history of philosophy lecture course, Hegel gradually reduced the time spent on the Orient, to more quickly approach that which for him is truly historical. For Hegel the birth of history, and of philosophy, is dependent on freedom of both politics and thought. The Oriental conception of the unity of Mind with Nature evidences a continuing enslavement, a theocratic binding of *Geist*: 'The oriental consciousness raises itself, indeed, above the natural content to what is infinite; but it only knows itself as accidental in reference to the power which makes the individual fear'.[9] The Oriental Mind, then, is beginning to be historical without being historical. It is on its way to Philosophy, but remains not quite even philosophical. Hegel continues:

> In the East, Mind indeed begins to dawn, but it is still true of it that the subject is not presented as a person, but appears in the objectively substantial, which is represented as partly supersensuous and partly, and even more, material, as negative and perishing. The highest point attainable by the individual, the everlasting bliss, is made an immersion into substance, a vanishing away of consciousness, and thus of all distinction between substance and individuality – hence an annihilation. A spiritually dead relation thus comes into existence, since the highest point there to be reached is insensibility. So far, however, man has not attained that bliss, but finds himself to be a single existent individual, distinguished from the universal substance. He is thus outside the unity, has no significance, and as being accidental and without rights, is finite only; he finds himself limited through Nature – in caste for instance. The will is not here the substantial will; it is the arbitrary will given up to what is outwardly and inwardly contingent, for substance alone is the affirmative. (HP,97–8)

The subject is the individual in its consciousness of the universal, interiority for itself. In the Orient, Hegel argues, the individual is immersed in contingency. This situation is elevated to the 'highest point', thereby installing a 'spiritually dead' understanding at the centre of the Oriental Mind. At least that would be the situation if this immersion were to be achieved. Hegel notes that this has not happened, so even this inferior insensibility is denied to the Oriental individual, who is forced by expectation into a certain relation with the arbitrary by the denial of such aspiration. This leads to Oriental despotism. Oriental philosophy, for Hegel, is more or less the religious mode of thought that he has already excluded from his study. Overcoming the evidence of individual forms in religious thought, Hegel argues that this 'individuality is not real, but merely superficial'(HP,118). Subjectivity is the recognition of necessity, the 'turning inward' that differentiates itself from contingency. In the Orient something almost opposite occurs: it is not the universal but the illimitable that governs. Graeco-Christian religions conceive individual freedom in and for itself, whereas in Oriental thought all is relative to God: 'the individual neither can have within himself, nor can he attain to any value in as far as he maintains himself against the being in and for itself'(HP,118). For Hegel, the reputation of the Chinese, like that of the Indians, is diminished by increased knowledge. So, initial studies suggest that although formally comparable to European thought, the content is immediately obviously inferior. After insisting on the abstract quality of Oriental thinking, Hegel presents brief engagements with various standard strands of that thought. Confucius, argues Hegel, is merely a moral philosopher, and not a good one, whose thought never broaches the speculative. The categories of the *Yi Jing*, for Hegel, are only abstract and therefore superficial. He understands the *Dao-de Jing*'s adherence to the dictates of reason as being to a non-philosophical reason. Hegel identifies the common abstraction he has already outlined in these forms of thinking: Chinese thought, he suggests, sees the universally abstract proceed to the concrete without any 'sensuous', 'internal' order, and it therefore remains abstract. One brief gesture points to a larger question, that of writing, and that gesture is Hegel's explication of Yin and Yang, and their further division. Hegel suggests that despite the superficiality of these categories, there is something at work here which is recognizable as philosophical beginning: 'All symbols have the advantage of indicating thoughts and of calling up significations, and in this way such are likewise present there. Thought thus forms the first beginning, but afterwards it goes into the clouds, and Philosophy does likewise'(LPH,123). Hegel has outlined his understanding of Chinese philosophy at such length that this should be no surprise – what almost gets started is arrested at the origin. That Hegel should note the Chinese association of the *Gua* (the sixty-four hexagrams constituting the original *Yi Jing*) with the origin of their characters points us away from these general reflections to more specific moments where Derrida, for one, identifies a difficulty in the dialectic's movement. Perhaps this gesture, specifying moments of difficulty in Hegel's dialectical vision, is not in itself making much of an argument; maybe all that has been established is an ethnocentric vision of philosophical development, one that might easily be dismissed precisely because of its ethnocentrism. Against this historical vision is a Hegelian logic that anticipates the nature of that which it accompanies: finitude always contains the implication of error.

To bring these problems into focus we might pass from the history of philosophy into the philosophy of history, although as already indicated, the overlap is considerable. Again the progress of *Geist* is outlined simply: 'the Eastern nations knew only that *one* is free; the Greek and Roman world only that *some* are free; while *we* know that all men absolutely (man *as man*) are free'.[10] In these lectures Hegel derives this development of the principle of freedom from the characterization of historical, political, and religious contexts, interpreted with a degree of license at times bordering on the indefensible. It is notable that Hegel thinks through the cartography of Spirit in terms that modify Kant's demonstration and derivation of principles from the body and orientation. Whereas Kant, in 'What is Orientation in Thinking?',[11] thinks of orientation as a basis for judgment, Hegel acknowledges a nominal relativity before transforming it into a historical demonstration:

> World history travels from east to west; for Europe is the absolute end of history, just as Asia is the beginning. World history has an absolute east, although the term is wholly relative; for although the earth is a sphere, history does not move in a circle around it, but has a definite eastern extremity, i.e. Asia.[12]

Once again Hegel outlines a certain beginning of, in this case, historical consciousness, but a beginning which is caught in a position whereby there is no sublation of a patriarchal principle. There are different kinds of theocracy traced by Hegel through India and Persia, but essentially the Chinese theocratic stasis is characteristic of the Orient. This moment of *Geist* is one that combines both arbitrariness and permanence. All of this is familiar from the account given in the history of philosophy. The same principles are identified and judged in both accounts. In the philosophy of history, however, these principles are clearly connected to both geography and supposed racial characteristics. The developmental narrative that takes the form of the growth from child to adult is framed by two governing principles: the 'nations of history' are both spiritual and natural.

At this point Hegel raises a question about language to which I will return through Derrida's reading of Hegelian linguistics, and which has a direct bearing on the geopolitical questions raised by Hegel. In the midst of the continued re-statement of strong developmental spatialised narratives of philosophical and historical progress, Hegel pauses to reflect on a curious phenomenon. He notes that the progress toward spiritual perfection is accompanied by a degeneration of language, specifically in grammatical functions. There is attenuation of linguistic structures that accompanies a movement toward perfection. The world-historical status of nations, dependent on the realization of the principle of freedom, before which the contingent 'vanishes away', is seemingly compromised by an imperfection not present 'earlier'. At the level of Philosophy this kind of temporalisation has no place:

> Those moments which the spirit appears to have outgrown still belong to it in the depths of its present. Just as it has passed through all its moments

in history, so also must it pass through them again in the present – in the concept it has formed of itself.[13]

Change in *Geist* is teleological progress toward perfection, an end which for Hegel is indeterminate. This teleology is one whose history is both inconceivably compressed and infinitely stretched. But as is unavoidable, this change accompanies change in *Natur*, which for Hegel is cyclical. Geographical determinations follow from this emphasis on the natural. The cartography of *Geist* seems, then, to necessitate the insertion of the temporal into the conceptual, no matter how much Hegel may dismiss the everyday opinions expressed about, for example, the influence of climate on thought. As it is, Hegel proposes a theory of partial climactic determination which leads to difficulties in any East-West narrative. In arguing that extremes of climate restrict the beginning of philosophy, Hegel subscribes to a theory comparable to that of Rousseau. Essentially, Hegel has recourse to climate because nature is the basis for the opposition of *Geist* and the external world. In extremes of nature, he argues, where nature is too powerful, there is limited scope for the internal reflection that is the dialectic's motor. Basic needs must be fulfilled before reflection, so in extreme climates man is always directing attention outwards, to nature. Hegel situates Europe within the North/South division of his (and our) moment, arguing that the compression of Europe within temperate climes provides just the context for the beginnings of proper philosophy. He argues that this geographical compression has led to a richness and diversity of florae and faunae supposedly unrivalled; a little later he will note that even New World tigers and crocodiles are weaker than their Old World counterparts. Hegel is able to offer detailed determinations of various locations, particularly derived from the opposition of land and sea: it is a comprehensive climactic determinism, and seemingly a necessary aspect of any Philosophy.

Rousseau elaborates a similar argument, in Derrida's presentation, by deriving development from 'needs' and 'passions'. In Rousseau's understanding, suggests Derrida, 'neither the orient nor the occident is privileged'.[14] Rousseau transforms the geography of the structure of language, with its insistent questions of orientation and disorientation, into a polar question, deriving his schemes from a seasonal model. So, Rousseau thinks in terms of the North aligned with need, the South with passion. Derrida identifies need already present in passion, particularly in the outlines of Europe as 'balanced'. According to Rousseau, European ethnocentrism derives from a lack of travel; but because of his non-extreme locality, the European is naturally more open to that travel, to the universal. It is between difference, between extremes, that such difference may be properly understood, and so Europe for Rousseau is, as Derrida observes, a 'privileged place of observation'(OG,223). From this privileged position, Rousseau is able to propose a counter-ethnocentrism that may merely reverse ethnocentric terms or install a more pervasive ethnocentrism in its place. Derrida summarizes the central thesis of the *Essay on the Origin of Languages* in this way: 'the more a language is articulated, the more articulation extends its domain, and thus gains in rigor and in vigor, the more it yields to writing, the more it calls writing forth'(OG,226). In Rousseau's scheme, the progress of history is towards the north, towards the death he has inserted at the heart of life. Rousseau thereby associates the 'tyranny of harmony' with science, and with writing, all 'proper' to Europe. So his anti-ethnocentrism appears complicit with the terms it seems to oppose, in the same way as Lévi-Strauss's denial of writing to the Nambikwara: it accepts the proposition that Europe has a monopoly on science, merely suggesting that this monopoly is evidence of European inadequacy. Derrida's larger argument is that Rousseau describes what he cannot declare: that, '[t]he becoming-writing of language is the becoming-language of language'(OG,229). This understanding will recur in Derrida's treatment of Hegel's linguistics, and helps guard against simply reversing Hegel's terms without interrogating them.

Such an understanding is important because Hegel makes roughly the same argument as Rousseau about climate, in terms of a North/South divide, placing it in the service of that East-West narrative. There is no failing on the part of the European by the moment of Hegel, and this clearly does not relate to a sudden increase in world travel within the fifty-year period since Rousseau. Indeed, Hegel is able to insert implications about physiology and *Geist* into reports of European activity in the New World:

> We do have information concerning America and its culture,[...] but only to the effect that it was a purely natural culture which had to perish as soon as the spirit approached it [...] For after the Europeans had landed there, the natives were gradually destroyed by the breath of European activity.[15]

It is almost as if *Pneuma* literally conveys *Geist*: *Pneumatologie* become philosophy, 'breath' referring to the voice, to that charmed repository of *Geist* that is speech. This suggestion relates to that deterioration of grammar Hegel identifies in European languages, which has already been remarked on and will be investigated in Derrida's reading of Hegel's linguistics. The comparison between Hegel and Rousseau on language will again help to outline a resistance to Hegel that asserts more than the sublatable nothingness of scepticism.

At this point it seems worthwhile summarizing Hegel's historical narrative: Africa proper is without history. China has history, but no development. India has history, but no order. Egypt has history and stability, but can only pose the problem of self-understanding. Beyond that is the realm of philosophy and history properly conceived: Europe as the land of science. Further west is the New World, which may be, as Hegel notes, 'of the future', but which currently (and necessarily, on Hegel's map) is weak and child-like. This historical narrative is open to easy ridicule, particularly because it clearly portrays non-Europeans in a more or less simply racist manner. Therefore, Hegel's philosophy of history *might* simply be dismissed. However, as already noted, many commentators find a pre-programmed persistence of Hegelian logic, and an in-built prediction of its writer's own fallibility.[16] Consequently, the Hegelian system might be reconstituted distinct from Hegel's own demonstration of that system; as Michael Forster suggests,

> [W]hen we read Hegel's texts, we should always keep in mind the possibility of *reconstructing* their application of the dialectical method, or even of modifying the method itself in ways consistent with its performance of the philosophical functions for which it was designed.[17]

So, opposing Hegel requires more than simply opposing him, and one place to mark a real break with Hegel is the overlap between the logic and the racist philosophy of history. In *Glas*, Derrida notes the necessity of narrative in Hegel's pedagogy,[18] in that there is always reference forward to a projected moment of completion, so that what we say now is always what the system *will have meant to say*. Perhaps, however, there is something in Hegelian logic that necessarily allows the system to have *meant to be* Eurocentric.

Language and situation

Breaking with Hegel requires a grasp of the situatedness of language, which is connected with the situatedness of any investigating subject. It also requires a grasp of the consequences of these forms of situatedness for our explanations of our critical approaches. Again, Derrida has much to offer us on these matters. He approaches the difficulty of justifying a critical approach in the following terms:

> If words and concepts receive meaning only in sequences of differences, one can justify one's language, and one's choice of terms, only within a topic [an orientation in space] and an historical strategy. The justification can therefore never be absolute and definitive. It corresponds to a condition of forces and translates an historical calculation. (OG,70)

Derrida always insists upon this: we begin only where we are, and we cannot choose the terms of our argument in some final or absolutely justifiable sense. The idea that one can or must step outside contingency into the realm of necessity is the dream of logocentrism. This dream would be the purging of contingency in the pursuit of science, of scientific status, that which Derrida explicitly denies grammatology: 'Graphematics or grammatography ought no longer to be presented as sciences: their goal should be exorbitant when compared to grammato*logical knowledge*';(OG,74) '[T]o think the history of the system, its meaning and value must, in an *exorbitant* way, be somewhere exceeded'(OG,85). The terms strategy, contingency, and writing are organized together. However, it is immediately clear that this organization implies no simple valorisation of these terms as interruptive, disjunctive, or deconstructive. The non-scientific nature of grammatology is, Derrida notes, a 'perilous necessity'(OG,74). Contingency and necessity are not being straightforwardly driven apart, to the long-overdue benefit of chance, the non-scientific. This point is made at length:

> The absolute parousia of the literal meaning, as the presence to the self of the logos within its voice, in the absolute hearing-itself-speak, should be *situated* as a function responding to an indestructible but relative necessity, within a system that encompasses it. That amounts to *situating* the metaphysics or ontotheology of the logos. (OG,89)

This is a renunciation we cannot renounce; in *Of Grammatology* he asserts that, 'In the deconstruction of the arche, one does not make a choice'(OG,62). 'Relative necessity' might be a fitting name for deconstruction, and how it works as a non-resistant resistance to Hegelian logic. This relative necessity is locatable in various contexts. The context of the interplay between Hegel's logic and philosophy of history is a dramatic example of the potential for resistance and its counters (both logical (as antithesis) and as commodity). We can return to the question of writing in Hegel, specifically Derrida's reading of Hegel's linguistics. Thematic context drawn from Derrida's thought will be useful. In 'Of grammatology as a positive science', Derrida finds one theme especially significant, the 'Chinese prejudice'. This theme coincides with the elaboration of his general critique in terms of ethnocentrism. Within a certain history there is a unity among ethnocentrism, primitivism, and logocentrism. Derrida's reading of Lévi-Strauss implies the preservation of these structures, not contingently but necessarily. We cannot simply step outside these structures into a realm of pure difference or absolute specificity. Rather, we can and must make this gesture, but this too would be caught in the logic of authenticity and originary presence. This gesture would constitute the desire to preserve the singular, and for Derrida singularity is, from the beginning, caught up in totalization.

This structure is translated into chronological terms by one primitivism. This is the structure that Derrida identifies in Rousseau's critique of ethnocentrism. For Claude Lévi-Strauss, it is as if the Nambikwara are drawn into history by the introduction of writing. They represent a kind of purity from which industrialized Europe can learn, and which must be protected from Europe. In this structure, Europe is associated with the technical and scientific, and what he calls a 'proliferating and overexcited civilization'; meanwhile, the 'primitive' is associated with the natural and pure, or 'the silence of the seas' and 'the pristine freshness of human beings'.[19] The formal correspondence with ethnocentrism is striking, and is in fact the structure that Derrida identifies in Hegel's linguistics. Derrida identifies the word, the name, and most especially the proper name, as ideal repositories of the logocentric urge: 'The word, and the name, which with its categorem is the word par excellence, functions in this linguistics as the simple, irreducible and complete element that bears the unity of sound and sense in the voice'.[20] The word and name constitute miniaturized universes, totalities on the way to idealization. The name operates as irreducible in the Hegelian philosophy of language. This irreducibility is linked to a certain familiar privileging of speech, and further, alphabetic writing. In Hegel's understanding, the voice is the most proper signifying substance. Speech makes the internal existent on the outside, in contrast to writing, which removes the internal from the place of its externalization, as if the presence of the writer might still elevate writing. Derrida suggests that this exteriorization (essentially a materialization) – refers to an anthropological discipline already in place before Hegel's object, psychology. Ultimately this relates to psychophysiology, and from this is derived the specific justification for privileging voice. Hegel's argument would be that there must be an in-built, originary, non-resistance to idealization at work in the sensory. In vision and audition there is the ideal non-resistance to this idealization, more so in audition, as hearing sublates sight:

> The teleological concept of sound as the movement of idealisation, the *Aufhebung* of natural exteriority, the *relève* of the visible into the audible, is, along with the entire philosophy of nature, the fundamental presupposition of the Hegelian interpretation of language, notably of the so-called material part of language, lexicology.[21]

From this Hegel derives his privileging of voice. Derrida focuses on Hegelian linguistics, but as has already been established, geography and anthropology also work together in a deterministic theory of philosophical development; Hegel's reference to the breath of the Europeans destroying the resistance of the Americans implies a network of nineteenth century racist biological anthropology intertwined with this logocentrism.

Derrida interrogates this racially determined theory of language through Hegel's understanding of writing. In *Of Grammatology*, Derrida argues that there has been a consistent understanding of certain writing systems as inherently less like writing than others: all writing systems displace and distort the living presence of speech, but some systems produce more distortions than others. Derrida suggests that even within the bounds of European knowledge of other writing systems; certain exclusions were performed that enabled an elevation of alphabetic writing as closest to living speech. For instance, research on the Aztecs and the Mayans had already (in the eighteenth century) revealed the presence of phonetic elements in their systems. Certainly Hegel was well aware of the work of Thomas Young and Jean-François Champollion on the Rosetta Stone, to which he makes reference in his discussion of Egypt in the philosophy of history. Whilst the deciphering of the Rosetta Stone did maintain some understanding of hieroglyphics as partly ideogrammatic, it destroyed the assumption that they were simply icons, and also revealed the extent to which they are phonetic: Champollion's major insight was to see that

Coptic derived from the language of the hieroglyphs. Despite some knowledge of the work of Young and Champollion, Hegel, as has already been indicated, tends to an understanding of the Egyptians as having a different kind of language which implies the occupation of a different (earlier) phase of history. This is not simply a judgment, from Hegel, of inferiority in certain writing systems: as has already been indicated, he sees the development of *Geist* as accompanied by the deterioration of grammar. However, this apparent ambiguity appears to be resolved by the superiority conferred by the more direct expressiveness of more simple grammatical form.

Similarly, Derrida notes a general tendency to view Chinese characters as constituting an 'unfulfilled alphabet',(OG,91) despite the knowledge available to Leibniz *et al.*:

> The concept of Chinese writing thus functioned as a sort of European hallucination. This implied nothing fortuitous: this functioning obeyed a rigorous necessity. And the hallucination translated less an ignorance than a misunderstanding. It was not disturbed by the knowledge of Chinese script, limited but real, which was then available. (OG,80)

He later adds that,

> [W]e have known for a long time that largely non-phonetic scripts like Chinese or Japanese included phonetic elements very early. They remained structurally dominated by the ideogram or algebra and we thus have the testimony of a powerful movement of civilization developing outside of all logocentrism.(OG,90)

The first sentence seems at least a qualification of the second. In fact it is more accurate to think of Chinese characters as morphemic rather than ideogrammatic. All of which emphasizes the fact that Derrida, in *Of Grammatology*, has an apparent tendency to reverse the evaluation of supposedly ideogrammatic script, making it a radical disturbance to logocentrism. He suggests that this 'necessary decentring' cannot be scientific or even philosophical. Through Mallarmé and Pound the ideogram is thought to be *poetic*. Writing and literature are again ranged against logocentrism. Despite appearances, this is not the prelude to a banal celebration of the literary over the philosophical. There is no escape (or indeed regression) to the pre-scientific: access to the experience of difference occurs only in knowing the trace, reserve, or *différance* within philosophical or scientific discourse. It is no accident that Derrida translates his elevation of the ideogram (as above, associated with the algebraic) into an opposition of mathematics to Hegelian thought: 'In arithmetic calculation [...] thought would come face to face with its other'.[22]

This emphasis on the scientific is given clear expression in Derrida's reading of Hegel's linguistics, in which Hegel outlines the kinship of alphabetic writing and speech, in contrast to the more proper *writtenness* of ideogrammatic writing. Two points from *Of Grammatology* frame this argument usefully: first, the purely phonetic is an impossibility, and second, phoneticisation has always already begun. Hegel must recognize the first point but, for Derrida, is unwilling to concede the second, conceiving a 'teleological hierarchy of writings'. Unsurprisingly, such a teleology follows the structures already seen in Hegel's philosophy of history. Returning to the materialization of interiority, Hegel argues that this materialization is most effectively enacted by speech. Yet, as already noted, Hegel also argues that with increased civilization comes a deterioration in grammar: there is an in-built exteriority and inferiority of spatialised language. In a familiar gesture, Derrida notes that writing can be seen as the concept of this spacing, not just an example. From orality there is an essential movement through writing on the way to idealisation. This movement implies a privileging of alphabetic writing, which is seen as more open to idealisation than other forms of writing precisely because of the phonetic. It is, therefore, unlike other forms of writing, not an obstacle to history. The ideogram therefore has, for Hegel, the quality of the empirical signature, and of the autobiographical. The voice is opposed to the autobiographical – the voice is science. If philosophy depends on the expulsion of the contingent for its progress towards science, this expulsion is matched by the supposed universalisation (again, not abstraction) constitutive of alphabetic writing. The ideogram retains in its very stroke form the trace of its contingency. So, in contrast to alphabetic script, ideograms are precisely obstacles to the movement of history. Egyptian hieroglyphs, specifically in their immersion in nature (the 'brutes'), exclude the voice (the 'face') and therefore impede the movement of Spirit. Chinese characters, likewise, for Hegel have three predicates: immobilism, exteriority, and naturality. Derrida suggests that, 'Following the classical framework of the Hegelian critique, Chinese culture and writing are reproached simultaneously for their empiricism (naturalism, historicism) and their formalism (mathematizing abstraction)'.[23] For Derrida this is a moment of denegation in the dialectic. He continues, implying a distinct thought of difference in this dry formulation of Hegelian procedure:

> A typical movement of the Hegelian text: speculative dialectics sets on its course a sometimes quite precise piece of historical information, but without precautions. A certain number of very determined effects result from this, and in the very form of that which Hegel elsewhere criticizes: the juxtaposition of an empirical content with a henceforth abstract form, an exterior form superimposed on that which it should organize. This is manifest particularly in unnoticed contradictions, contradictions without concepts and not reducible to the speculative moment of contradiction.[24]

For Derrida these contradictions appear to fundamentally destabilize the dialectic, in that they constitute pure loss, the non-sublatable. Somehow the mired inadequacy of all east of Europe comes to be associated with mathematics, science, and the mechanical: Hegel's narrative of Western superiority performs certain strange manoeuvres that lead to denegation. Of course the location of these non-dialectical moments is not accidental. Geospatially distant, China recurs as a figure of the non-sublatable. Egypt, as already established, performs a very specific function in the cartography of Spirit, enabling the transition from the Orient to the Greek world. Along with the excluded sub-Saharan Africa, these locations of non-sublatable contradiction function importantly in the Hegelian philosophy of history. Derrida considers these moments within a certain framework. He is concerned to identify the *Aufhebung* with logocentrism. China would then be 'outside' logocentrism, either disrupting the dialectic or confirming metaphysics in its dialectical movements. However, we cannot simply reverse these hierarchies. We cannot access some realm of the non-philosophical, or rather we do not choose to access this realm; we cannot choose to think in a radically different way, that way supposedly figured by Chinese characters. This impossibility is not just a question of empirical fact (Chinese is not a totally alien script), but is necessary philosophically. So far the following terms have been associated: writing, literature, autobiography and the machine. They function in apparent opposition to speech, philosophy, science and thought. But the opposition is only apparent; as Derrida suggests, 'Making explicit the evaded *question* always and necessarily keeps to the system of what is evaded'.[25] Yet this does not state enough, implying as it does that Derrida is just 'the same' as Hegel. It is not that Derrida identifies a certain moment in Hegel, before admitting that such a moment is merely empirical error, already allowed for by Hegelian logic; Derrida is not Hegel, not quite, but the difference remains to be elaborated.

To summarize the argument so far: Hegelian logic appears, in its very weakness, to have ready answers to any correct accusation of racism in Hegel's writings. So, Hegel may argue that non-Europeans are at different moments of stasis on the way to an idealisation that is 'present' to the European, but this is already predicted by Hegelian logic. In principle, Hegel's philosophy is just another philosophy of its day, although in its case what is sublated is mainly the unfortunate empirical example, leaving Philosophy. The name of Hegel disappears from view. So, Derrida and Marx, for instance, are able to identify errors that compromise specific historical mappings of the dialectic, but that do not compromise the logic. As the *Science of Logic* determines it:

> Difference in itself is self-related difference; as such, it is the negativity of itself, the difference not of an other, but *of itself from itself*; it is not itself but is other. But that which is different from difference is identity. Difference is therefore itself and identity. Both together constitute difference; it is the whole, and its moment. It can equally be said that difference, as simple, is no difference; it is this only when it is in relation with identity; but the truth is rather that, as difference, it contains equally identity and this relation itself. Difference is the whole and its own *moment*, just as identity

equally is the whole and its moment. This is to be considered as the essential nature of reflection and as the *specific, original ground of all activity and self-movement.*[26]

Every proposition implies Hegelian speculative thought. As is stated earlier, 'identity, not externally, but in its own self, in its very nature, is this, to be different'.[27] The corollary is that every assertion of difference is, of course, identity. But is there another way of thinking about what is different from difference? In other words, do those moments of racist empirical error point to a more fundamental problem in the Hegelian system? It might seem that the previously remarked immersion in the autobiographical that, on one reading, distinguishes Hegel from Kant, highlights a problem of supposed systemic infallibility.

To express this point at the level of cultural politics, many critics have emphasized the perils of humanisms as conceived into this century. This criticism identifies one gesture central to humanism: scratch the surface of humanity, of any given culture, and underneath 'we' are all the same. This assertion of an abstract humanity has functioned to distract attention from the continued inequalities at the level of specificity. Gayatri Chakravorty Spivak, for one, accuses existing projects of liberal multiculturalism of providing an alibi for globalization: 'Liberal multiculturalism without global socialist awareness simply expands the U.S. base, corporate or communitarian'.[28] Existing forms of liberal multiculturalism function, Spivak suggests, as public relations gestures to win support from developing countries for global financialisation. She further asserts that the pursuit of civil justice in the West can function as an alibi for the refusal of that same justice in other locations. To return to Hegel, a system that is able through its very weakness to assimilate any contradiction has unfortunate parallels with similar agencies of colonialism, neo-colonialism, and globalization. Identity in its endless recognition of difference is on this reading an endless assimilation of difference. What Derrida provides is a model for writing *through* the necessary totalization that is Philosophy. This writing is a mode which can persuasively be called 'autobiographical'.

Chance and autobiography

The kind of resistant non-resistance to Hegelian Philosophy acted out by Derrida's writing can be named in various ways. One particularly apt name for this resistance is 'autobiography', because of the general context in humanities disciplines in which autobiography has come increasingly to the fore. Yet at the same time this autobiography, even when it is thematised or demonstrated by more or less traditional autobiographical writing, is not quite equivalent to the 'autobiographical turn' of much recent cultural studies writing. The kind of 'deconstructive autobiography' to which I refer is as much about the reader as the autobiographically inclined author; rather, the reading moment is exemplary of a structure present in all I have so far discussed.

Paul de Man frames the following argument suggestively, in his widely discussed and often rather simplistically dismissed 'Autobiography As De-Facement'. In that important essay he writes that,

> From specular figure of the author, the reader becomes the judge, the policing power in charge of verifying the *authenticity* of the signature and the consistency of the signer's behavior, the extent to which he respects or fails to honor the contractual agreement he has signed.[29]

Expressed in this manner, we might be forgiven for taking de Man's argument as marking an equivalence of the name (sign) and the actuality of the author (referent). At the same time it is clear that the text is the action that is to be judged, as well as being that which provides the framework for judging. With this in mind we can return to Hegel, through Derrida once again:

> Hegel presents himself as a philosopher or a thinker, someone who constantly tells you that his empirical signature – the signature of the individual named Hegel – is secondary. His signature, that is, pales in the face of the truth, which speaks through his mouth, which is produced in his text, which constructs the system it constructs. This system is the teleological outcome of all of Western experience, so that in the end Hegel, the individual, is nothing but an empirical shell which can fall away without subtracting from the truth or from the history of meaning. As a philosopher, he seems to be saying basically that not only is it possible for his signature and his proper name to disappear without a loss, to fall outside of the system, but that this is even necessary in his own system because it will prove the truth and autonomy of that system. Thus, my exclusion from what I am saying – the exclusion of my signature from the text produced through me – is absolutely essential and necessary if my discourse is to be a philosophical, ontological one.[30]

It is possible to contest this reading, although only at the expense of something in the whole idea of the system in general. The system (as philosophy) is specific to a time, place, and even an individual, but the logic itself (Philosophy proper) is the exclusion of those specificities. Again, this is to assume that the logic can be isolated, but one of the consequences of Derrida's argument is to disallow such isolation. This relates to a further point about readership, and the kind of reading involved in Derrida's suggestion. Although Derrida's characterization of Hegelian thought has the appearance of a judgment, as de Man's suggestion implies, that would be a drastic simplification of the argument. De Man's suggestion is comparable to Derrida's argument that *it is the ear of the other that signs*. This argument does not entail a relativistic belief that readers make texts mean whatever they please because, as de Man argues, the signing takes place within certain rules invoked, transformed, or invented by the author. This suggestion emphasizes that what makes texts at least minimally readable is their openness to interpretation beyond their original context (if we could consensually identify that context). If the ear of the other did not sign then the text would be by definition unreadable. The signature moment sends a text in search of countersignature. However, this might initially imply that the reader always judges on the basis of pre-established rules. De Man frames his argument in suitably juridical vocabulary, and the judgment is that of a test case, each and every time: *legislation.* This is because reading a text cannot rely solely on objectively determinable principles, but involves the judgment of the autobiographical, the idiomatic, or the empirical. It is a kind of rule-less judgment, one searching for or inventing the rules by which it was made, and therefore postmodern.

Returning to Derrida's reading of Hegel, it implies that the dialectic is the ultimate form of reason that denies the necessity of contingency. From the 'moment' of its completion, projected or otherwise, it would be precisely a system that appears necessary. Of course Hegel literally signs 'Hegel' constantly, and this literal sense parallels the philosophical sense by which excess over totality is understood. For this reading of Hegel, the writing of philosophical rationality is unavoidably autobiographical. Hegel insists on the necessity of subjective 'moments' on the way to reason; for Derrida these moments are as destructive as they are necessary, and rather than being sublated, they invade the dialectic in its entirety. This is ruination, through which what is necessary for reason inevitably deconstructs that same reason. There is a return of the autobiographical, what Robert Smith cautiously calls, 'the dehiscence of the literary into the philosophical'.[31]

Now this sense of the autobiographical is analogous to the general structure of writing as determined by de Man, which frames this section. As in de Man's argument, autobiography becomes a general feature of writing rather than a consequence of psychology or subjectivity. So, what could be described as the mixing of 'life' and 'work' in a familiar psycho-biographical sense loses the specificity that has always been its preserve and accordingly loses some of its force. Another way of putting this 'loss' is to suggest that its weakness constitutes its force: it is parasitical on the body of philosophical reason. If traditional conceptions of philosophy associate 'desire' with the inessential and incalculable (chance), and 'necessity' with reason (philosophy), this structure that Derrida finds essential to the dialectic proposes at least a reversal of this polarity. Desire would then be associated with philosophy and necessity with the elusive: chance. Consequent to this is the recognition that we cannot escape the necessity of the a-systemic. Further, it appears that contingency will necessarily become indistinguishable from the transcendental truth that philosophy invents 'for' itself. Chance enables system yet denies its possibility. Being hardly present at all, chance is irreducible and non-negotiable. One understanding of Derrida's project sees him writing against desire through necessity rather than choice, for we cannot choose to step outside reason.

For philosophy to be scientific it must set limits and therefore must be legislative. Legislation in philosophy aims to eliminate the contingent: this is Hegel's remit for philosophy. The contingent must be eliminated from the field to be conceptually organized. Additionally, the contingent must be eliminated from philosophy so it can *be* philosophy. In being contingent, the contingent appears to disqualify itself necessarily from philosophy. However, the very nature of contingency is that it always might surprise us, or surprise philosophy; as Smith notes,

> It is *always possible* that contingency will startle philosophic anticipation; it takes the form of the future and opens historical change. And, being *always* possible, it amounts in its invariant categoriality to a necessary condition or a priori; therefore *also* taking the form of the (absolute) past.[32]

Chance is the limit but also the precondition of philosophy. Derrida's reading of Hegel enables a writing of philosophy that becomes more idiomatic, more strictly singular. Not that philosophy could ever become idiomatic, not strictly, not without forfeiting its readability as philosophy, something that remains vital for Derrida. In Derrida, chance is anticipated, but with the anticipation that it is precisely what disallows anticipation – strictly philosophical anticipation. Chance is the unique generality, which again links it to the autobiographical. If the only necessity is that there is no necessity, and every text is necessarily (counter-)signed by the other, then 'I' too am signed by the other, or 'completed' by the other: 'The ear of the other says me to me and constitutes the *autos* of my autobiography'.[33] Likewise, surprise always comes, and is in this general sense one of the least surprising phenomena imaginable.

Rephrased, chance and necessity are endlessly co-implicated, implying an ultimate emphasis toward the nobility of philosophical effort. Smith describes this situation as one of 'original sin'. In the structure of an original sin it must appear that events could have been otherwise. In the case of philosophy it would appear that the contingency installed at the heart of reason could be and ought to be identified and expelled. And this would be partially achieved through the expulsion from the start of the signature, which would by definition also confound the necessity for countersignature. As Smith puts it: 'In principle, a philosophical text should not be signed. Its pretensions being toward universality any blot of specificity compromises it'. However, as he continues: '[W]ithout the signature no philosophical text could exist at all'.[34] There are two explanations given for this: 1) specificity is essential to philosophy, without which it would not get started at all and 2) the signature guarantees copyright. Of course, the signature is a name like any other, subject to the structure of iterability, requiring the fixity of legislation to avoid the confusion of chance. That legislation is what happens does not detract from the inherent possibility of appropriation and interpretation: this is a necessary possibility. To be read at all of course is to risk necessarily being countersigned in a conflictual way. What can be seen in these texts is the fact that reading simply is countersigning. Derrida's autobiographical writing is an honouring of texts, its ruses and styles the attempt to demonstrate the experience of difference. In almost inhabiting the texts Derrida reads, his texts mimic the parasitical nature of contingency, almost leaving everything just as it was. However, this repetition is each time discrepant.

Autobiography, then, exemplifies a necessary openness of reading. In *Archive Fever* Derrida writes that, 'To have a concept at one's disposal, to have assurances with regard to it, is to presuppose a closed heritage and the guarantee sealed, in some sense, by that heritage'.[35] Openness in philosophy is not something that we maintain until, one day, philosophy is complete, but is an absolute value. Derrida suggests that the archive should pose the question of futurity, in a minimal sense at least in terms of what the archive has been: 'The archive: if we want to know what that will have meant, we will only know in times to come. Perhaps. Not tomorrow but in times to come, later on or perhaps never'(AF,36). Here this is cast in terms of writing the history of psychoanalysis: to assert that one examines the archive of psycho-analysis without reference to the concepts of psychoanalysis is to posit an untenable distinction between an inside and an outside of that archive. The archive creates the event just as much as it gathers it up, carefully formalizing that which is singular. The problem is posed clearly near the beginning of the text. Psychoanalysis *opens* archivisation onto new and radically *open* terri-tory. A science of the archive is caught in an initial aporia: to 'include' Freud or to 'apply' Freud. Including Freud seems rather too confident of exclud-ing his methods. And of course, psychoanalysis as an aspirant 'theory of the archive' is also part of that archive. The openness to psychoanalysis that transforms the concepts of the archive must pose the question of how one writes within the loop of psychoanalyzing psychoanalysis. So, for Derrida, Yerushalmi's insistence that he writes a-psychoanalytically about the history of psychoanalysis shows an unwillingness to 'hear anything about it'(AF,55). This is all the more problematic because psychoanalysis is precisely that dis-course that has taught us the dependence of the scientific rational mind on its excluded but structurally essential other. Historiography, scientific discourse that it is, is yet structured by the radically non-scientific, that which is singular and radically non-repeatable. The mutual implication of historiography and psychoanalysis is exemplary of a general structure:

> In the *classical* structure of their concept, a science, a philosophy, a the-ory, a theorem are or should be intrinsically independent of the singular archive of their history. We know well that these things (science, phi-losophy, theory, etc.) have a history, a rich and complex history that carries them and produces them in a thousand ways. We know well that in diverse and complicated ways, proper names and signatures count. But the structure of the theoretical, philosophical, scientific statement, and even when it concerns history, does not have, should not have, an intrinsic and essential need for the archive, and for what binds the archive

in all its forms to some proper name or to some body proper, to some (familial or national) filiation, to covenants, to secrets. (AF,45)

This is a general requirement that can never be fulfilled, but to assert this structural impossibility is not to reduce theory/philosophy/science to some absolute specificity, to the autobiographical, because historiography is not reducible in this way. Nor is the philosophical reducible to a mere reflex of history or socio-economic context. This structure does not entail the renunciation of the search for truth; rather, truth is made spectral, and Derrida writes of a structural spectrality of the archive. The motion of the quasi-transcendental matches the motion of 'historical truth' in the writing of Yerushalmi: it 'resists and returns' (AF,87) as spectre. The singularity that makes the archive impossible also makes it necessary:

> With the irreplaceable singularity of a document to interpret, to repeat, to reproduce, but each time in its original uniqueness, an archive ought to be idiomatic, and thus at once offered and unavailable for translation, open to and shielded from technical iteration and reproduction. (AF,90)

Psychoanalysis attempts to dissolve this trouble, but at the same time necessarily heightens it; psychoanalysis insists on what is necessarily and originarily there. Singularity can be respected but cannot be simply maintained; it is necessarily gathered up, totalized, and this gathering up is necessarily violent. When there is singularity then there is necessarily, 'murder, wounding, traumatism'(AF,78). 'The one, alas, or happily, is the condition of the other. And the Other is the condition of the One'(AF,79). That there is archivisation presupposes the continuance of the archive, and openness onto a future *à-venir*. Again singularity, autobiography, is seen to presuppose violent totalization, the totalization of the concept, history, philosophy, science: in a word, *theory*. But perhaps the name 'autobiography', in its weakness, which for Robert Smith grants it force, has begun to look rather too general, with perhaps only tenuous connection to what we usually understand by that term. We need to hold onto a definite connection between the two senses, between 'autobiography' (strong) and the 'autobiographical' (weak). We can do this by pursuing the apparently rather enigmatic theme of violence, which can be related to that of a certain death at the heart of life. Derrida elaborates this notion:

> Only the name can inherit, and this is why the name, to be distinguished from the bearer, is always and a priori a dead man's name, a name of death. What returns to the name never returns to the living. Nothing ever comes back to the living.[36]

To make sense of this enigmatic declaration it is necessary to understand how autobiographical discourse, despite appearances, exemplifies the presence of 'death' at the heart of 'life'. To return to the signature, we might ask how it is the exemplary name, the name of names: why, as Derrida puts it in 'That Dangerous Supplement', and as discussed elsewhere, the name is the question of questions.

This question can be framed once again by de Man's argument in 'Autobiography As De-Facement':

> Death is a displaced name for a linguistic predicament, and the restoration of mortality by autobiography (the prosopopeia of the voice and the name) deprives and disfigures to the precise extent that it restores. Autobiography veils a defacement of the mind of which it is itself the cause.[37]

De Man installs death at the heart of life in his understanding of the language of tropes as 'the specular language of autobiography'.[38] De Man's reading is filtered through specific moments in the poetry of Wordsworth, but the projected generality of the argument is clear. What is identified at the level of reference is symptomatic of a more primal level of linguistic arrangement. We can recall Derrida's argument about necessary possibility, iterability, and death: to be readable at all a text must function beyond the presence of its signatory, beyond (as the maximal example) therefore the signatory's death, in fact as if the signatory was dead already. Iterability means death, in this sense. In being necessarily possible, this death is installed from the beginning at the heart of all texts. For de Man, signatures and therefore autobiography are exemplary of this structure. It is then worth recalling to what extent de Man elsewhere, particularly in *Allegories of Reading*, considers the connection between autobiography and politics. Here he confines himself to noting that, 'Writers *of* autobiographies as well as writers *on* autobiography are obsessed by the need to move from cognition to resolution and to action, from speculative to political and legal authority'.[39] Autobiography might be said even to propose itself as the solution to a set of problems of which it is the most consistent cause, if causality had any real purchase on the situation.

Traditionally conceived, autobiography would surely be riddled with doubt and confusion as to the wider implications of its claims. More recent theories of autobiography reverse this evaluation, to the point where we might wonder why anyone ever wrote any other kind of text. This reversal at the level of genre accompanies a more philosophical reversal, when all this ought to teach us that such a simplistic move is not only theoretically impossible but also politically undesirable. This point can be illustrated by considering the implications of the various arguments outlined about the Hegelian system. On the one hand, autobiography is what complicates a supposed desire to become purely philosophical, to purge the irrational and the contingent. On the other, autobiography is always on the way to becoming philosophy. Resisting the conflation of logic and history will not quite do the trick, because each is necessarily invaded by the other. What happens in autobiographical theory opens us onto openness in general. We could suggest that the philosophical system in fact allows for the persistence of signature, thereby disallowing the possibility of a self-thinking thought, but also resisting the reduction of truth to signature. Consider Derrida's enigmatic argument that *infinite difference is finite.* If everything is a question of difference, then there is a danger that everything will be flattened, undifferentiated, and so difference will blur into *in*difference. For infinite difference to be infinite one would have to survey a field from an impossible external position – by contrast, autobiographical theory talks to us from the interior of any context, differentiating, sorting and insisting on the singularity of any event. Autobiography is accordingly less my own than that of the other, even the non-human other, animal or machine. Autobiography has been spirited away by writing, my written self only guaranteed by its being read, or signed, by some other, and so I have always been ghostwritten.

References

1. In his *Philosophical Papers Volume Two* (Cambridge: Cambridge University Press, 1991) Richard Rorty discusses Derrida and writes that, 'Many responsibilities begin in dreams, and many transfigurations of the tradition begin in private fantasies.' (p.121) However, it might be better to say that all such 'responsibilities' begin in dreams, or the autobiographical, etc.: Derrida's daydream is, of course, an explicit form of the kind of remainder he describes.
2. Derrida, *Dissemination*, trans. B. Johnson (Chicago: University of Chicago Press, 1983), p.49.
3. *Hegel After Derrida*, Barnett (ed.) (New York & London: Routledge, 1998).
4. Foucault, 'The Order of Discourse' in Young (ed.) *Untying the Text* (London: RKP, 1981), p.74.
5. Hegel, *Lectures on the History of Philosophy. Volume One*, trans. E. S. Haldane and H. Simon (London: RKP, 1996), p.1. Further refs. to LHP in the text.
6. Rose, *Hegel Contra Sociology* (London: Athlone Press, 1981), p.215.
7. See Bernasconi, 'Hegel at the Court of the Ashanti', in Stuart Barnett (ed.) *Hegel after Derrida* (London: Routledge, 1998), pp.41–63.
8. Bernasconi, 'Hegel at the Court of the Ashanti', p.63.
9. Hegel, *Lectures on the History of Philosophy, vol. 1*, (trans.) E. S. Haldane and Frances H. Simon (London: Routledge and Kegan Paul, 1956) p.97. Further refs. to HP in the text.
10. Hegel, *The Philosophy of History*, (trans.) J. Sibree (New York: Dover, 1956) p.19.
11. Kant, In *Selections from the Political Writings*, H. S. Reiss (ed.) (Cambridge: Cambridge University Press, 1991).
12. Hegel, *Lectures on the Philosophy of World History* (trans. H. B. Nisbet) (Cambridge: Cambridge University Press, 1975) pp.196–197.
13. Hegel, *Lectures on the Philosophy of World History*, p.151.
14. Derrida, *Of Grammatology* (trans.) G. Spivak (Baltimore: Johns Hopkins University Press, 1976) p.216. Further refs. to OG in the text.
15. Hegel, *Lectures on the Philosophy of World History*, p.163.
16. In *Infinite Thought* (London: Verso, 2003) Alain Badiou, having mentioned Hegel's philosophy of history, makes the very different but important claim that,

'The literary in philosophy is the directed transmission, the vectoring, through an effect of sense, of the following: the relation of a truth to sense is a defective or void relation. It is this defection that exposes philosophy to the imperative of a localized fiction. The moment at which the argumentation fails imitates, amid the power of the argument itself, this, that truth causes the failure of knowledge'. (pp.104–105)

17. Forster, 'Hegel's dialectical method' in F. C. Beiser (ed.) *The Cambridge Companion to Hegel* (Cambridge: Cambridge University Press, 1993) p.153.

18. Derrida, *Glas*, (trans.) R. Rand and J. P. Leavy, Jr. (Lincoln & London: University of Nebraska Press, 1986) p.15a.

19. Lévi-Strauss, *Tristes Tropiques* (trans.) J. and D. Weightman (London: Jonathan Cape, 1973), p.43.

20. Derrida, *Margins: Of Philosophy* (trans.) A. Bass (London: Harvester Wheatsheaf, 1982) p.96.

21. Derrida, *Margins: Of Philosophy*, p.93.

22. Derrida, *Margins: Of Philosophy*, p.106.

23. Derrida, *Margins: Of Philosophy*, p.102.

24. Derrida, *Margins: Of Philosophy*, p.102.

25. Derrida, *Margins: Of Philosophy*, p.50.

26. Hegel, *Science of Logic* (trans.) A. V. Miller (Allen & Unwin: London, 1969) p.417.

27. Hegel, *Science of Logic* (trans.) A. V. Miller (Allen & Unwin: London, 1969) p.413.

28. Spivak, *A Critique of Postcolonial Reason* (Cambridge (MA.): Harvard University Press, 1999) p.402.

29. de Man, *The Rhetoric of Romanticism* (New York: Columbia University Press, 1984) p.71.

30. Derrida, *The Ear of the Other* (trans. P. Kamuf) (Lincoln and London: University of Nebraska Press, 1988) p.56.

31. Smith, *Derrida and Autobiography* (Cambridge: Cambridge University Press, 1995) p.4.

32. Smith, *Derrida and Autobiography* p.23.

33. Derrida, *The Ear of the Other*, p.51.

34. Smith, *Derrida and Autobiography*, p.35.

35. Derrida, *Archive Fever* (trans.) E. Prenowitz (Chicago: Chicago University Press, 1996) p.33. Further refs. to AF in text

36. Derrida, *The Ear of the Other*, p.7.

37. de Man, *The Rhetoric of Romanticism*, p.81.

38. de Man, *The Rhetoric of Romanticism*, p.80.

39. de Man, *The Rhetoric of Romanticism*, p.71.

5   Full disclosure and the native informant in postcolonial theory

Questioning narration

If one postcolonial critic in particular is associated with Derrida's work, it is his early translator Gayatri Chakravorty Spivak. Fittingly, there is much to be said about Spivak in relation to autobiographical theory. Three things need to be stated about Spivak's relationship with autobiography. First, she is extremely critical of what she sees as metropolitan diasporic intellectuals flaunting their difference as part of some dubiously careerist manoeuverings. Second, according to her critics she's not above flaunting her difference as part of some dubiously careerist manoeuvering. Third, her work displays an admirable honesty about how these two things co-exist, and a stern theoretical grasp of the necessity of this co-existence. Indeed, she remarks a necessity to staging identity: 'The stagings of Caliban work alongside the narrativization of history: claiming to *be* Caliban legitimises the very individualism that we must persistently attempt to undermine from within'.[1] Yet, according to Spivak, while we must accept this necessity of staging, we need simultaneously to hold on to the impossibility of controlling that staging in any absolute sense:

> As you may have gathered by now, I am guarded and watchful of the autobiographical impulse within postcoloniality. The line between aesthetics and politics is not necessarily programmed by the authority of the author. [...] Let us not read the text's desire as its fulfillment in the text. Let us not read the historical provenance of author/protagonist as if unmediated by the dynamics of class, institution, and affiliation. Let us remember the informant of the testimonial as we read autobiography.[2]

Such is clear enough in any moderately sophisticated analysis of life writing, but is perhaps less often put into practice when reading the autobiographical moment in any theory. And yet, at the same time, for Spivak we cannot simply stop doing what we are doing. It is not possible to forget the necessity of autobiographical staging, and this makes it yet another example of one of those things that Spivak describes in a way guaranteed to provoke as much as to inform: *something we cannot not want*. In her own words:

> One needs to be vigilant against simple notions of identity which overlap neatly with language or location. I'm deeply suspicious of any determinist or positivist definition of identity, and this is echoed in my attitude to writing styles. I don't think one can pretend to imitate adequately that to which one is bound. So, our problem, and our solution, is that we do pretend this imitation when we write, but then must do something about the fact that one knows this imitation is not OK anymore.[3]

Not only, then, is this something that has to be acknowledged at the level of concept. It must also be written into the theories we produce. In fact, it is only at this level of writing, we might say, that this impossible balance can be registered. This necessary but necessarily insufficient staging of situation might offer an explanation of Spivak's style. Which brings us to a fourth thing to be said about Spivak and autobiography: the fiercest criticism of her work tends to suggest that it is not only self-obsessed but also impenetrably suffused with jargon.

Cults of personality

British cultural critic Terry Eagleton's memoir *The Gatekeeper* at one point slips in a brief theoretical justification for its existence. It is, Eagleton writes, an 'anti-autobiography', aiming to, 'outwit the prurience and immodesty of the genre by frustrating your own desire for self-display and the reader's desire to enter your inner life'.[4] Eagleton refers elsewhere to the 'prolier-than-thou sentimentalism'[5] of Frank McCourt, so perhaps he is dismissively alluding to *Angela's Ashes*. The focus of this criticism is more likely, however, to be a supposedly American obsession with personality, rather than any apparently professional proletarian Irish-ness. If these remarks are put in the context of his theoretical work, in fact, they become clearly connected to his recent theoretical complaints about 'left criticism' in general and postcolonialism in particular. The obvious place to look at these complaints is Eagleton's review of Spivak's *A Critique of Postcolonial Reason*,[6] which has been discussed at length in many different places, but which should repay one more discussion. In that review he complains about academic culturalisms, which reduce complex phenomena to cultural questions. He sees this tendency also playing itself out in the autobiographical urges to which cultural theory has become prey. Spivak's autobiographical tendencies are, Eagleton suggests, on the one hand 'a satirical stab at scholarly impersonality', but on the other, 'a familiar American cult of personality'; ultimately, for Eagleton they are much more the latter than the former. Strangely enough, in a review of someone so widely associated with (let's call it) transnational cultural literacy, Eagleton is basically saying that Spivak is all too American, and this nowhere more than in her autobiographical stylings, for which read *poses*. She is or has *become* all too close to Stanley Fish, who is upbraided in a similar review in the same magazine for, 'typical American parochialism and self-obsession'.[7] Eagleton insists on the problematic nature of this convergence because it goes unremarked; his position puts an emphatically negative spin on the convergence of contexts, pressures and possibilities characteristic of confessional culture, as recently described by Leigh Gilmore.[8]

The problem is not just stylistic, but is, for Eagleton, a question of perspective lacking. According to him, our political positioning is directly connected with just how much of ourselves we put into our critical writings, but not in the way that many critics imagine. To insist on what David Simpson calls the *azza* sentence can be just as disabling as it is enabling, and in the present moment leads to what Eagleton provocatively diagnoses as a general American false consciousness.[9] To return to his review of Fish, Eagleton is essentially arguing that postmodern cultural particularism is a rather serious failure of perspective, basically occluding US specificity: on this view, bad universalisms are countered by bad particularisms. As Eagleton suggests in the review of Fish: 'the view from nowhere is inevitably countered by the view from us alone'.[10] Another way of putting this is to say that theory is replaced by autobiography. This, in brief, is one criticism of postcolonial theory, which in the shape of Spivak is taken to be all too autobiographical. The criticism, as I've implied, is thought to open up a large number of questions to which postcolonial theory has at best inadequate answers. However, this chapter will reconsider these questions and argue that what we get with Spivak's autobiographical theory is hardly full disclosure – and this 'failure' is quite deliberate. In the situation as described by Eagleton it seems we need rather more people writing anti-autobiographies; however, this is, whatever Eagleton may argue, something like what Spivak does. It should be said that she is also alive to the limits of anti-autobiography itself. Accordingly, we have to bear in mind many nuances when we read her work. Looking at Spivak in this more nuanced way is also likely to give a more rounded and less confrontational view of postcolonial theory generally.[11]

Opening arguments

Spivak's style, autobiographical or impenetrable or both, according to your taste, really does bring us directly to the centre of her work. In his discussion of *A Critique of Postcolonial Reason*, Brent Hayes Edwards explores Spivak's writing in terms of the trope of *parataxis*, pointing out that her withholding of connection and conjunction demands an active reading, which he understands in terms of the textile metaphors informing the book, and connects to 'the problem of autobiography in criticism'.[12] More generally, in his introduction to Spivak's work, Stephen Morton straightforwardly and persuasively insists that her, 'style of composition should be considered as an inextrica-ble part of her theoretical method'.[13] Accordingly, it will be useful to bring together this style and what is probably her most well known work, that on the question of the subaltern. As is well known and widely discussed, Spivak's position on metropolitan academic study of subalternity suggests that it is an extremely problematic category, at least insofar as anyone might claim to have isolated any pure, previously suppressed subaltern consciousness. What should be remembered is that Spivak, at least in some of her earlier work, makes clear distinctions between different approaches to subaltern conscious-ness. In her famous reading of Deleuze and Foucault, she makes it entirely clear that their micrological approach to power will continue to be insufficient when transferred to analyses of subalternity; as I'll discuss further later, she asserts that the macrological, ideological analysis best developed in Marxist writings is far less likely to make the kinds of error to which French theory has succumbed: in the revised version of 'Can the Subaltern Speak?' she says simply that French intellectuals can talk all they like about power and desire, but they cannot imagine the power and desire of Europe's Others. However, there are other approaches to subalternity that, again famously, Spivak sees as strategically essentialising. In 'Subaltern Studies', for example, Spivak outlines what looks like a double-bind (and is therefore by definition not a question of either-or, although this has often been overlooked) when it comes to representation and the subaltern:

> Reading the work of Subaltern Studies from within but against the grain, I would suggest that elements in their text would warrant a reading of the project to retrieve the subaltern consciousness as the attempt to undo a massive historiographic metalepsis and 'situate' the effect of the subject as subaltern. I would read it, then, as a *strategic* use of positivist essentialism in a scrupulously visible political interest.[14]

Such a strategic essentialism would be a phase through which to pass, per-haps, but at the moment there is an apparently stark choice which really must be resisted: 'The radical intellectual in the West is either caught in a deliberate choice of subalternity, granting to the oppressed that very expres-sive subjectivity which s/he criticizes or, instead, a total unrepresentability' (SR,209).

Spivak's warnings about the subaltern, even if they do not begin as such, tend to crystallize both in reception and in her later work into a rigorous logic of exclusion: the 'speaking' subaltern is no longer the subaltern. This logic is apparently in contrast with Philipe Lejeune, who writes of

> trying to break down the logic that maintains that, as soon as the working-class memory *is written*, it ceases to belong to the working class and circulates only among limited circles of militants or intellectuals (and, for all that, without reaching the general public).[15]

In Spivak's terms, as soon as subaltern memory is written it is no longer that of the subaltern – it belongs to the ex-subaltern, or more likely is packaged by the metropolitan migrant for consumption, however well-meaning. As she says in the interview 'Subaltern Talk', 'every moment that is noticed as a case of subalternity is undermined. We are never looking at the pure subaltern. There is, then, something of a not-speakingness in the very notion of subalternity'(SR,289). If that is so, then there is something perhaps grimly ironic in the extreme visibility of Spivak herself – or the staged and endlessly self-reflexive discussion of a vanishing Spivak, who becomes increasingly the topic of her writing. Rather than sound merely disapproving of this strangely self-denying autobiographical drive, this chapter will test its limits, convinced that there is some kind of connection between the tones and modes of Spivak's theories, and their themes and conclusions. The chapter will accordingly revisit what Spivak has to say about subalternity, testimony, about various (and conflicting) versions of French theory, and her thematisation and performance of autobiography. It's easy to be nervous about the difficulty of Spivak's writing (many are), or mocking about its clumsy jargon (many have been), but either way we will fail to get a good sense of her critical project and the possibilities it has opened (or those it closes down). This chapter will make an effort at debating with Spivak without domesticating her writing.

Identity politics

One thing that Spivak especially targets is what she calls 'chromatism', which may have its expressions in everyday life but is perhaps particularly troubling in the university. In an essay titled 'Being a White Male', published in 1992, Terry Caesar makes the point that, 'Everybody knows what a white male is, and nobody wants to be one'.[16] Discussing various stories of the white male in US academia, Caesar argues that such an identity has been the static given around which the active margins circulate, and on which they prey. It may or may not be comforting to Caesar to know that, ten years later, whiteness and maleness have both become academic growth industries in themselves – the catch being, that the result is less a making problematic of every identity, and far more a reification of every identity, so that now academics all *know* exactly what opinion colleagues will hold on any given issue, on the basis of whatever identities they assume in any given discourse. Of course it is not quite that simple, and the assumption of identities and their constant remaking, is a central theme in various critical cultural discourses, to the point that no assumption should be safe. However, that such reification is in fact what often happens seems difficult to dispute. Spivak names this tendency chromatism because, she argues, pigmentation is equated with political positioning. Such a phenomenon is centrally important to any investigation of the autobiographical writing of postcolonial theory. Returning to Terry Caesar's essay, he defends himself against any accusation of being *merely* anecdotal by asserting that there has been a 'feminist co-option of 'the personal' in the writing of discursive prose'.[17] There is a danger that the autobiographical nature of postcolonial theories might become merely the assertion of critical thinking rather than its actuality, if that co-option takes place, or if it is allowed to go unqualified.

Given that I've now introduced the question of critical thinking, and critical projects, an obvious thing to do is to look at how Spivak appropriates Kant, as her reading is one place to look for explicit and sustained theorization. This will focus the chapter more directly on postcolonial theory, particularly Spivak's theorization of the investigating subject. Not all of the texts she reads are anything like transparent, and some of what she has to say is (as she herself admits, although it sometimes looks less like an admission and more like a boast) nothing like orthodox. However, I'll keep things as simple as possible within the orientation of this book. In this section, for example, I'll be introducing what she has to say about Kant as it pertains to an autobiographical theory. Initially, I will consider Spivak's insistence on taking into account the *parerga* of Kant's text: the non-intrinsic, strictly that which does not belong to the object's whole presentation.[18] Spivak's main treatment of Kant (specifically the 3rd *Critique*) is found at the beginning of *A Critique of Postcolonial Reason*, and I want to use it to open a consideration of Spivak's general treatment of the limitations of the investigating subject. Spivak explicitly signals her debt to Lyotard's presentation of Kant, and her reading develops various points coming from the introduction of the body and its orientation; her general argument is that, 'The subject as such in Kant is geopolitically differentiated'.[19] The first point to note is that Spivak in the preface to the *Critique* refers to Kant, Hegel, and Marx as, 'remote discursive precursors', (CPR,3) a suitably non-committal choice of designation, which holds open from the start Spivak's sense that our investment in the notion of critique prevents any simple disavowal of Kant. In Spivak's narrative, the end of the eighteenth century sees the emergence of new narratives of self/otherness that soon become assimilated by narratives of empire, whilst still pretending to have universal applicability. Such a narrative, with precautions, is familiar and justifiable. What follows becomes steadily more enigmatic, and so I'll try to piece things together slowly. Indeed, Caroline Rooney suggests, in reading the same sections (albeit with a different emphasis) that, 'you would need to read all this for yourself for the summaries will be hasty'.[20]

Spivak begins her specific treatment of Kant with the assertion that, 'I write in the conviction that sometimes it is best to sabotage what is inexorably to hand, than to invent a tool that no one will test, while mouthing varieties of liberal pluralism'(CPR,9). *Sabotage* is apparently exactly what occurs in Spivak's reading, although perhaps she invites us to think this rather too easily, prefacing these passages with the insistence that her reading is a category error and 'mistaken' in the sense that it imports the empirical into the transcendental. Spivak suggests that her reading does not immediately amount to an appropriation, recalling Kant's own reintroduction of the empirical into the transcendental, which seems to be a necessity beyond any discussion of intention (*Absicht*).[21] Her reading claims to be, then, Kantian in an important sense. The reading itself appears straightforward, at least for a while. Her basic assertion is that there is, in this text as a specific example, an anthropomorphizing moment that is irreducible to the systemic and the philosophical. This anthropomorphizing moment, present in all texts, licenses Spivak to anthropomorphize the Kantian narrative, the better to access its close associations of violence, decision, and ethical programmatics. She does not argue that such an operation is a dismissal of Kant, insisting that this is merely marking what *cannot not* be in operation: 'Such [an anthropomorphic] moment is irreducible in [Kant's] text, as it is in any discursive practice, including, of course, de Man's or mine. The best we can do is to *attempt* to account for it'(CPR,16)[22]. How does she account for this moment in Kant's text, which as I implied earlier is hardly an accidental place to find this necessary contamination?

Spivak reconstructs Kant's argument in the following way. Reason (*Vernunft*) requires culture (*Kultur*) but is not solely produced by culture (culture here being cultivation – with precautions, *education*). One is naturally inclined to reason through the given-ness of sensibility (*Sinnlichkeit*), and sensibility is prior to cultivation. According to Kant some, however, are naturally uneducable, because they are not given this sensibility – for example, the poor or women. A more enigmatic term accompanies these categories – *dem rohen Menschen*, 'man in the raw' (as Spivak translates). Spivak expands this term to the *primitive*, and it might seem that her gesture almost repeats the central gestures of primitivist discourses in attempting to analyse one example. However, this point ought not to rely on locating the specific gesture 'in' Kant, and as I understand this section, Spivak is simply not interested in arguing about Kant's prejudices.[23] Spivak is more concerned to read a projected generality of imperialism through Kant. Following Kant, then, she argues that the educational task of imperialism is both impossible and necessary: the specifically Western phenomenon 'culture' is required to educate the raw man into moral feeling, but this education is apparently inherently unachievable. Spivak notes what she calls a 'proper' philosophical dismissal of the rhetorical invocation of the raw man (she backs her point through reference to homonyms in Kant's text[24]), but simply argues that this dismissal ignores a very real foreclosure, one that operates to deny speech and subjectivity. To the question, 'Who comes after (before) the subject?', the answer will have all too easily been, 'the Aboriginal'. For Spivak it is in this case facile and irrelevant to insist that the performance of Kant's text is deconstructed, since the 'real needs of imperialism' (CPR,30) are served precisely by that performance. In a way comparable to Foucault's analysis of Descartes as successful speech act, Spivak asserts the performative power of Kant's philosophy.

The extent to which this act is necessarily successful is up for discussion, but it can hardly be argued that imperialism did *not* have real needs, and that arguments like this did *not* serve such needs. In any case, if we return to the question of the *sensus communis*, in Spivak's presentation of Kant the *man* that would have this common sense, and therefore the man with whom one could communicate, and who would thereby become part of the community, is not up for debate. Spivak states clearly again: 'Kant's philosophical project, whether sublime or bourgeois, operates in terms of an implicit cultural difference'(CPR,32). To rewrite this argument following Derrida's critique of Hegel: the irreducible contingency surviving in philosophical systems will have had effects that are not, by their specific nature, reducible to marginal status. If (and this is one of the central themes to be drawn from rewritings of Kant) ethics is dependent on the individual's inability to cognize him- or herself[25] (a cognizance allowing the unchallengeable application of rules), then this insufficiency invades both the philosophical and the *practical*. Spivak accordingly suggests that, 'theory (analyzing the sublime) is always already normed by practice (having to assume a moral being)'(CPR,24). Yet, as needs re-stating, this necessary insufficiency or contamination at the projected source of our critical modes of thinking is not something we can simply wish away, or decide to leave behind by adopting defiantly novel ways of philosophizing, collating, and reproducing. Spivak's treatment of Kant comes at the beginning of a lengthy chapter on Kant, Hegel, and Marx. Whilst it is true that the chronological progression through this trio is accompanied by some kind of moral progression, one of the recurring themes is the continued complicity between what we might otherwise be given to believe are simply opposed blocks of thought.[26]

Subaltern testimony

During her discussion of Kant, Spivak refers at one point to, 'the prisonhouse of academic identity politics'(CPR,29). I want now to consider the necessities of acknowledgement and resistance that this Nietzschean echo implies, and to suggest how Spivak maintains the double gesture that her critique demands, not claiming to transcend such politics but simultaneously not subscribing to them. I will approach this through some of her more directly autobiographical passages, constantly referring them to more general questions of subjectivity and agency. Scattered throughout Spivak's essays are autobiographical interludes of a bewildering variety. The rest of this chapter will connect these passages to some of the broader controversial arguments present in Spivak's work. First, I will consider Spivak's perhaps most controversial argument: the following discussion considers Spivak's 'Can the Subaltern Speak?',[27] motivated by that essay's re-appearance as part of a chapter in her *Critique of Postcolonial Reason*. This appearance was announced some time ago: the editors of *The Spivak Reader*, Donna Landry and Gerald MacLean, note that Spivak refused its publication in that collection, in original or revised form, 'because of the importance of the revised version for her forthcoming book, *An Unfashionable Grammatology*, and because her revisions, although they leave her conclusions unchanged, have made the original version obsolete'.[28] That title went the way of many other Spivak titles, providing further easy jokes for her critics, and even foregrounding the extent to which the version in the *Critique* is in fact substantially the same. This discussion will try to bring out the apparently small difference made, the way Spivak has demonstrated an argument without stating it. In response to the first question in 'Subaltern Talk', about the reception of 'Can the Subaltern Speak?', Spivak notes that, 'It has even been suggested by some that I will not *allow* resistance to speak';[29] whereas of course it is precisely the stance of *allowing resistance to speak* that is under scrutiny. I find Spivak's revised conclusion to this essay central to the *Critique*. On the assertion that the subaltern cannot speak, Spivak later notes that, 'It was an inadvisable remark'.[30] I will argue that – inadvisable as it may have been – this remark remains central to the essay, especially in its recontextualised appearance in the *Critique*.

First, I will reconstruct the argument of 'Can the Subaltern Speak?' as it appeared in its longest stand-alone form, but interspersed with quotation from the revised version, especially where such quotation expands or emphasises the connections to Spivak's most general arguments. In introductions to post-colonial studies, this essay invariably assumes prominence in discussions of Spivak, and has led to significantly differing readings. It does appear to have a reasonably straightforward, if lengthy, argument. The argument is some-thing like the following: 'Can the Subaltern Speak?' is an anti-foundationalist critique of the concept of a subaltern subject constructed as accessible and rep-resentable by the disinterested intellectual. Noting that, 'I don't think there is a non-institutional environment',[31] Spivak questions the possibility of recover-ing the subaltern voice in a way which is not an essentialist fiction. The project of giving a voice to those written out of history in conventional accounts has both emotional and political (strategic) validity, but proves theoretically problematic according to Spivak's account.

As in her 'Subaltern Studies: Deconstructing Historiography',[32] Spivak focuses on Ranajit Guha's 'Subaltern Studies' project, which of course aims to displace elite history. Spivak praises the recognition of the colonial sub-ject's heterogeneity, and gives qualified support to the attempt to construct a 'politics of the people'; however, she finds serious problems in the con-struction of a speaking position for the subaltern. Wanting to acknowledge the continuity and vigour of postcolonial practice, its ability to transform and resist colonial incursions and definitional/exclusional strategies, she argues that the poststructuralist mode of the 'Subaltern Studies' project disguises its essentialism – this much I summarized earlier. How, Spivak asks, can one construct a category of the subaltern with a 'voice' which is audible clearly and unproblematically above the constant multiple echoes of its inevitable heterogeneity? To demonstrate this general argument, Spivak introduces gen-der into the colonizer/colonized polarity: using the example of *sati*, she argues that the gendered subaltern is controlled by both traditional patri-archal authority and by the colonizing power. Spivak's conclusion has been received with most reservations, perhaps because it has been widely miscon-strued, or perhaps because its scope and specificity seem at best imprecise, and possibly confused. She appears to argue that the true subaltern, with an identity constructed (in the 'Subaltern Studies' project) through difference, cannot be a knowing and speaking subject. Accepting this impossibility (in a signalled and specific context) the intellectual should not reconstruct the subaltern as yet another unproblematic field of knowing, which would confine its effects to the very form of representation to which the project is explicitly opposed. Regarding the construction of true subalternity, she concludes: 'Subaltern historiography must confront the impossibility of such gestures'.[33]

This outline covers the essay's broadest arguments, but obviously schematically. To understand further what Spivak's text argues and performs, I will approach it through the opening discussion of Deleuze and Foucault. Spivak contrasts their understanding of the transparency of the investigating subject with the writings of Derrida: I will sharpen this contrast later, in this chapter and the next, by discussing Spivak and Derrida in terms of autobiographical theoretical texts. Spivak's discussion of Foucault and Deleuze focuses on their 'Intellectuals and power: a conversation between Michel Foucault and Gilles Deleuze'.[34] Her argument is that they unknowingly substitute various primitivised subjects for the sovereign subject they explicitly critique. Further, they systematically ignore their own ideological positioning, understood in an Althusserian sense, in that they (implicitly) identify other positions as ideological, but are silent on their own (necessary) ideological marking. For Spivak, when Deleuze refers to '*the* workers' struggle', this demonstrates a tendency (in this specific context) to homogenize various key discontinuous concepts, resulting in the treatment of global capitalism entirely in the terms of Western capitalism. At the same time Spivak wants to generalize her suspicions of Deleuze's contribution, suggesting that this problem with ideology can be found in Deleuze and Guattari's theories of desire, which fail to consider relations of desire, power, and subjectivity: they have no theory of ideology, or of interests. This inattention to ideology manifests itself, in Spivak's reading, in the utilization of an undivided subject, which for Spivak re-empowers a subject that is specifically *European*. She suggests that the operation of this essentialism within poststructuralist modes of thought relies on notions of 'concrete experience' constitutive of positivisms of various kinds. And as Foucault and Deleuze apparently assume the disclosure of reality through the intellectual, their inattention to their own (unavoidable) complicity with international capitalism is disabling.

Spivak shifts focus at this point in 'Can the Subaltern Speak?', considering more general questions of representation arising from the analysis of Deleuze and Foucault. In the *Critique* she exasperatedly corrects those who take Marx's description ('they cannot represent themselves ...') to be a prescription, or those (like Deleuze, in her presentation) who apparently introduce continuity into discontinuous senses of representation. Deleuze, Spivak argues, conflates two discrete senses of representation: representation as *speaking for*, and representation as *re-presentation*. The Foucault-Deleuze conversation constructs a sequence of unproblematic subalterns, implying their own investigative transparency, accordingly privileging a specifically Western mode of investigative subjectivity. It is worth re-emphasizing here that this mode of subjectivity is precisely what Deleuze and Foucault are apparently critiquing, and is a major symptom, in their reading, of the insufficiency of Marxist analysis. Deleuze, for instance, argues that, 'The thrust of Marxism was to determine the problem [that power is more diffuse than the structure of exploitation and state formation] essentially in terms of interests (power is held by a ruling class defined by its interests)'.[35] Their target is any monolithic understanding of power, an understanding that they want to associate with monolithic constructions of subjectivity. Foucault's later writings on sexuality, as I indicated earlier, notoriously put forward a highly dispersed model of power as necessary in the reading of specifically *micrological* operations of power. For Deleuze and Foucault, Marxism (as we have seen in its brief treatment in *The Order of Things*)[36] is conceived as continuous with (or even consequent upon) the very modes of existence it supposedly critiques. For Spivak, such an understanding is insufficient to the workings of global capitalism, workings unjustifiably bracketed in this analysis. For example, the complexity of the relationships between global capitalism and nation-state alliances is simply too macrological to be explained by micrological readings of power, although this problem is reversible; Spivak in fact does not dismiss the Foucault-Deleuze emphasis, clearly arguing that, 'the relationship between global capitalism (exploitation in economics) and nation-state alliances (domination in geopolitics) is so macrological that it cannot account for the micrological texture of power' (CPR,263). However, Foucault and Deleuze *merely* reverse the terms of the analysis, neglecting the macrological, and Spivak not only wants to maintain this macrological analysis, but also implicitly to account for its neglect. A theory of ideology is therefore necessary, something clearly lacking in the Foucault-Deleuze conversation. So, their analysis will have been inadequate from its inception. Further than that, however, their accompanying critique of subjectivity is incomplete:

> The S/subject, curiously sewn together into a transparency by denegations, belongs to the exploiters' side of the international division of labor. It is impossible for contemporary French intellectuals to imagine the kind of Power and Desire that would inhabit the unnamed subject of the Other of Europe. It is not only that everything they read, critical or uncritical, is caught within the debate of the production of that Other, supporting or critiquing the constitution of the Subject as Europe. It is also that, in the constitution of that Other of Europe, great care was taken to obliterate the textual ingredients with which such a subject could cathect, could occupy ('invest'?) its itinerary – not only by ideological and scientific production, but also by the institution of the law.[37]

Spivak insists that localized resistances supplement Marxism, in practice, with all the Derridean implications of that supplementarity intact. The privileging of the micrological is specific to the First World. This argument coincides with my concerns about primitivism and exoticism, dangers apparent in some treatments of postcolonial autobiography. Also coinciding with my argument about what I have called autobiography, Spivak wants to connect this argument to a concern with subjectivity and 'textual ingredients'. I find 'Can the Subaltern Speak?' straightforward enough up to this point, although there is some ambiguity (for example, in the final sentence of the passage quoted immediately above, which conceivably covers a disparate variety of the positions I am considering) and a lack of sympathy towards some of the texts involved. Of course the essay has provoked extensive and emotional response from a multitude of critical positions, mostly concerning what *follows* the critique of Foucault and Deleuze. However, to ignore this initial analysis is to decontextualize the sections on the subaltern and Bhubaneswari Bhaduri, and also significantly to misconstrue Spivak's distinction between Foucault-Deleuze and Derrida, who is introduced later in the essay. I will therefore continue to reconstruct the argument of 'Can the Subaltern Speak?', connecting the various sections, but also looking forward to the essay's recontextualization as part of chapter three of the *Critique*, a recontextualization that expands Spivak's concern over the question of textuality and subjectivity.

Continuing, Spivak highlights the incompleteness of a 'poststructuralist' account of both intellectual and subaltern agency. She finds Foucault's account of the emergence of 'modern' forms of knowledge glaringly incomplete. As others have suggested, the epistemic violence of the redefinition of sanity at the end of the eighteenth century can be seen as intimately related to the constitution of the colonial subject as Other: 'What if the two projects of epistemic overhaul worked as dislocated and unacknowledged parts of a vast two-handed engine?'.[38] The omissions of Foucault's account, for Spivak, are not derived from blindness to facts. Foucault, like Deleuze (at least, Deleuze in this context), relies on an explanatory totalizing 'desire', writing in terms of libidinal instead of social being. But the result of a theory of libidinal being is still, for Spivak, a posited form of 'pure consciousness', its content different but form identical: 'pure consciousness' is surreptitiously relocated in the unconscious or the *subject-in-oppression*. Spivak further develops this account, suggesting that Deleuze exemplifies benevolent first-world appropriation and re-inscription of the Third World as Other, whilst Foucault is apparently unaware of the topographical re-inscription of imperialism and therefore consolidates its effects through his accounts.[39] The self-contained West is a creation of the imperialist project, and Foucault re-inscribes this idea: 'The clinic, the asylum, the prison, the university –all seem to be screen-allegories that foreclose a reading of the broader narratives of imperialism'.[40]

By way of contrast, Spivak introduces Derrida (very briefly, in the revised version) in order to think about the *mechanics* of constitution of the Other, in contrast to appeals to a notional authenticity of the Other. The emphasis placed on mechanics remains perhaps enigmatic: are these mechanics a necessary feature of discourse on the other, insofar as it sets off from a subject-object split? When Spivak refers to the 'positionality of investigating subjects',(CPR,283) there is some hesitation over the extent to which this can be overcome, and whether or not such an overcoming would necessarily entail the transformation of a practical positioning (a gesture Spivak elsewhere dismisses as further primitivism) or could be accounted for and worked through in theoretical terms. Spivak's invocation of Derrida occurs more directly in many other texts, but it is at this moment in 'Can the Subaltern Speak?' that her reading makes most sense. Specifically, she recalls Derrida's references in *Of Grammatology* to various 'prejudices' – specifically around the question of the search for the perfect language, and the supposedly arithmetical qualities of Chinese characters. There is much to be said about Derrida's careful warnings against simplistic reversals and primitivisms, as I have already suggested. At this point in her essay, however, Spivak introduces Derrida to think about what might be called a feminist issue, although that would instantly delimit its bounds restrictively. This section of Spivak's essay provoked the most heated responses, and therefore allows me to strategically slice into what is at stake.

These issues arise from an apparent meeting point of Marxist, feminist, and postcolonial concerns. To recall the final section of the essay, intact in the *Critique*, which considers questions of 'gender and development' through an analysis of *sati*, Spivak there notoriously reduces her (specific, but generalisable) argument to, 'White men are saving brown women from brown men' (CPR,284). She notes that, 'my insistence on imperialist subject-production as the occasion for this sentence discloses a politics that I cannot step around' (CPR,284)[41]. This 'I' is to be generalized, as I will suggest later. Additionally, the generalisability of the argument has been questioned. Spivak introduces this example of *sati*, then the specific example of (the non-subaltern) Bhubaneswari Bhaduri. In both cases, the justification for the specific example remains enigmatic. However, the case of *sati* is a particular example of a certain mode of subject-production which Spivak will generalize in the *Critique*, and the empirical example (and its relation-production) are specific kinds of rewriting this subject-constitution. The generalisability is not absolute, but then one consequence of the models of exemplarity to which Spivak seems to subscribe is that final generality is an objectivist illusion, and that examples' wider application (further, their potential exemplarity) is always to be produced.

What is this specific mode of subject-constitution that Spivak is challenging, both thematically and formally? Once again Spivak invokes Foucault's account of the epistemic delineation of the scientific, which depends upon the declared shift from private to public. What in abstract terms can be viewed as the elevation of the 'masculine' at the expense of the 'feminine' here is (only slightly) re-cast as the colonial codification of Brahminical law. There are two narratives of *sati*: the British narrative (the sentence quoted above) and the nativist narrative that 'They wanted to die'. In neither case is there even the beginning of a counter-sentence, the minimal testimony necessary to the production of the counter-example. It is clear that the counter-example is required to challenge both narratives. However, in common with the essay's implied concern (and that of the *Critique*) Spivak focuses on the British narrative, which quickly stands in for an intuitively larger mass of knowledge, ethics, and law. The protection of women by men is commonly invoked as a moment transitional towards a 'good society', and this moment exceeds legal equality; Spivak argues that, 'Imperialism's (or globalization's) image as the establisher of the good society is marked by the espousal of the woman as *object* of protection from her own kind'(CPR,291). It is almost as if the British codification of *sati* operates to conceal a general effacement of gendered positioning: 'the broader question of the constitution of the sexed subject is hidden by foregrounding the visible violence of *sati*'(CPR,300). The *Critique* makes clear the exemplary status of *sati* in Spivak's analysis of a particular mode of subject-production.

There are various ways that this subject-production or -constitution is challenged. The section of the essay that thematically considers one example of challenge has been the most provocative, particularly its blunt assertion that the subaltern cannot speak. This has been an assertion that has consistently been literalized, although perhaps understandably, as I will argue. Spivak's argument is, however, concisely enough expressed:

> The case of *suttee* as exemplum of the woman-in-imperialism would challenge and reconstruct this opposition between subject (law) and object-of-knowledge (repression) and mark the place of 'disappearance' with something other than silence and nonexistence, a violent aporia between subject and object status.[42]

What is this *something other than silence*? Spivak insists that it is necessary to use an example in order to think about interventionist practice, but this necessity remains unargued: I take it that an example is the minimal condition for the production of counter-sentences. Her relation of the example of Bhubaneswari Bhaduri is concerned with the *blocking* of such counter-production by those who elevate a supposedly pure 'native' consciousness. Like Deleuze and Foucault, who render themselves transparent and produce (whilst disclaiming any production whatsoever) a pure working-class consciousness, there is something of disavowal in the operations of the 'liberal multiculturalist academy'. Recounting (in the *Critique*) a discussion of the example with a colleague, which ended in casual dismissal, Spivak writes that, 'I was so unnerved by this failure of communication that, in the first version of this text, I wrote, in the accents of passionate lament: the subaltern cannot speak! It was an inadvisable remark'(CPR,308). However, the sense in which 'speaking' has been misunderstood around this essay needs to be sharpened: this is not merely a question of mistaking 'speaking' for 'talking'. What Spivak seems to argue (and what remains only implicit, despite her use of speech-act theoretical vocabulary) is that texts, whilst signed, are necessarily also countersigned. In the case of Bhubaneswari Bhaduri, her embodied speech act (her *use* of menstruation) has almost not been countersigned at all. And, to return to the analysis of Foucault and Deleuze, there appears to be an *ideological* explanation for this lack.

It is this ideological explanation to which the *Critique* is dedicated, and it is a question of autobiography, examples, and their transformation within given contexts. 'Can the Subaltern Speak?' concerns, on one level, the transformation (and suspicion) of psycho-biographical models, specifically in the context of subaltern studies and the production of a pure subaltern consciousness. However, the ideological explanations Spivak implies and sometimes states pertain to the psycho-biographies and auto-expositions of the First World feminist i.e. the investigating subject. Accordingly, I will now consider the ways in which Spivak's own texts countersign and produce counter-examples, but also the ways that they resist the straightforward equation of certain textual gestures with oppositionality. So, clearly Spivak wants to produce 'a deconstitution of the colonial subject', and to displace 'Europe's preferred autobiography as history';[43] at the same time, however, she insists that there is no easy substitution of some other autobiographical 'I'-'We', and therefore constantly stages an insufficiency of her autobiographical gestures. For example, in 'Acting Bits/Identity Talk' Spivak produces, 'a series of citations of "myself" engaged in identity talk' in order to consider the position – found by Spivak in Assia Djebar's *Fantasia: An Algerian Cavalcade* – that, 'to achieve autobiography in the double bind of the practice of the conqueror's writing is to learn to be taken seriously by the gendered subaltern who has not mastered that practice'.[44] It is this sense of a precarious metropolitan autobiography, which is an autobiography that is made precarious, that Spivak's work at least attempts to maintain, if not always successfully.

Deconstruction as impossible autobiography

What Spivak's work is constantly gesturing toward is an impossible autobiography, which is, as she herself might put it, something we cannot *not* want. The sense in which we exist within this double-bind needs to be explored, and to do so I will reiterate one context for Spivak's intervention in the *Critique*, her most sustained attempt at exploring the double-bind. To really understand what is happening in this text, however, certain responses that refuse the double-bind should be explained. So, postcolonial theory has been for some time under criticism, accused of neglecting macrological economic analysis, of playing dangerous identitarian political games, and of promoting textuality to an absurdly overstated position, overall constituting a form of intellectual neo-colonialism. There is a certain renewed self-construction of Marxist analysis taking place in these criticisms, evident in the analyses of Aijaz Ahmad, Neil Lazarus, and Benita Parry.[45,46] Perhaps the most concise example of this tendency is Eagleton's review of the *Critique of Postcolonial Reason*, which I discussed in my introduction. Eagleton, renowned for his capacity for crystallizing critical positions, forcefully suggests that Spivak is exemplary of the problems inherent in poststructuralist materialisms, specifically those hailing from the US. He argues that Spivak's writing is entirely predictable in the context of capital's radical mobility, and that her autobiographical style accompanies an unwillingness to actually perform the critique announced by the book's title. Eagleton's review was the occasion for several issues' discussion on the letters page of the *London Review of Books*. This chapter considers in more depth one aspect of Eagleton's argument against Spivak, generalized to postcolonial theory in its projected entirety – the autobiographical style. What I will find Spivak most often implying or demonstrating, but sometimes explicitly arguing, is apparently the opposite of what this style is taken to show: Spivak demonstrates that identitarian claims (claims to alterity) are severely problematic at best, and dishonest on occasion. The constant claim, repeated by Lazarus and Brennan recently, that Spivak is, to be generous, an inconsistent Marxist, is apparently challenged by an attention to critical form and a mimicry of critical styles. But this mimicry is not simply mocking, and I will also find Spivak repeating a certain resistance of feminist analysis to a supposedly encompassing materialism – *A Critique of Postcolonial Reason* does, after all, announce itself in its preface as a *feminist* book.[47]

To think about Spivak's autobiographical style, I want to quickly recall Derrida's 'Circumfession', and Spivak's discussion of that text in 'Three Women's Texts and Circumfession'.[48] She is specifically *not* arguing that Derrida is 'the postcolonial autobiographer' (e.g. p.11), but Derrida's texts offer extremely powerful ways to think about theory and autobiography together. Many of Derrida's texts argue and demonstrate a particular logic of exemplarity, and set up an understanding of singularities as simply what call for translation, being therefore only quasi-singularities. A quasi-singularity is, in terms that Peter Hallward's book *Absolutely Postcolonial*[49] introduces to postcolonial theoretical debate, relational, and therefore specific; my point is not quite Hallward's, but I'll return to that later, as it'll sharpen what this book has to say generally. Regardless, this apparently more abstract level of description will help to demonstrate what is taking place in autobiographical translation. Later, I discuss Derrida's *Monolingualism of the Other*.[50] This text shares with his earlier *Spurs*[51] a perhaps curious insistence on the misunderstanding of Derrida's term *dissemination*: in both texts there is the assertion that, contrary to standard interpretation, dissemination is at least as much about singularity as plurality.[52] This insistence can be related to the occasions for these texts: *Spurs* considers the place of 'woman' in Nietzsche, *Monolingualism*, the status of the autobiographical instance of 'the colonized'. These brutal simplifications miss much of what takes place in these texts, and much of what I will discuss later, but do at least have the virtue of suggesting two contexts to which Derrida is, despite certain claims to the contrary, more or less sensitive: women's studies and postcolonial studies. So, I will be suggesting that something in the theorization of singularity, and in the demonstration of autobiography, retains a sense of the precariousness of institutional identities whilst celebrating the potential for continued 'poetic' reinvention. I will find Spivak attending to the same set of questions, perhaps drawing slightly different conclusions, conclusions addressed to a particular set of institutional contexts, but also concerned to remember the non-saturability of context and the always already broken-ness of institutional frames.

To approach the most far-reaching arguments of the *Critique of Postcolonial Reason* I will consider certain recurring themes and modes of discourse present in *In Other Worlds*. I return to Spivak's earlier work, in preparation for consideration of the more recent text, in order to trace the continuities present alongside the radical departures C. L. Innes identifies in the *Critique*.[53] Spivak's work, despite its fragmentary qualities, is united by an immense coherence of argument, which extends further than the rewritings of earlier essays that constitute much of the *Critique*. The later text may be the first full statement of the argument, an argument signalled by various mutations of its title over the years, but Spivak has constantly written to and about the metropolitan feminist intellectual. Shadowing Spivak's argument that *we* must learn to see ourselves as *others* would see us, and imagining Aijaz Ahmad's response to that argument, Innes suggests that, 'Ahmad would no doubt reply that "we" have been all too prone "to see ourselves as others would see us"';[54] Ahmad might make this response, but the response appears to talk past Spivak's argument (in the sense that the 'we' in question has not until recently acknowledged or even been aware of what it was up to), but the rest of this discussion will attempt to address its apparent criticism.

I will begin with the translator's preface and translation of 'Draupadi', in order to explore Eagleton's charge that Spivak fails to attend to the language of literature – to the literary qualities of language. If I am correct in my presentation of Spivak, in claiming that her writing is a demonstration of a certain argument, then we might also expect to find explicit thematization of such concerns. Thematization is given early in the translator's preface:

> When we speak for ourselves, we urge with conviction: the personal is also political. For the rest of the world's women, the sense of whose personal micrology is difficult (though not impossible) for us to acquire, we fall back on a colonialist theory of most efficient information retrieval.[55]

This argument is certainly familiar from the *Critique*, which finds the continued invocation and then foreclosure of the native informant perspective (rather, Spivak finds a simultaneity of invocation and foreclosure). That argument is the specificity of the later text. Here, however, Spivak is concerned to read Devi's story as allegorical, and to find its villain, Senanayak, to be a useful expression of 'first world' benevolence, 'the closest approximation to the First World scholar in search of the Third World' (IOW,179):

> In *theory*, Senanayak can identify with the enemy. But pluralist aesthetes of the First World are, willy-nilly, participants in the production

of an exploitative society. Hence in *practice*, Senanayak must destroy the enemy, the menacing other. He follows the necessities and contingencies of what he sees as his historical moment. There is a convenient colloquial name for that as well: pragmatism. (IOW,179)

Spivak uses 'enemy' advisedly, and it is the only term appropriate to Devi's story. She notes the rather brutal simplicity of this reading, but it is a reading licensed by the text – as translated, of course, by Spivak. The story does apparently play with the violence of an asserted discontinuity between theory and practice, the necessary undoing of such an opposition in pursuit of revolutionary change. Towards the story's close, Spivak renders a brief moment of free indirect speech from Senanayak, considering the perceived dangers of the tribal peoples: 'One can shoot and get rid of the ones whose only recourse is extrinsic book learning and sincere intrinsic enthusiasm. Those who are working practically will not be exterminated so easily'(IOW,191). Sections of the story are broken down into an insistent if inconsistently-fulfilled ontological demand – a 'what is?' that confirms Senanayak in his mastery of the situation, even as the situation is beyond his control. His knowledge is of what Spivak here as elsewhere terms the 'self-consolidating Other', on the one hand a theory and on the other, a practice. Most significantly for my argument, however, is Spivak's diagnosis of the causes of this break:

> The assumption of such a clean break in fact depends upon the assumption that the individual subject who theorizes and practices is in full control. At least in the history of the Indo-European tradition in general, such a sovereign subject is also the legal or legitimate subject, who is identical with his stable patronymic. (IOW,185)

Explicitly Spivak makes this discontinuity between theory and practice a question of the sovereign subject, and more specifically of a certain 'masculist' version of that subject, should that constitute a qualification. This argument will be revisited in the *Critique*, and consistently Spivak will argue that there is an increasing tendency for metropolitan women to occupy this position, valuing 'efficient information retrieval'. In perhaps her most succinct expression of this concern, 'French Feminism in an International Frame', Spivak simply writes that, 'the First World feminist must learn to stop feeling privileged *as a woman*'(IOW,136). That essay also focused on displacing the centrality of the 'investigator as subject'(IOW,15). So there is, then, a recurrence of a certain argument about the metropolitan (female) writing subject, one that will certainly be re-invoked in the *Critique*. But, as I indicated previously, whilst this question is certainly made into a question, thematised and posed, there is another question that is apparently elided here, and that is the question of language, a question that will attain specific weight when it comes to the rewriting of theory that Spivak recommends and undertakes in much of her work but especially in the *Critique*. In the context of Devi's story, we might wonder about the translation itself – which I am not qualified to judge, an excuse that Spivak might find evasive – and the concomitant allegorical reading. This questioning marks the limit of thematic reading. Such questions I will recall in my discussion of Derrida's *Monolingualism*, a text explicitly concerned at certain junctures with the question of a *poetic* invention.

Here I will continue tracing continuities in Spivak's work between *In Other Worlds* and *A Critique of Postcolonial Reason*. I have raised certain questions about Spivak's attention to form, language, and theme; now I wish to consider the strong thematisation given to intellectual production in 'Scattered Speculations on the Question of Value', which of course frames its discussion of a generalised Value in Marx in the context of contemporary literary critical production, particularly the revision of canons. Her central argument about Marx, however, is that value is less *representation* than *differential*, and that use-value is something of a theoretical fiction – questions of origin become questions of process, a familiarly Derridean gesture. Perhaps most interestingly in the context of Derrida's *Monolingualism*, Spivak recalls Marx's analogy of money and a foreign language (or perhaps the foreignness of language). Here ideas always require translation into a foreign language prior to exchange, an originary difference that Spivak recalls from Saussure, a complication of both use-value and originary accumulation together, although clearly with use-value cast as a *useful* fiction of origin.

These general comments on Marx's theory of Value are worked into the essay's most specific treatments of global financialisation, to the point where this essay appears to be a concentration of the *Critique*'s argument, fifteen years in advance, perhaps unsurprisingly in the light of the later work's considerable use of Spivak's earlier pieces. Concerned to defend economic analysis of neo-colonialism in (in both senses) cultural studies, she writes that, 'A 'culturalism' that disavows the economic in its global operations cannot get a grip on the concomitant production of barbarism'(CPR,168). Further, Spivak suggests that the then prevalent discourse of postmodernism just is neo-colonial: 'the post-modern, in spite of all the cant of modernization, reproduces the 'pre-modern' on another scene'(CPR,169). Specifically, towards the close Spivak criticises Frederic Jameson's work on 'cognitive mapping' in the context of postmodernism, a criticism that is reworked and expanded at the opening of chapter four of the *Critique*, in which Spivak gives fullest expression to the text-ile,[56] textual economic cultural analysis put forward in 'Scattered Speculations'. Most importantly for my discussion, Spivak again elaborates this criticism in the context of the investigating subject. Spivak considers Dominick LaCapra's notion of historiography-as-transference,[57] which she finds rather naïve on questions of power in transference, and, therefore, prone to a certain primitivism comparable to that she finds in Kristeva's *About Chinese Women*.[58] It is this distrust of broadly primitivist gestures that informs Spivak's autobiographical practice, a practice deeply ambivalent toward the possibility of autobiographical (personal) criticism: mimicking but not mocking, as already suggested.

I have tried to outline some of the broad arguments in Spivak's work that I find rewritten in the *Critique*, and I have suggested that these arguments and their redeployment may be usefully understood within the context of an autobiographical critical practice. Before I return to the *Critique*, I should again stress Spivak's ambivalence concerning this autobiography; in the *Critique* she writes that: 'Calling the place of the investigator into question remains a meaningless piety in many recent critiques of the sovereign subject. Although I attempt to sound the precariousness of my position throughout, I know such gestures can never suffice'(CPR,247–8). I will concentrate my discussion around Spivak's criticisms of Jameson at the beginning of chapter four, in which she takes issue with his staging of Marxism against deconstruction. I will concentrate my discussion here because at this point in the text Spivak begins to fulfil the project announced by the title, and draws together some of the dispersed arguments from the first three chapters (which, to reiterate, consist largely of reworked earlier pieces). Here Spivak points to a 'general US ideological subject'(CPR,319) present in Jameson's postmodernism work. It is an interesting section of Spivak's text in that she takes issue with a theoretical position to which we might assume she subscribes. The position to which I refer is expressed famously in Jameson's *Postmodernism*:

> The end of the bourgeois ego, or monad, no doubt brings with it the end of the psychopathologies of that ego – what I have been calling the waning of affect. But it means the end of much more – the end, for example, of style, in the sense of the unique and the personal, the end of the distinctive individual brush stroke (as symbolized by the emergent primacy of mechanical reproduction). As for expression and feelings or emotions, the liberation, in contemporary society, from the older *anomie* of the centered subject may also mean not merely a liberation from anxiety but a liberation from every other kind of feeling as well, since there is no longer a self present to do the feeling.[59]

This passage is fairly self-explanatory, with Jameson finding postmodernism necessarily accompanying the latest stage of multinational capitalism, in which interchangeability of subjectivity entails the *dispersal* of subjectivity, something to be tackled through the previously-mentioned 'cognitive mapping'.[60] Spivak's response to this diagnosis is to suggest that Jameson has converted what is (in Derrida, for example) a philosopheme into a narrateme,[61] and that this chronology and becoming-postmodern of the subject is the latest self-consolidating gesture of the neo-colonialist cultural interpreter. Spivak writes that:

> Rather than prove that the subject has disappeared in postmodernism, the entire analysis hangs on the presence of a subject in a postmodern hyperspace where it *feels* that old-fashioned thing: a loss of identity.

The postmodern, as an inversion of the modern, repeats its discourse.
(CPR,319–20)

What appears to be a rupture, albeit a 'bad' deteriorative one, is figured
by Spivak as a repetition. In her reading of the decentred subject, the effect
of centring is irreducible; as she suggests in 'Scattered Speculations', there
is an originary co-implication of materialist and idealist predications of the
subject.

I want to emphasise not only Spivak's scepticism about a nominally decentred subject of late capitalism, but also her further and related concerns
about the kind of discourse Jameson has produced. Spivak suggests that
Jameson's diagnosis of the late capitalist subject in some senses produces
that subject: 'This apparently descriptive gesture is, alas, a performative:
the thing is done with words; culture is cultural explanation; to say everything is cultural is to make everything *merely* cultural'(CPR,334). Within the
text's broadest argument – that the native informant perspective is simultaneously invoked and foreclosed – this criticism of Jameson finds his text
to be not only incorrect but also irresponsible. In this sense, Spivak's argument bears comparison with Aijaz Ahmad's response to Jameson:[62] Ahmad's
objection to his production by Jameson as a third world subject is not only
that this production is historically and geographically dubious, but also that
it is pressed into the service of a particular kind of self-constitution. Spivak
suggests that, 'like most periodizing and culturally descriptive or explanatory terms in the pre- and post-imperialist West, what is *not* postmodern
shares with the postmodern a manipulation of the geopolitical other in
its production'(CPR,336–7). This argument finds the production of postcolonial subjects in the metropolitan university to be, at least partly, further
manipulation of self-consolidating otherness: 'the privileged inhabitant of
neo-colonial space is often bestowed a subject-position as geo-political other
by the dominant radical'(CPR,339).

The sometimes barely-present shape of Spivak herself is apparently that
privileged inhabitant of neo-colonial space, but this fact has never been
in doubt; the question might be, as Innes ventriloquises Ahmad, to what
extent and in what ways does Spivak challenge this representation of her
own subject-position? I have focussed on Spivak's concerns about the kind
of text constituted and produced by Jameson's *Postmodernism* specifically to
lead into the question of Spivak's own writing in the *Critique*. I have already
indicated that I find a certain mimicry of apparently dominant modes of
academic discourse in Spivak's writing, but that this mimicry is not simply dismissive.[63] That said, nor is it empty in its over-literal repetition: it
does produce a rupture of sorts, and is therefore on the parody side of
Jameson's parody/pastiche divide.[64] Nor does Spivak fall prey to the kind
of objection that is found in Eagleton's characterization of postmodernism as
parodying precisely the art works of the classical avant-garde;[65] this claim
is crucial, because I find greater complexity in the *Critique*'s deployment

of autobiography than Eagleton allows when he dismissively suggests that (as I've already quoted) the, 'work's rather tiresome habit of self-theatricalising and self-alluding is the colonial's ironic self-performance, a satirical stab at scholarly impersonality, and a familiar American cult of personality'.[66].

We might assume from interventions such as 'Who Claims Alterity?'[67] or 'Lives'[68] that Spivak is wholly opposed to the kind of self-constituting autobiographical practice that would claim marginality. In 'Lives', for instance, she writes that, 'I at least found myself constructing Gayatri Spivaks who "represented" various historical and geographic cases'. If this does not sound of itself dubious, later she suggests that, 'These two pieces respond, of course, to the current demand that every interesting person show some marginality, some minimally nondominant class or ethnic origin, some otherish gendering. I remain unconvinced of my particularized and differentiated marginality, alas'.[69] Spivak is sceptical about such claims to marginality, at least to the extent that such claims, if heard, are heard within a privileged context. This reading would not be false, but nor would it be entirely accurate, as is evident from Spivak's response to Benita Parry in *Outside in the Teaching Machine*. This brief response led to the exchange of various polemics on questions of ethnic, national, and political identities,[70] but has perhaps not been examined for its own marked and hardly accidental ambivalence on these questions. Responding to the charge made by Parry (and pointed out to Spivak *by* Parry) that Spivak (with Homi Bhabha and Abdul JanMohamed) silences the native voice, Spivak first quotes herself: 'When Benita Parry takes us to task for not being able to listen to the natives or to let the natives speak, she forgets that the three of us, post-colonials, are "natives" too'. On the same page, Spivak refers to the 'identitarian ethnicist claims of native or fundamental origin'[71] implicit in Parry's criticisms, contrasting these claims with political claims. The two gestures come on the same page, and appear to sit rather awkwardly, despite the scare-quotes Spivak inserts around *natives* (scare-quotes pointedly absent in the equivalent section of the *Critique*). Spivak goes on to claim (and here we should recall the section on Jameson in the *Critique*, where Spivak suggests that the individual's sense of the 'subject' is *catachrestic*) the following:

> Within the historical frame of exploration, colonization, decolonization – what is being effectively reclaimed is a series of regulative political concepts, the *supposedly* authoritative narrative of the production of which was written elsewhere, in the social formations of Western Europe. They are being reclaimed, indeed claimed, as concept-metaphors for which no historically adequate referent may be advanced from postcolonial space, yet that does not make the claims less important. A concept-metaphor without an adequate referent is a catachresis. These claims for founding catachreses also make postcoloniality a deconstructive case.[72]

In Derrida's work there is a paleonymic strategy, the re-appropriation of terminology, which often takes the form of a putting to work of previously

unremarked or marginalized meanings. However, Spivak's notion of catachresis would seem to be a catachresis of catachresis, and the term *concept-
metaphor* itself might be a source of some confusion. What occurs in this
catachretised catachresis is a confusion of claims to the originary status of any
given rhetorical term, theory, or revolutionary model. Accordingly, when
Spivak refers (in an essay on Derrida's debate with John Searle) to 'revolutions that as yet have no model', we are in the space of the postcolonial as
a deconstructive case: an example, but also more than mere example – a
model, exemplary, without being foundational, original or privileged. When
she refers to these revolutions, Spivak is discussing Derrida's 'Limited Inc.: a
b c',[73] which re-elaborates and demonstrates the argument that speech acts,
even when they do succeed, are still marked by the necessary possibility
of their 'failure'. Failure in this context can be understood as what allows
the translation of revolutions between contexts that necessarily vary, however minimally. Failure is the possibility, then, of another kind of success.
Aijaz Ahmad, however, suggests that Spivak's gesture is a form of historical
amnesia that elides the acts of revolutionary heroism constitutive of anti-
colonial struggle: there are, Ahmad insists, historical referents (examples)
to be found in the history of anti-colonial action.[74] That word, *referent*, may
help to explain the misunderstanding here, implying as it does that there
have been no historical instances of the political concepts in question. We
might wonder about the difference between referents and reference; Kalpana
Seshadri-Crooks writes the following concerning Ahmad's 'literalist' critique
of Spivak:

> Spivak's insistence that, insofar as socialism, nationalism, etc. function as
> regulative political concepts, they effectively resituate struggle within the
> frame of imperialism and that this is not a denial of history but a comment
> on the limits of historiography itself. But the literalism permits Ahmad
> to read ideological critique here as free-floating dehistoricizing postmod-
> ernism, thus reenacting, in the name of Marx, what Spivak problematizes:
> ideological regulation.[75]

Ahmad's insistence that Spivak is disallowing all reference to historical
instances of postcolonialism takes her to be arguing that there have been
literally no postcolonial examples of these political concepts in action. Insofar as these political concepts have been regulatory in a certain sense (to the
extent that they have regulated all political talk in terms of *proper*, original
examples, i.e. insofar as they have been owned), they have been limited in
application to postcolonial contexts. So, the literal instances Ahmad cites
were not actually instances of those concepts in action – rather, they transformed those concepts in the instant of enaction in a colonial or postcolonial
context. In parallel, there is the example of 'Can the Subaltern Speak?', as
I have already discussed. We can re-approach that essay with the reference-
referent distinction in mind, and see that Spivak has not really helped her

own case through her choice of certain terms. In one interview, Spivak says that,

> Problems arise if you take this 'speak' absolutely literally as 'talk.' There can be and have been attempts to correct me by way of the fact that some of the women on the pyres did actually utter. Now I think that is a very good contribution, but it really doesn't touch what I was trying to talk about.[76]

Again, it happens that some critics take Spivak as arguing that subaltern women *literally* could not speak (although Spivak might be somewhat exaggerating this misunderstanding); and again, this might come down to the choice of terms subjected to Spivak's catachresis. *Speaking* does not seem a particularly good choice for a catachretised term, at least not without some more elaborate and explicit justification.

All of these questions of terminology, and the invention of language adequate to its object, inspire more consideration of Spivak's position as a literary critic. Much of the autobiographical turn in social science and humanities writing has been traced back to literary studies, not always admiringly. There does seem to be some kind of connection, although this will always be impossible to situate with precision, and many who attempt to situate precisely will be doing so in order to dismiss or disavow. Nonetheless, that Spivak is both a literary critic and autobiographical critic is clearly important. I will here return to the question of Spivak's attention to language, and her transformation of modes of academic discourse, which bears comparison to Derrida's writing. But just as the term 'poetic' stands rather uncertainly in Derrida's *Monolingualism* (as I will discuss in conclusion), so the reader of Spivak is left to wonder at the short-hand references in the *Critique* to literature's singularity. Caroline Rooney expresses concern about Spivak's occasional cavalier dismissals of literature in favour of more serious business, e.g. government archives.[77] However, if the uncertainty around the poetic *is* uncertainty, that might not indicate deficiency in the arguments of Derrida and Spivak, for as is obvious, the literary-poetic is obviously not of itself beneficial or revolutionary. And, as is evident from their shared concern with the necessary and ongoing invention of identity, particularly for certain national, social, and political groupings, Derrida and Spivak look toward a future that will never arrive, not finally, not knowably. This structural openness is written into their auto-expositions. In Derrida's case, on a deliberately denuded level he suggests that *Monolingualism* is an account of why he will never be able to write an autobiography. Spivak's *Critique*, similarly, is structured by a certain self-displacement implied by its subtitle ('Toward a History of the Vanishing Present'), a displacement which suggests that the text constitutes a history of a vanishing Spivak, absent not only to her readers, but also to herself. Further than that, written into Spivak's account is the displaced presence of her readers, a displacement effected by the text, entailing that we cannot take the final specification of the book's implied readership (the university-educated daughters of the disenfranchised diasporic subject) as *final* at all. In making an example of herself, Spivak tests our general sense of exemplarity,[78] what makes a good political example, and accordingly our sense of what makes a good political intervention. I have mentioned that Spivak, like Derrida, finds a constitutive insufficiency in a specific form of auto-exposition. Spivak specifies a context that remains implicit in Derrida's account, naming 'the liberal multiculturalist metropolitan academy' as the 'new mainstream'(CPR,309). It is too simplistic to suggest that there is an *affectation* of subalternity at work in this metropolitan context, and yet Spivak apparently maintains that the affectation of an embattled marginal chromatism is exactly what betrays the supposed empowerment conferred by (post-)subaltern affect. The 'waning of affect' that Jameson finds particular to postmodernism is apparently resisted by metropolitan materialist discourses, discourses that insist on the limitations of postmodern diagnoses, their specificity to a certain context; yet even as the subaltern consciousness is allowed to speak against this previously generalized postmodern subjectivity, this *allowing to speak* begins to look like a *putting forward* that effaces its own context and effects.

Spivak's singularity

Many critics have come at Spivak's writing on subalternity ready to point to examples of speaking, talking, and otherwise articulating subalterns, and she has side-stepped them. Perhaps we should look at someone quite prepared to take on Spivak philosophically (although as I see it, the argument in question suggests that philosophical debate is not quite what her writing invites, either). Peter Hallward, in his *Absolutely Postcolonial*, argues that, 'the only precise and useful meaning of the label 'postcolonial' is one that makes explicit its singularizing implications'.[79] All that hybridity talk is, for Hallward, the very definition of a flattened, non-relational plane, one that denies the legacies of the colonialisms and neo-colonialisms presently playing themselves out (and likely to do so for the foreseeable future). Postcolonialism is a singularizing formation, as in the following: '*The singular acts without criteria,* or – it is the same thing –, its criteria are wholly immanent to its action (its self-actualisation)'(AP,7). Hallward's book is an important intervention, to which I will return in my conclusion, but for the moment I want to see what he says about Spivak, who is an obvious choice for discussion, particularly in that he implicitly elevates and definitely produces a certain model of critical writing that insists on clarity, however complex, and invites reasoned relational critical debate – i.e. his writing is quite unlike Spivak's. Returning once more to the question of subalternity, Hallward takes Spivak at her word about the self-dissolving subaltern: any subaltern 'speaking' is no longer subaltern, and this is desirable, of course. Hallward seems quite justified in drawing his pointed conclusion: 'The subaltern [...] is the theoretically *untouchable*, the altogether-beyond-relation'(AP,30). Whatever her talk of responsibility, Hallward's Spivak thinks we can only be responsible (*discursively*, of course – other interventions are another perhaps more important matter) to the subaltern by leaving alone.[80]

If Hallward is correct in his presentation of Spivak, then her responsibility for the subaltern is pushed so far that it becomes an irresponsibility. Hallward summarizes his case like this:

> It is because the postcolonial critic entertains *no relation with* the (unpresentable) subaltern object of inquiry that the critic's self-reflexive discourse 'about' the subaltern obtains effectively unlimited prescriptive power – unlimited, that is, by the burdens of transitive explanation or interpretation. (AP,32)

We can think of his position like this: Hallward grants Spivak the truth of her self-questioned privilege, but simply wonders if such privilege might be better extended rather than disowned. And, importantly for this chapter, Hallward directly connects his criticisms with the kind of writing Spivak produces – autobiography – whatever doubts she may have about autobiography. As he makes clear:

> Whereas militant political mobilization has always depended upon the power and validity of essentially *anonymous* statements – statements that *anyone* could have made, articulating principles that compel agreement for their own sake – Spivak grabs every opportunity to foreground the complex subjective inflection and orientation of her own idiosyncratic discourse. (AP,31)

Idiosyncratic is Hallward being polite, I think, because he's more robust elsewhere. But perhaps it opens a good way of re-phrasing his point, which is that Spivak's writing is strictly idiosyncratic, extremely difficult to engage in give and take reasoned debate (as this chapter may well be demonstrating) – it is, then, in Hallward's terms a singular form of writing, creating the terms of its own judgment, along the lines of Lyotard's *postmodern*, judgments always in search of the rules by which they were made, future anterior (that tense invoked on occasion by Spivak herself). Spivak's writing is, then, non-relational – like literature, but in a negative sense in that one would never quarrel with literature for its failures to guide us in the creation of counter-globalizations, whereas one would be quite right to look for some sense of direction from Spivak's project. The writing is itself a performance, intentional or otherwise, of the non-relational descriptions of the world it contains; further, as Hallward indicates, this is some kind of *pre*scription, again intentional or not (the idea of an unintentional prescription being a little peculiar, but useful here I think). What he describes as the 'postcolonial agenda' is the just barely discerned, singularly encountered, impossible ethical justice.

A little earlier I quoted Spivak referring to literature's singularity, and in a certain way Hallward's position is rather similar. Indeed, Hallward makes a reasoned traditional case for the relative autonomy of literary study, remarks that postcolonial studies seem peculiarly uninterested in literature even though they are literary studies themselves, and firmly suggests that all the singularizing talk that comes with literature probably will not be directly helpful when we are trying to formulate the kinds of universalisable principles necessary in contemporary social and political contexts. To put it another way, in Hallward's terms (although he does not argue this explicitly), Spivak's autobiographical performances might be pertinent (or may be, at most, merely harmless) in a more strictly literary context, but her texts tend to roam much further afield and apply their singularizing logics in quite unsuitable places. This position is clearly a strong one, and I may be pushing Hallward a lot further than he would wish to go, but I think this position is consistent with his objections to Spivak's writing, and also seems to express something of the anti-postcolonial mistrust of autobiographical statements. By way of conclusion I should, then, indicate the extent to which these statements are performing other important works beyond or even in opposition to simple statements of self-situation.

Partial disclosure

Most recently, Spivak has presented her auto-expositions as not quite fully present links in various, contingent chains. Whatever Hallward might argue about the banality of difference and the non-identical (and he says this forcefully about postcolonialism generally, as I'll pick up again later), there is a coherence to this new emphasis. Postmodern academic culture has made us all familiar with those chains of signifiers with no beginnings or ends and no centres from which all is regulated. Now for many unsympathetic critics, these chains have sounded rather homogenizing, as if every link in the chain was equivalent to every other. 'Postmodernism', or whatever else one wants to call it (if it ever existed), was assumed to privilege no signifier, and certainly did not pay much attention to the signified, let alone the referent. This has, of course, always been a caricatural perspective. Terry Eagleton's many discussions[81] identify a general postmodern atmosphere, which is unfortunately just as much a straw man as the positivism supposedly targeted by postmodernism. Nevertheless, the caricature offers a way into thinking about autobiography and difference that illuminates some of Spivak's more recent essays. Derrida's contention that infinite difference is finite, something I discussed in the conclusion of the previous chapter, is again useful here. If everything is a question of difference, as is commonly understood in cultural theory, then there is a danger that everything becomes flattened and undifferentiated, and so difference will blur into indifference. For infinite difference to be truly infinite, I suggested, one would have to survey any given field from an absolutely external position.

To recall what Eagleton says about bad universalisms and bad particularisms (discussed at the beginning of this chapter), it actually seems that an absolute insistence on cultural particularity requires the external position usually associated with universal theories. In theoretical terms, however, autobiographical theory talks to us from the interior of any context, differentiating, sorting, and insisting on the specificity of any event. Autobiographical theory would not be, then, hand-in-hand with many of the confusions so often attendant on relativism. To put it another way, I would argue that this theory will not, in principle, necessarily lead to the kind of singularizing vision Hallward criticizes, even if *in practice* this is precisely what has resulted.

The argument up to here might be granted, and yet you might still wonder if Spivak's writing is really anything like my presentation of it. A final word should be given, then, to one of her recent essays, so much concerned with disclosures partial or really virtual (*spectral* might be pushing it, but nonetheless the connection is there). The recent essay 'Moving Devi' recalls me to 'Can the Subaltern Speak?', the link between them in play from the very first sentence, and tantalizingly named a 'life-link'.[82] The essay seeks to position Spivak as but one link on a chain of displacements, albeit right now the most important link. Still, the whole point is that her position is not final, and any making-speak that takes place is open to challenge or at least gentle revision. To this extent her apparent visibility is not quite all it seems. On the one hand, I think Spivak's readership will, generally, be amused to read her initial comparison between the two essays: 'I am no longer beset by the need to occlude the traces of the irreducibly autobiographical in cultural speculations of this sort'. I will not labour the immediately apparent irony, but the thought of Spivak at some point rigorously excising personal reference from her writing is certainly intriguing. On the other hand, 'Moving Devi' really only makes the earlier essay more mysterious, not less, for example the following: 'The essay itself was a resolute suppression of the autobiographical, in more ways than I can yet reveal'.[83] Differences between the initial version of 'Can the Subaltern Speak?' and the version in the *Critique* have already alerted various readers to the enigmatic qualities of that essay,[84] some of which begin to look more complex than merely theoretically expedient omission, but which have become even jealously guarded tokens of personal lives not for discussion. In such a situation, matters will not become any more susceptible to debate, and Spivak's singularizing text will continue to perplex as much as it stimulates. It is not that we should demand full disclosure, but that the injunction to 'work my agenda out' (given by Spivak in the *Critique*) looks like leading to endless deferrals and muted incomprehension when the text in question is so tortuous and elusive: Spivak is vanishing just as fast as the present, in fact. With its object moving at such velocity, this chapter has just barely completed its argument, if it has a single argument to complete. Certainly its assessment of one aspect of Spivak's work has traced its implications for other elements of her project, but its conclusions remain difficult to generalize across that project.[85] Some of what I've argued supports Hallward's position on the singularizing nature of Spivak's work, but I do not find this position applicable to her work in its entirety, let alone the last word on postcolonialism generally. Any project is likely to be divided, intentionally or otherwise, and Spivak's attention to the various double-binds of her critical position should not be dismissed as lightly as it has previously been.[86] The double-binds she identifies around questions of autobiographical theory do look, superficially, as if they are overridden in practice; few critics are apparently so self-expressive. However, this chapter has advanced the position that what is given with the one hand is deftly spirited away by the other, both in theme and form, theory and practice.

References

1. Spivak, *A Critique of Postcolonial Reason* (Cambridge MA: Harvard University Press, 1999), p.118.
2. Spivak, 'Three Women's Texts and Circumfession' in *Postcolonialism & Autobiography*, Hornung and Ruhe (eds.) (Amsterdam: Rodopi, 1998), p.21.
3. Spivak, *The Post-Colonial Critic* (London: Routledge, 1990), p.38
4. Eagleton, *The Gatekeeper* (New York: St. Martin's Press, 2002), p.57.
5. Eagleton, *Figures of Dissent,* (London: Verso, 2003), p.231.
6. Eagleton, 'In the Gaudy Supermarket', *London Review of Books* 13 May 1999, pp.3–6. The title refers us to Spivak's 'Subaltern Studies: Deconstructing Historiography', where she writes that, 'Since one cannot accuse this group of the eclecticism of the supermarket consumer, one must see in their practice a repetition of as well as rupture from the colonial predicament: the transactional quality of inter-conflicting metropolitan sources often eludes the (post)colonial intellectual' (p.202).
7. Eagleton, *Figures of Dissent,* p.173.
8. See Gilmore, *The Limits of Autobiography* (Ithaca: Cornell University Press, 2001), pp.16–17.
9. Simpson, *Situatedness, or, Why We Keep Saying Where We're Coming From,* (Durham: Duke University Press, 2002). To recap, Simpson is referring to sentences like 'As a straight white male...'; his book is rather more circumspect than Eagleton's position, viewing the rhetoric of situatedness as many faceted.
10. Eagleton, *Figures of Dissent,* p.177.
11. Interestingly, Simpson's brief discussion in *Situatedness* implies that Spivak pushes to another extreme, in her criticisms of the 'meaningless piety' of calling the investigative subject into question (pp.29–30); this is not far from the position advanced in this chapter.
12. Edwards, 'Selvedge Salvage', *Cultural Studies* 17(1) (January 2003), p.34.
13. Morton, *Gayatri Chakravorty Spivak* (London and New York: Routledge, 2003), p.20.
14. From *The Spivak Reader* (London: Routledge, 1996), p.205. Further refers to SR in the text.
15. Lejeune, *On Autobiography,* (trans.) K. Leary (Minneapolis: University of Minnesota Press, 1989), p.212.

16. Caesar, *Conspiring with Forms: life in academic texts,* (Athens: Georgia University Press, 1992), p.104.
17. Caesar, *Conspiring with Forms: life in academic texts,* p.105.
18. See § 14 of *Critique of Judgment*; trans. W.S. Pluhar (Indianapolis: Hackett, 1987), pp.69–72.
19. Spivak, *A Critique of Postcolonial Reason: Toward a History of the Vanishing Present* (Cambridge, MA: Harvard University Press, 1999), pp.26–27. Refers to CPR in the text.
20. Rooney, *African Literature, Animism and Politics* (London: Routledge, 2000), p.97.
21. This necessity allows the generalization of the faculty of judgment; to Lyotard, for example, reflection as critique's main weapon is 'a kind of transcendental pre-logic' (Lyotard, *Lessons on the Analytic of the Sublime,* trans. E. Rotternberg, (Stanford: Stanford University Press, 1994), p.32).
22. The reference to de Man implies that his writing opens the kinds of readings of itself demanded by his war-time journalism, rather than denying history, as might be supposed.
23. Her reading is therefore distinct from Paul Gilroy's, which does not clearly elaborate an argument about what exactly is at stake in the *example* of Kant; see *Between Camps* (London: Allen Lane, 2000), esp. p.60.
24. The terms in question are *Neuholländer* and *Feuerländer,* which to Spivak are not accidental choices, and cannot be explained away as merely euphonic; see the long footnote 32 on pp.26–29.
25. In her *Critique,* Spivak suggests that, 'The crucial antinomy is that we *must* think a final purpose and yet we *can* not know it' (p.22).
26. So, Spivak suggests that, 'One task of deconstruction might be a persistent attempt to displace the reversal, to show the complicity between native hegemony and the axiomatics of imperialism' (p.37). She does something of the sort in 'Can the Subaltern Speak?', which I consider later, but also in the problematic reading of Hegel which follows this reading of Kant.
27. In Laura Chrisman and Patrick Williams (eds.) *Colonial Discourse and Post-Colonial Theory: A Reader,* (London: Harvester Wheatsheaf, 1994), pp.66–111.
28. Landry and MacLean, Introduction to 'Subaltern Talk: Interview with the Editors', in *The Spivak Reader* (London: Routledge, 1996), p.287.
29. Landry and MacLean, *The Spivak Reader,* p.287.
30. Spivak, *A Critique of Postcolonial Reason: Toward a History of the Vanishing Present* (Cambridge, MA: Harvard University Press, 1999), p.308.
31. Spivak, 'Can the Subaltern Speak?' In *Colonial Discourse and Post-Colonial Theory: A Reader,* Patrick Williams and Laura Chrisman (eds.), (New York: Harvester Wheatsheaf, 1994), pp.66–111.
32. *In Other Worlds: Essays in Cultural Politics* (London: Routledge, 1987), pp.197–221.
33. 'Can the Subaltern Speak?', in Williams & Chrisman (eds.) *Colonial Discourse and Post-Colonial Theory: A Reader* (New York: Columbia University Press, 1994), p.82.
34. In Foucault, *Language, Counter-Memory, Practice: Selected Essays and Interviews,* trans. D.F. Bouchard and S. Simon (London: Cornell University Press, 1977), pp.205–217.
35. Quoted in 'Can the Subaltern Speak?', in Williams & Chrisman (eds.) *Colonial Discourse and Post-Colonial Theory: A Reader* (New York: Columbia University Press, 1994), p.74.

36. Foucault, *The Order of Things. An Archaeology of the Human Sciences*, trans. A. S. Smith, (London: Tavistock, 1970).
37. 'Can the Subaltern Speak?', p.75.
38. 'Can the Subaltern Speak?', p.76.
39. Homi Bhabha argues that Foucault's spatialisation of time is complicit in 'colonial-ist' dispersal; see 'In a Spirit of Calm Violence', in G. Prakash (ed.) *After Colonialism*, in G. Prakash (ed.), (Princeton: Princeton University Press, 1995), esp. pp.327–28.
40. 'Can the Subaltern Speak?', p.86.
41. In the earlier version, she simply notes that, 'my insistence on imperialist subject-production as the occasion for this sentence discloses my politics'. (p.92)
42. 'Can the Subaltern Speak?', p.102.
43. Spivak, 'Speculations on reading Marx: after reading Derrida', in *Post-structuralism & the Question of History*, Attridge, Bennington and Young (eds.), (Cambridge, Cambridge University Press, 1987), p.58.
44. Spivak, 'Acting Bits/Identity Talk', *Critical Inquiry* 18 (Summer 1992), p.770, 771.
45. See, for instance, Ahmad, *In Theory: Classes, Nations, Literatures* (London: Verso, 1992).
46. Lazarus, *Nationalism and Cultural Practice in the Postcolonial World* (Cambridge: Cambridge University Press, 1999).
47. Colin Wright points out that, 'the place of woman is meticulously elided by Eagleton, despite the fact that three of the four chapters in Spivak's book are directly addressing the subalterneity of woman, in and out of the Imperial context'. See 'Can the Subaltern Hear?: The Rhetoric of Place and the Place of Rhetoric in Postcolonial Theory', accessed at http://www.scholars.nus.edu.sg/post/poldiscourse/casablanca/wright.html on September 27, 2006.
48. In *Postcolonialism and Autobiography*, Hornung and Ernstpeter (eds.), (Amsterdam: Rodopi, 1998), pp.7–22.
49. Hallward, *Absolutely Postcolonial*, (Manchester: Manchester University Press, 2001).
50. Derrida, *Monolingualism of the Other* trans. P. Mensah (Stanford: Stanford University Press, 1998);
51. Derrida, *Spurs: Nietzsche's Styles* trans. B. Harlow (Chicago: Chicago University Press, 1979).
52. In *Spurs* the 'I have forgotten my umbrella' section (pp.123–143), along with note 21, makes this point; in *Monolingualism* see p.26 for a more direct statement.
53. Innes, review of Spivak's *A Critique of Postcolonial Reason*, *Wasafiri* 31 (Spring 2000), pp.67–69.
54. Innes, review of Spivak's *A Critique of Postcolonial Reason*, p.68.
55. Spivak, *In Other Worlds*, p.179. Further refs. to IOW in the text.
56. Brennan responds to Spivak rather as Ahmad responds to Jameson by writing in 'The Illusion of a Future', that, 'the work of Gayatri Chakravorty Spivak [in the 1980s] was a mixture of Derrida and a textualized Marx – although this may only be a way of saying a Derridean Marx'.(p.567) 'Scattered Speculations' repre-sents Spivak's most concise and explicit thematic justification of this textualization, which appears to be a way of finding Marx everywhere, always where he ought not to be. Spivak wants to undo 'the binary opposition between the economic and the cultural', (p.166)
57. See, for example, LaCapra 'Is Everyone a *Mentalité* Case? Transference and the "Culture" Concept', in *History and Criticism* (London: Cornell University Press, 1987), pp.71–94.

58. Kristeva, *About Chinese Women*, trans. A. Barrows, (London: Marion Boyars, 1977).
59. Jameson, *Postmodernism, or, The Cultural Logic of Late Capitalism* (London: Verso, 1991), p.15.
60. In 'Scattered Speculations on the Question of Value', Spivak says she hopes never to meet this cognitively-mapped subject, (p.173).
61. See also 'Speculations on reading Marx: after reading Derrida'; 'My move cannot represent itself as a political programme, for it cannot consider "deconstruction", named as such, as *realia* or assume that the political – or ethico-personal – narrative can adequately represent the philosopheme'.(p.30)
62. 'Jameson's Rhetoric of Otherness and the 'National Allegory''; *In Theory* (London: Verso, 1992), pp.95–122.
63. Bhabha's notion of mimicry might be usefully deployed here, although one might object that such a form of self-reflexivity would become *merely* self-regarding.
64. Jameson writes in *Postmodernism* that, 'Pastiche is, like parody, the imitation of a peculiar or unique, idiosyncratic style, the wearing of a linguistic mask, speech in a dead language. But it is a neutral practice of such mimicry, without any of parody's ulterior motives, amputated of the satiric impulse, devoid of laughter and of any conviction that alongside the abnormal tongue you have momentarily borrowed, some healthy linguistic normality still exists', (p.17)
65. Eagleton writes, in 'Capitalism, Modernism and Postmodernism': 'What is parodied by postmodernist culture, with its dissolution of art into the prevailing forms of commodity production, is nothing less than the revolutionary art of the twentieth-century avant-garde'; (p.385) in *Modern Criticism and Theory: A Reader*, David Lodge (ed.), (London: Longman, 1988), pp.385–397.
66. Eagleton, 'In the Gaudy Supermarket', p.6. The rather loose play with 'irony' might be related to the debate between Laura Chrisman and Robert Young occasioned by Young's review of Spivak's *Outside in the Teaching Machine*; see Chrisman, 'Questioning Robert Young's post-colonial criticism', and Young, 'Response to Laura Chrisman', *Textual Practice* 11(1), pp.39–50.
67. 'Who Claims Alterity?', in *Remaking History*, Barbara Kruger & Phil Mariani (eds.) (Seattle: Bay Press, 1989), pp.269–92;
68. 'Lives', in *Confessions of the Critics*, H.A. Veeser (ed.) (London: Routledge, 1996).
69. 'Lives', p.205, 214.
70. Although, perhaps curiously, not between Parry and Spivak, and in the end shifting the focus away from Spivak: Chrisman explicitly brackets Spivak, instead focusing on Young, as indicated previously.
71. Spivak, *Outside in the Teaching Machine* (London: Routledge, 1993), p.60. This passage of self-quotation is to be found in similar form in the *Critique*, p.190.
72. Spivak, *Outside in the Teaching Machine*, p.60. Aijaz Ahmad takes issue with this catachrestic post-colonial identity in his 'The politics of literary postcoloniality', *Race & Class* 36(3), pp.1–20. For a simple explanation of Spivak's (unorthodox) use of *catachresis* in this specific sense, see her 'Translation as Culture', *Parallax* 14, pp.13–24.
73. Derrida, *Limited Inc*, trans. S. Weber, (Evanston: Northwestern University Press, 1988).
74. See Ahmad, 'The Politics of Literary Postcoloniality', *Race and Class* 36(3) (1995), pp.1–20.

75. Seshadri-Crooks, 'At the Margins of Postcolonial Studies: Part 1' in *The Pre-Occupation of Postcolonial Studies*, Afzal-Khan and Seshadri-Crooks (eds.) (Durham: Duke University Press, 2000), p.14.

76. In Landry and Maclean (eds.) *The Spivak Reader* (London: Routledge, 1996), p.291.

77. See Rooney, *African Literature, Animism, and Politics* (New York and London: Routledge, 2000).

78. As does Derrida: Irene E. Harvey argues in 'Derrida and the Issues of Exemplarity', that, 'That examples function otherwise or could function in a variety of ways that are not incessantly bound or re-bound between the universal (laws) and particular (cases) seems never to have crossed Derrida's mind here [*Of Grammatology*] or elsewhere in the later works' (*Derrida: A Critical Reader* (Oxford: Blackwell, 1992), p.215). Such a suggestion, however, does not seem adequate to either *Monolingualism* (mid 1990s) or *Spurs* (mid 1970s), to name only these two exemplary cases.

79. Hallward, *Absolutely Postcolonial* (Manchester: Manchester University Press, 2001), p.329. Further refs. to AP in the text.

80. Spivak has nuanced her position in recent times: for example in 'A Conversation with Gayatri Chakravorty Spivak: Politics and the Imagination', she says the following: 'There's nothing particularly good about penetrating into subalternity. I'm not in search of the primitive or anything. But if we are going to talk about it, then I will say that if one manages to penetrate in there, and it's not easy, then I think what we have to do is take a moratorium on speaking too soon.' (*Signs: Journal of Women in Culture and Society*, 28(2), p.619).

81. See, for example, Eagleton, *The Illusions of Postmodernism* (Oxford: Blackwell, 1996).

82. Spivak, 'Moving Devi', *Cultural Critique* 47 (Winter 2001), p.120.

83. Spivak, 'Moving Devi', p.120.

84. Bart Moore-Gilbert, *personal communication*.

85. For example, Spivak's representation to the international public hearing on Crimes against Women Related to Population Policies, Cairo, Egypt, Sept 1994 begins, 'I am a South Asian who lives and works in the United States as well as South Asia', and continues to discuss testimonies from an earlier session. However, the perspectives I've investigated in this chapter would likely be unproductive in that context.

86. In more specific terms, Caroline Rooney writes the following: 'Idealist philosophy seems to aim for the perfection of a self-consistency; the truth as the elimination of self-contradiction: and, that is perhaps in its nature. If contradictions arise in Spivak's work, this may be an effect of struggling for other truths. Self-consistency might be admirable, but risking contradictions is life-affirming'.(Rooney, *African Literature, Animism and Politics* (London: Routledge, 2000) p.122)

6 Singularity and postcolonial exemplarity

In conclusion, I will discuss responsibility in postcolonial criticism, in relation to categories of the singular and the universal. All the way through this book I've suggested that, like other forms of criticism, postcolonial criticism appears to have become more literary through becoming more autobiographical: a literary form of criticism about literature, and of course about other things, because postcolonialism has to be interdisciplinary (or at least it usually is assumed that it must be). We might then argue that this makes postcolonial criticism more responsible through self-situation and contextualization, undermining the urge to universalize and so cancel difference. Autobiographical theory is one means by which we can maintain and respect differences, and so is a central part of a postcolonial philosophy of difference. As soon as I refer to such a philosophy, it is possible to see that I am actually referring back to the French philosophers from whose work methods of maintaining or creating difference have been drawn. Now, while there have been many challenges to these philosophers' influence on postcolonial theory, and many other forms of theory, Foucault, Derrida, Deleuze and others do enjoy a kind of theoretical dominance, and this is something that this book has generally defended. If nothing else, this book has pointed to all the ways that this apparent influence is complex and divided, something inevitable given the differences between the various thinkers. All of them, however, have relevance to the idea of autobiographical theory. If I have depended most upon Derrida it is because, among other things, his work's relevance to autobiographical theory is often rather explicit, with the autobiographical often a most insistent element in his own writing.

The Universal and the same

However, in conclusion I will re-approach the idea of autobiographical theory through current challenges to this philosophy of difference, particularly the challenge posed to Deleuze by Alain Badiou. I will do this by considering how Badiou's translator Peter Hallward, who I've already discussed in the context of Spivak's work, has brought this philosophical challenge into the context of postcolonial criticism, particularly postcolonial literary criticism.

This is in his book *Absolutely Postcolonial*, itself a major challenge to postcolonial theory generally, which is he believes politically irresponsible. To explain the pertinence of Hallward's philosophy to this book, I'll begin with the following comment on postcolonial insistence on the located-ness of critical subjectivity:

> Nothing is more orthodox in the domain of postcolonial studies than an insistence on the multiple, specific, heterogeneous nature of contexts and subject positions. But even here, how exactly this theoretical insistence is to be turned into critical practice remains a matter of vigorous debate.[1]

As Hallward suggests, how to convert a principled insistence on such multiple locations *is* a matter of debate, but in very broad terms postcolonial critical practice has become autobiographical, and I take this to be how it translates its theory of multiple location into a way of writing about those locations. This has various implications, which we can think about by briefly invoking Wittgenstein, who writes the following regarding *value*: 'The sense of the world must lie outside the world. In the world everything is as it is, and everything happens as it does happen: *in* it no value exists – and if it did exist, it would have no value.'[2] We might say that, if there is no meaningful outside to this world, at least no absolute outside, then such sense as there is must be brought to the world *as if* from outside, as if *at least for a time* there might be an external perspective enabling order and sense. The autobiographical turn in postcolonial theory often appears to demand an immersion in a lack of sense, or at least a lack of overriding sense: such sense as there is *is* mine, or is specific to my culture or community. The autobiographical turn in theory therefore fits quite well the discourse of respect for otherness and difference. This has been an entirely appropriate turn for the discourses of theory to take, given that they for a long time seemed to imply prescriptive universal methods. It will have been necessary to take the autobiographical detour in order for theory to become theories, and to divest itself of devalued value, narrow universalisms, and the like. However, in conclusion I want to recall that it is possible to challenge the emphasis on otherness, and accordingly on autobiographical theory, in the name of new universalisms. Such a challenge is what we can see in recent theoretical engagements with postcolonial theory, like Hallward's, or theoretical arguments against multiculturalism, like Žižek's.[3] Despite its claimed introduction of anti- and post-colonial politics into literary and cultural discourse, if we follow the challenges to the philosophy of difference there is serious doubt as it whether postcolonial theory is adequate to contemporary political questions, and this doubt has been focused around the convergence of alterity and theory.

In his assault on contemporary notions of ethics, for example, Alain Badiou develops his argument based on assumptions fundamentally alien to much literary and cultural theory. For example, he writes that, 'Infinite alterity is quite simply *what there is*. Any experience at all is the infinite deployment of infinite differences.'[4] In order to think about what there is, we cannot simply affirm this infinity of differences. Thinking and truth require more than straightforward description:

> Against these trifling descriptions (of a reality that is both obvious and inconsistent in itself), genuine thought should affirm the following principle: since differences are what there is, and since every truth is the coming-to-be of that which is not yet, so differences are then precisely what truths depose, or render insignificant. No light is shed on any concrete situation by the notion of the 'recognition of the other'. (E,27)

Badiou's idea of thought is here explicitly posed against much of contemporary theory: the criticism of 'recognition of the other' is fairly clearly directed as Lévinas, Derrida, and all of the literary, cultural and philosophical criticism that is, however indirectly, in their debt. Against this recognition, Badiou poses the active creation of the same:

> The Same, in effect, is not what is (i.e. the infinite multiplicity of differences) but what *comes to be*. I have already named that in regard to which only the advent of the Same occurs: it is a *truth*. Only a truth is, as such, *indifferent to differences*. (E,27)

So, differences must be genuinely put to one side, we might simplistically say. Truth cannot be 'my truth' or 'our truth', it must simply be truth: 'Every invocation of blood and soil, of race, of custom, of community, works directly against truths'(E,76). It is well known that for Badiou the matheme is what gives us our most privileged example of such a truth, which is more than an example, given the identification of mathematics and ontology. This truth is one from which the speaker is subtracted, as Badiou writes in *Infinite Thought*: 'the matheme is that which, by causing the Speaker to disappear, by removing any mysterious validation from its site, exposes argumentation to the test of autonomy and thus to the critical or dialogic examination of its pertinence.'[5] For a theory really to be worthwhile, it cannot be tied to its situation, despite the fact that it necessarily arises in a time and a place: therefore, a theory certainly cannot remain autobiographical.

Badiou's challenge is to contemporary thinking generally, but certainly has great relevance to postcolonial theory, perhaps the single most 'alteritist' field in literary and cultural theory. As I have suggested, this challenge is given most far-reaching expression in the work of Peter Hallward. As I outlined when I discussed Spivak's work, Hallward considers postcolonial theory in relation to the categories of the singular and the specific in his book *Absolutely Postcolonial*. Hallward's argument draws on Badiou, and has general relevance to theory, as he suggests by stating that, 'To move from the specified to the specific, without yielding to the temptation of the singular: this is perhaps the only general goal that can be ascribed to a critical theory as such.'[6] Theories come from times and places, which means they can be specified. Nonetheless, this does not mean that they are *only* in relation to their time and place, or that their time and place can only be explained through reference to them. They do not have singular and privileged explanatory power, nor do they create their own terms of evaluation. Theories must be made to work, made in fact universal through, most likely, coordination rather than a laissez-faire respect for difference. Such respect for difference leads to rather *un*critical theory, as Christopher Norris might say.

This is Hallward's argument, directed at theory in general. Postcolonial theory, however, is his specific example, and he contends that it operates on an entirely singularizing logic, creating its own terms of evaluation and becoming therefore non-relational. It may appear to be politically responsible, but its lack of relationality consigns it to irresponsibility. Postcolonial theory seems to him mired in singularity, and therefore unable to contribute to contemporary political questioning: 'Postcolonial critics generally prefer "malleable situational lessons" to hard matters of general principle'(AP,176). Indeed, while it is important to contextualize phenomena, there is a danger of over-contextualization that (we might infer) is particularly clear in the ways theory has become autobiographical:

> That everything exists as specific to a situation does not mean that its significance and complexity is reducible to a function of (or in) that situation; that every event has its specific occasion does not mean that its significance is exhausted by that occasion. (AP,39)

Theories cannot be explained or explained away simply by reference to their location, or their origin, or whatever else we might call their situation. There is a need for *subtraction* of situation from theory, and this process is one that postcolonial theory in particular seems unwilling to carry out. Hallward's position is simple:

> [P]ostcolonial theory in general can only obstruct what is arguably the great political task of our time: the articulation of fully inclusive, fully egalitarian political principles which, while *specific* to the particular situation of their declaration, are nevertheless *subtracted* from their cultural environment. We must strive to prescribe principles whose coherence does not rely upon *any* notion of community, any kind of *cultural* proximity, any cultural criteria of sharing or belonging. All progressive politics must presume the cultural despecification of its participants as much as it resists the singular transcendence of a simply *sovereign* legitimation. (AP,126)

Hallward's position draws heavily on Badiou's thought, focused here on post-colonial theory. A theory cannot create its own terms of evaluation, for it will then be exclusive and accordingly ineffective in the face of a genuinely global hegemony. When counter-hegemony is required, utter fragmentation hardly seems adequate. The specified locales of thought are what lead to this fragmentation, and they are what must be overcome. Autobiographical theory is a stage on the way to a critical theory; or, as Hallward asserts, 'Though every truth certainly proceeds *through* a specified tangle of local interests, institutions and constraints, the truth-affirming mechanism is itself fully 'subtracted' from this tangle'(AP,185). This subtraction entails an important understanding of the subject, in particular perhaps the subject of theory: 'The specific presumes a fundamentally *militant* conception of the subject, understood as a decisive and divisive process of despecification'(AP,248). Autobiographical theorists seem to be specified subjects, their theories therefore limited; the militant theorist is specific, relational, in short political.

This argument constitutes a serious challenge to theory that elevates its autobiographical qualities. However, Hallward's position also undermines the idea of cultural politics, something so important to postcolonial theory. Indeed, of course cultural politics and the cultural turn are closely connected with autobiographical theory and the autobiographical turn. For Hallward, there can be no cultural politics: at least every instance of a cultural politics that remains wedded to a singular culture is thereby depoliticized, or has in fact never been truly political. This idea can be illustrated by discussion of Homi Bhabha's work, particularly on the creativity of the postcolonial subject. in other words, that subject's *agency*. Hallward notes that Bhabha asks the question that so many critics demand of him: what does the absolutely prior deconstruction of the sign mean for subjects? If this deconstruction implies indeterminacy, then Bhabha's answer is essentially that postcolonial subjects '*incarnate* this indeterminacy pure and simple'(AP,24). According to Hallward, then, 'Specific individuals are here always derivative, a result'(AP,24).

> Rather than simply treat historical or social situations as linguistic or rhetorical ones, it would be more accurate to say that Bhabha equates Creative agency with the precise moment of this differing enunciation as such, the moment 'behind' or productive of language itself. (AP,25)

This behind-ness operates as an absolute *singularisation*: 'Escaping from a situated position relative to other positions, the postcolonial slips between *every* possible position because it refers back, immediately, to that *one* logic that positions every possibility'(AP,26). This is of course a rather abstract way of thinking about postcolonial agency.

From Hallward's perspective, the category of difference in Bhabha licenses a de-contextualized theory. It produces the conditions of judgment as a singular plane, within which it is impossible to make sense of what actually happens under a specific example like Apartheid. This singularized critical perspective produces only the illusion of agency, or of criticism as such, making the categories of the colonial and postcolonial entirely self-serving and self-confirming. If colonialism is all a matter of denying the splitting of agency at the origin then the postcolonial can smoothly enter the stage to save the day:

> The colonial enterprise can then be figured as an *inevitably* unsuccessful effort to reduce enunciation to the relation of distinct (i.e. static) identities; the post-colonial enterprise appears, in turn, as the triumphant (and no less inevitable) dissolution of these distinctions through a return to the real process of enunciation. (AP,26)

Such a perspective really would tell us little of value about the real histories and ongoing struggles of anti-colonialism. The prior agency or creativity necessarily undoes the authority of colonial power, and yet this tells us absolutely nothing about the *actuality* of colonial power, because it takes place in a *virtual* realm. If we associate postcolonial theory with this emphasis, then it is emphatically virtual rather than actual, and this is a very strange position for such an apparently interventionist form of criticism to occupy.

It may of course be objected that Hallward is taking Bhabha as too representative, and that postcolonial criticism is full of varied and conflicting critical perspectives. Bhabha of course has been criticized for different things by just about everyone. And yet I think Hallward has a serious point in that whether or not postcolonial critics believe in the prior deconstruction of the subject, or whatever else we might associate with Derrida *et al.*, there is a general tendency to think in terms of cultural politics, and these politics must seem irresponsible from the hard universalist perspective. So, Robert Young writes that, 'There is nothing to apologize for in the idea of cultural politics – it has always been central to the practice of liberation.'[7] But of course the idea of cultural politics has been criticized for being *more* culture and *less* politics – a form of cultural*ism*, and while culture is on any estimate important, politics is really taking place elsewhere. And yet the idea of cultural politics remains important, and serves as the very justification for cultural studies. The idea of hegemony, which is really the central category in cultural studies, forces us to see cultural politics as perhaps *the* most important kind. Certainly, ideas like the *expressive community*[8] make clear the force of cultural politics, and imply that such politics create their own terms of reference, principally because of course the cultures in question have been historically excluded from politics per se. Indeed, postcolonial criticism has a tendency in this direction; otherwise we would all be discussing *only* the economic determinations of neo-colonialism and globalization.

We can draw these specific remarks on postcolonial theory back into more general philosophical debates. Hallward is really concerned about the ability of any philosophy to contribute to transforming actual situations. This is a particular concern when we think about philosophies of difference, which seem to hold onto to these actual situations rather than subsuming them into more general categories. Hallward wonders if such philosophies are really as attuned to these real situations as they seem: does respect for difference and otherness enable any form of politics that might transform situations that need it? Like Badiou, he wants to contest Deleuzian philosophy in particular, or at least contest readings of Deleuze that find in his work transformative political potential. There are indeed many such readings, in particular perhaps the works of Michael Hardt and Antonio Negri, who adapt Deleuze in order to see Empire as the manifestation of 'a concrete universal itself'.[9] This reading of Deleuze allows Žižek to write with considerable scepticism that, 'Deleuze more and more serves as the theoretical foundation of today's anti-globalist Left and its resistance to capitalism.'[10] Deleuze seems to hold this position because of his very irresponsibility, his embrace of the thinker's transvaluing and declarative manner, as opposed to the dutiful accounting of the philosopher. If we look back through his work, we find that, in his book about Nietzsche, Deleuze writes: 'Irresponsibility – Nietzsche's most noble and beautiful secret'.[11] Of course for Deleuze this irresponsibility is a desirable quality, being the thinker's irresponsible fidelity to difference rather than the philosopher's responsible fidelity to the same. Hallward, like Badiou, might respond that this idea of irresponsibility must be wrested back from Deleuze's appropriation, and seen for what it is, a genuine irresponsibility in our everyday sense because it is a refusal to enter into the relational thinking that politics requires.

On this view, if cultural politics is going to transform actual situations, it will have to stop thinking about the virtual and the singular, and start thinking about the actual and the specific. Even though forms of cultural politics might well intervene in such actual situations (say, the situations characterizing neo-colonialism or globalization), their constitutively non-universal nature precludes their being responsible politics. The whole idea of the *body without organs*, so influentially appropriated from Deleuze and Guattari,[12] puts emphasis on the pre-existent *creating* rather than the actualized *creature*. Rather like postcolonial theory, then, Deleuzian philosophy forgets the specificity of things as they are. This forgetting even leads to the dismissal of the subject, as subjects as actualized creatures. Any autobiographical theory that put such a thought to work might then be involved in a problematic and paradoxical enterprise. Hallward's recent book about Deleuze makes the following argument:

> Since what powers Deleuze's cosmology is the immediate differentiation of creation through the infinite proliferation of virtual creatings, the creatures that actualise these creatings are confined to a derivative if not limiting role. A creature's own interests, actions or decisions are of minimal or preliminary significance at best: the renewal of creation always requires the paralysis and dissolution of the creature per se. The notion of a constrained or situated freedom, the notion that a subject's own decisions might have genuine consequences – the whole notion, in short of *strategy* – is thoroughly foreign to Deleuze's conception of thought.

Deleuze obliges us, in other words, to make an *absolute* distinction between what a subject does or decides and what is done or decided through the subject. By rendering this distinction absolute he abandons the category of the subject altogether.[13]

The actuality of situation, agency, relation, and politics is therefore of at most secondary importance to Deleuze. Anyone that follows him on this path also demotes these categories. For this reading, although Deleuze may seem to be a philosopher of difference, he is really a philosopher of the One-All.[14] In terms drawn from *A Thousand Plateaus*, we can say that although Deleuze writes of both planes of movement and planes of rest (planes of consistency and planes of organization) it is always the former that draw his interest. As Deleuze and Guattari write, 'Being expresses in a single meaning all that differs'.[15] According to this reading, it is the single meaning that matters more than the difference. This is more than a dispute over the reading of Deleuze, and is beyond argument about Deleuze's theory of creation, having also political implications. Immediately, Hallward draws them out:

> Deleuze writes a philosophy of (virtual) difference without (actual) others. He intuits a purely internal or self-differing difference, a difference that excludes any constitutive mediation between the differed. Such a philosophy precludes a distinctively relational conception of politics as a matter of course. The politics of the future are likely to depend less on virtual mobility than on more resilient forms of cohesion, on more principled forms of commitment, on more integrated forms of coordination, on more resistant forms of defense. Rather than align ourselves with the nomadic war machine, our first task should be to develop appropriate ways of responding to the newly aggressive techniques of invasion, penetration and occupation which serve to police the embattled margins of empire.[16]

The virtual level of creating on which Deleuzian thought insists coincides with that singular plane of immanence Hallward identifies as the postcolonial. His critique of Deleuze therefore repeats his critique of postcolonial theory. The politics of the future will not be postcolonial, on this view: postcolonial criticism is to be understood as singular criticism. It must be said that Hallward questions Badiou's thinking on precisely the issue of relation, writing that, 'my guiding assumption is that an individual has no being outside of its relations with other individuals, so what matters is the conversion of oppressive relations into liberating ones.' Nonetheless, Hallward's reading of Badiou is what allows him to define his own categories, and he goes on to suggest the following:

> As long as philosophy is defined as singular rather than specific, as long as it preserves itself in its pure *déliaison*, as long as it retains a strictly

axiomatic integrity, it will not be able to provide a fully convincing account for the shift from withdrawal to intervention, from subtraction to transformation, from prescription to production.[17]

Indeed, despite their slight differences, Hallward's reading of Deleuze follows Badiou, and sees a fundamentally virtual element to Deleuze's thinking. Žižek, by contrast, finds much the same kind of virtuality privileged over actuality, but insists that this is Deleuze being led astray in his collaborations with Guattari. For Hallward, in the same way that, despite apparent disagreements, postcolonial thinkers are all singular, Deleuze's work in general thinks a singular creating. Such a philosophy of difference is not really anything to do with difference, it would then seem. The reading of Deleuze put forward by Badiou and Hallward is controversial, and is likely to remain so. In its challenge to an unthinking celebration of difference, it is extremely significant, and in the context of postcolonial criticism it poses a serious challenge to autobiographical theory.

All of this works against the image of postcolonial criticism as meaningfully related to colonialism, and therefore also postcolonial criticism as politically engaged. Instead of autobiography being a mark of principled and politicized self-situation, it becomes more the assertion governing its own world of legislation, creating its own terms of reference. And given the reminder that postcolonial criticism began as a form of literary criticism, we should ask what this all means for literature and literary criticism. This perspective might require a serious re-thinking of the aims and claims of postcolonial criticism. But of course postcolonial criticism has been from the beginning, whenever you want to say that was, a divided enterprise, and could not have been any other way. Aijaz Ahmad's stress on literature as among the signs of our times reminds us that many critics might want to argue that literary criticism should not bear the kinds of political responsibilities imagined in postcolonial criticism. It is possible to insist on a rather traditional sense of literature's relative autonomy. In fact, Hallward says that postcolonial criticism has divested itself of an interest in literature: in a rush to become interdisciplinary, postcolonial critics have less and less to say about the literary, or specific instances of language. This is ironic because many dismissals of postcolonial criticism forget that it really is a kind of literary criticism (or a form of *culturalism*) and should not be expected to apologize for this fact. And yet apologize is what a lot of postcolonial criticism has done. Returning to Robert Young's point about *not* apologizing for cultural politics, given that cultural politics were such a vital part of liberation movements, we might see that as part of its historical moment, something appropriate to certain contexts. Should 'we' now be more satisfied with more modest postcolonial literary criticism, and stop worrying about the political responsibility or otherwise of that criticism? We should perhaps excise ourselves from the texts we produce, given that autobiographical self-situation tends to distract from the texts we are supposed to be reading. At the start of this book I suggested that postcolonial theory had become in many respects autobiographical. At the start of this chapter I converted this into the suggestion that autobiographical criticism appeared to be more literary. It might now seem that it is in fact *less* literary. We might be better served by being responsible to the literary text.

But we should look again at this position, and return to another of Hallward's examples. Looking at a specifically Deleuzian form of postcolonial theory, Hallward also challenges the work of Édouard Glissant, whose thought of errantry, directly drawing on Deleuze and Guattari, seems to be *all* about relation. So, Glissant writes that, 'Rhizomatic thought is the principle behind what I call the Poetics of Relation, in which each and every identity is extended through a relationship with the Other'.[18] Hallward argues that although Glissant's earlier work has an appropriately national and genuinely relational sense of identities, his later work dissolves this specificity in the whirlwind of the *Tout-monde*: for Hallward, Glissant privileges identities which are post-national, beyond relation, and strictly singular. Hallward writes that, 'The equation of subject and world as a single process of Relation obliterates all 'in-between' space, the space of "development" and "conflict"'(AP,124). Again, although the privileged terms of postcolonial theory seem to be politically engaged, in fact they set up a singular frame of reference within which difference is effectively cancelled. Hallward seems to have a point, in that when Glissant discusses epic, he interprets the classics of national foundation as paradoxically telling of that community being surpassed and of the temptation of errantry. According to Glissant, in the epic the intransigent is qualified by the uprooted. However, this is not quite the dissolution of intransigence in uprootedness, because there is a dialectic of totality evident in Glissant's writings, working through a kind of *circular* nomadism. Importantly, Glissant cautions us against associating the nomad too quickly with any kind of simple freedom. Accordingly, when we read his comments on totality, we should not imagine that difference amounts to that freedom either. So, the following may appear a straightforward dismissal of the universal, but the qualifications near the end are central:

> Errant, he challenges and discards the universal – this generalizing edict that summarized the world as something obvious and transparent, claiming for it one presupposed sense and one destiny. He plunges into the opacities of that part of the world to which he has access. Generalization is totalitarian: from the world it chooses one side of the reports, one set of ideas, which it sets apart from others and tries to impose by exporting as a model. The thinking of errantry conceives of totality but willingly renounces any claim to sum it up or to possess it.[19]

To conceive but not to possess? That might be, in terms of circular nomadism, in effect to possess in a temporary manner, something like the consequence of David Simpson's idea of a situated critical historicism. In an essay from the same work, Glissant reads Saint-John Perse as demonstrating a kind of rooted errantry, given the clash between his orality and his metropolitan totalizing emphasis. His poetry, says Glissant, does incompatible things, and so we have the idea of a rooted errantry. Despite political differences, there is a poetic kinship here, and I wonder if this rootedness is the necessary aspect of relation that stops Glissant's thought from being singular in the way Hallward outlines. Perhaps, then, we can say that Glissant's work constitutes a postcolonial supplement to Deleuze, just as we might say that postcolonial discourses very often supplement postmodernism or post-structuralism.

Autobiographical universals

Whatever future readings of Deleuze may bring, it's possible to focus this now by looking back instead to Derrida, because his thinking about restricted and general economy can help us to understand Glissant's idea of a circular nomadism. We should look at Derrida's *Monolingualism of the Other*,[20] which begins with a quotation from Glissant's writings. In *Poetics of Relation*, Glissant links the necessary twisting of French into forms adequate to his conceptual objects, and so he places emphasis on *métissage*, writing adequate in particular to the clash of oral and literate cultures.[21] Derrida quotes Glissant on this theme, talking about the necessary 'critical revision' of French. In the context of postcolonial autobiographical theory, *Monolingualism* can be introduced by looking at the terms Derrida uses to discuss Bataille,[22] as mentioned earlier. Derrida reads Bataille's 'resistance' to Hegel, his laughter, in terms of Bataille's general thought of economy. The calculable expenditure of the restricted economy cannot contain excess and the force of general economy. However, such general economy is always gathered back, pure expenditure always already returning to restricted economy. Derrida asks,

> [H]ow, after having exhausted the discourse of philosophy, can one inscribe in the lexicon and syntax of a language, our language, which was also the language of philosophy, that which nevertheless exceeds the oppositions of concepts governed by this communal logic? Necessary and impossible, this excess had to fold discourse into strange shapes. And, of course, constrain it to justify itself to Hegel indefinitely.[23]

Folding discourse into strange shapes might seem one way of describing autobiographical theories, and so an obvious place to look is *Monolingualism*, with its apparent staging of autobiographical identity. Like Derrida's *Spurs*, *Monolingualism* insists that *dissemination* is about singularity rather than plurality. In this case, however, Derrida more directly risks his singularity in a kind of autobiographical text setting off from his own colonial childhood in Algeria. Beginning with these early Algerian experiences (languages, religions, French-ness), the text's theme might be reduced to the following: there is a generalisability of the enigmatic statement, 'I have only one language, yet it is not mine'.[24] On the one hand, the text elaborates what such a statement might mean, addressing accusations of performative contradiction; on the other hand, there is a line of argument on the essentially colonial quality of culture that, however explicit it becomes, bears still perhaps mysteriously on questions of postcolonialism. Derrida pushes reflection on testimony into more general elaboration of the logic of exemplarity. The unique is attested to in a universal language, and this universal structure is 'more vividly' (MO,20) readable because of exemplarity: this argument has intuitive plausibility. Derrida further wants to argue for the exemplarity of the Colonial in this context: 'All culture is originarily colonial'(MO,39). Now while Derrida insists immediately that this should not be taken to efface the specificity of colonialisms, this generalization of the colonial appears to risk a levelling of difference unacceptable to postcolonial studies, although as we have seen the subtraction of difference is exactly what Badiou recommends. It remains to be demonstrated that Derrida's thought of exemplarity in communication with the specificity of *this* autobiographical example (in other words, the strategic calculation Derrida has made) work to give difference a chance generally, for instance in multiculturalist discourses.

Clearly *Monolingualism* is in various ways autobiographical. However, this intervention into the practice of multiculturalist or postcolonial discourse is ambivalent toward the autobiographical urge,[25] in much the same way as Spivak's *Critique*. As Jane Hiddleston writes,

> By stressing the excentricity of the philosopher's own disjointed voice, and by allowing the autobiographical element to disrupt the philosophical argument in the text, Derrida preserves the ongoing singularisation of the singular in the hope of preventing his philosophical reflection from generalising, and thus mythologising, the very processes of marginalisation he explores.[26]

However, as in Spivak's work, the risking of singularity is always already underway, whether we know it or not; that Derrida should be an exaggerator (he exaggeratedly claims: 'I always exaggerate'(MO,48)) accompanies an over-literal mimicry of claims to alterity,[27] together pausing over the sense of autobiography as a mode, both like and unlike the Nietzschean double style he discusses and performs in *Spurs*.[28] *Monolingualism* in fact performs a kind of mimicry, and this mimicry is incalculably dividing Derrida's text. My use of the term mimicry recalls Homi Bhabha, of course, and so this autobiography certainly guards against generalization and totality, but also guards against the theorizing of anti-theory, or a theory of the margins. So, this autobiography is concerned to make certain claims about the simultaneous impossibility and possibility of autobiography. Such a formulation appears straightforwardly contradictory, but conveys the circumspection of an argument that might otherwise seem reductive, both of autobiography generally (to incomplete philosophy or science) and of different autobiographies to a general undifferentiated stream. Derrida suggests towards the close that

Monolingualism is, 'an account of what will have placed an obstacle in the way of this auto-exposition for me'(MO,70). The future anterior is not accidental. Or, again, a little later: 'A Judeo-Franco-Maghrebian genealogy does not clarify everything, far from it. But could I explain anything without it, ever?'(MO,71–2). To return to the possibility and impossibility of autobiography, this last quotation should not be taken to imply that autobiography only ever offers partial explanation, if that is taken to imply the later assumption of interpretation's burden by a philosophy purged of such contingency. This latter conception would allow for the necessary contingency of philosophy's genesis, with the philosophical structure supervening at a moment to be assigned, whereas Derrida is apparently concerned to put forward a co-implication of contingency and necessity at the origin: the *prosthesis of origin* of the translation's subtitle.

As I have indicated, this prosthesis of origin is a theme of Derrida's work from its earliest stages, and has often been taken to be in some sense a necessary corrective to 'myths of origin' of various kinds.[29] On this construal, deconstruction is taken to have an implacable suspicion of essentialisms, origins, etc. Indeed, this is not a misreading, although it is a partial reading. Assuming as it does a neglect in Derrida's work of socio-political reality, a response that cautiously defends nationalisms, for instance, points out that essentialisms function in circumscribable and beneficial ways in specific contexts; Derrida would (on this reading) elide differences in search of a projected generalisable neutrality of philosophy. However, it is clear from other contexts that Derrida would insist, in the case of certain terms like 'the colonial' or 'the feminine', that there is a necessity to the patient, laborious, perhaps implicitly boring, establishment and sustaining of a concomitant institution. These terms do not function in the same way, and they all have specificities to be respected, even if such respect is already tempered by appropriation. In *Monolingualism*, Derrida advances an apparently more striking claim, that accompanying the impropriety of each monolingual's relation to his or her language is a law that the originary language *must* be invented, with further implication that this is, in some sense, desirable or beneficial. This suggestion follows from many themes developed in earlier works, as is indicated by Derrida's parallel insistence on singularity in *Spurs*.

The text approaches the question of singularity through the already mentioned autobiographical exemplarity. Derrida refers to the perhaps commonplace recognition that rigid distinctions of idiom, dialect, and language quickly become untenable with increased detail of description. This is not Derrida's point, however, as such external descriptive criteria ought to retain the mark of their provisional nature. Derrida focuses rather on that which actively crosses or blurs the descriptive boundaries. Here, with his invocation in this context of creolisation,[30] we are again reminded of the extra-descriptive force of such boundaries. Derrida approaches this blurring through the *most purely* disordered of examples: he himself as the most pure of Franco-Maghrébians. The specificity of the Franco-Maghrébian context here is patiently outlined, putting forward a general precariousness of citizenship and identity generally: Derrida sketches the 'choice' of languages at school, the 'solely' French oppression, and more generally the relation to metropolitan France. This France (Paris) is the otherness via which Franco-Maghrébian identity must journey. Such circuits of alterity are specific and only generalisable with precautions. French (metropolitan French) is the 'forbidding-forbidden' language that must be *to be* appropriated, and must be *to be* constructed. Within the problem of one's mother tongue, a question continually posed within our political culture, there is the possibility of situating (*constructing*) oneself in relation to that tongue in an explicitly uneasy, dislocated manner. In Derrida this situating would be that torsional and tense syntactic form of argument above the lexemic level. It can be countered that this intentional distancing from one's language is a privilege, but perhaps what is important about privilege is not its existence but its use. Derrida surrenders to an impure purity that is his (and others', for example Cixous) privilege: '[to] speak in good French, in pure French, even at the moment of challenging in a million ways everything that is allied to it'(MO,49). Derrida here puts in place all possible precautions guarding against generalization without respect, whilst simultaneously demonstrating (in 'this other scene of demonstration'(MO,6)) that singularity is always from the start on its way to totalization, is created by the law, like Derrida's French. So, while the claim that there is originary alienation is also the claim that this alienation is *within* the language of the master as well as the of colonized, there is no sense in which this of itself disallows its further exploration, or of itself constitutes resistance. So, in this context, the circuit of reference via alterity is specifiable to, for instance, the colonial schoolteacher, referring always *elsewhere*. The 'colonial impulse'(MO,40) is ultimately the recitation of the law as if it was autonomous rather than heteronomous, but each time the law of law produces singularity anew, always to be translated.

   If there is something specific about the demonstration of this argument that is formalisable, it is in Derrida's 'incineration' of philosophy and literature, and French, his intention, 'to make something happen in this language' (MO,51). In his autobiographical sketch, Derrida remarks on the institution of French literature, and French literature as something not quite institutional. If entrance into French literature is guaranteed by losing one's accent, he has not quite lost his, and so is not quite within: it is a double non-belonging, then. But this is not a straightforward celebration of such non-belonging (playing the card of the exile, perhaps) or disavowal of privilege. Derrida's 'I' is the *last defender* (that exaggeration again) of French, even against himself, 'forcing the language then to speak itself by itself, in another way, in his language' (MO,51). Yet this defence would not quite be merely the confirmation of that privilege, its cosy continuation at the expense of its excluded other: as has been indicated, in confirmation there is a general circuit via the other. Derrida calculates this structure, which is a structure of translation, as a virtue, and in this particular context suggests that, 'One would have to construct oneself, one would have to be able to *invent oneself* without a model and without an assured addressee'(MO,55). The exemplary situation of the Franco-Maghrébian is of being 'thrown into absolute translation'. The monolingual deprived of his or her own language has only *target* languages ('events without arrival') from which is derived the desire for an absolutely originary language (MO,61). Whilst this language is, 'a future language, a promised sentence'(MO,62) of the other, it is, despite formal equivalence, not necessarily of the master; however, the undecidability remains in a structure of radical openness familiar to readers of Derrida. There is a necessary possibility that such a future language always *might* be the language of the master; that is the possibility of it being otherwise.

In other terms, the 'miracle of translation'(MO,72) is necessarily inscribed with the possibility of its failure. Such a formulation can help work through arguments about incommensurability as the degree zero of intercultural contact, a move again pertinent to multiculturalist debate, and to the kinds of argument given such clear expression by Badiou. Derrida puts forward the patient and laborious work of translation, implying the precariousness of that translation, but also staging the openness that gives it its chance: the 'messianicity without messianism' that is structural opening, as elaborated generally in *Specters of Marx*. Idioms are always undergoing invention without end, as witnessed and demonstrated by the exaggerated call Derrida sends out to addressees that always might not exist, always might not receive it, or in fact are produced by it:

> Compatriots of every country, translator-poets, rebel against patriotism! Do you hear me! Each time I write a word, a word that I love and love to write; in the time of this word, at the instant of a single syllable, the song of this new International awakens in me. I never resist it, I am in the street at its call, even if, apparently, I have been working silently since dawn at my table. (MO,57)

There is a clear anticlimax (critics would say bathos) at work in this passage, perhaps in *Monolingualism* generally, that operates to deflate the assertion of credentials, especially in institutional terms, but also in linguistic and literary terms. Yet still this demonstration of 'weaving some veil from the wrong side'(MO,70) constitutes a political event, is a *démonstration*, 'A street scene without a theater, yet a scene all the same'(MO,2). At least, Derrida continues, it always might have been, the uncertainty acknowledged, the risk run. Derrida's insistence on this radical openness is discomforting as it emphasizes that the chance of just such a critique is also the chance of its object; that, for instance, Marx's text did not accidentally (although not necessarily) lead to various totalitarianisms; and that, in the terms of *Monolingualism*, the future language necessarily might be that of the master as much as that of the oppressed: this means that the poetic idiom to-come always might be the idiom of oppression. As Derrida suggests in *Specters of Marx*,

> [D]econstruction has never been Marxist, no more than it has ever been non-Marxist, although it has remained faithful to a certain spirit of Marxism, to at least one of its spirits for, and this can never be repeated too often, there is *more than one* of them and they are heterogeneous.[31]

In the same way France is spectral, and Derrida remains faithful to a spirit of France, and a spirit of French.[32] The meaning of these phenomena, to be meaning at all, must be open to re-inscription in new contexts: according to a logic of necessary possibility, it must be readable otherwise.

We can redescribe this necessary possibility in the following way. There is a doubleness, even a duplicity, to the concept of the example. And in this context, Derrida presents himself, on the one hand, as exemplary in the sense of the *very best* example, indeed more than an example, a model; and, on the other hand, as no more than one example among others, exemplary of this disruptive question of language but no more so than other possible examples. This doubled structure, inhabiting as it does Derrida's work generally, appears to take this particular example beyond mere expediency, perhaps suggesting that it is intuitively most possible to put *oneself* forward as exemplary. But this structure of exemplarity, translating a historical strategy, will inevitably suggest a certain stance toward the questions of rights and credentials as they present themselves in post-colonial criticism. Still, one can imagine principled objection to the strategy justifying the use of 'colonial', indeed an argument that this structure of exemplarity should not always be risked, by every term, in every imaginable context. Just as the question of risking essence is (and will continue to be, perhaps indefinitely) problematic for feminism, or women's studies, so it is not clear that the structure of reference that enables 'colonial' to function at all is yet ready to be faced in more classical practical terms. These structures are not in themselves about to level differences, but of course we need to guard against any slippage through which Derrida might become exemplary of every possible instance of what 'colonial' might mean. Thus it might be argued that we need to ensure that the singular is made specific, in given contexts and for given purposes: that is, in the end, postcolonial strategy.

Conclusion

It is arguable, then, that the singular is always already the specific, in Hallward's terms, but that this prior relational quality is denied in any equation of autobiography and bounded situation, or of culture with identity. While language is, on any estimate, an extremely important aspect of identity and politics, it is not any basis for the delineation of general political principles. And yet any language, with all its singularity and difference, is never in and of itself complete, and is always on its way to translation, with the singular becoming the specific. Just so, identities, in their relationality, take us beyond cultural particularity or relativism. These movements towards universality or translation are never, of course, final; they always receive their justification in a given context and for a certain time, which in principle cannot be predicted. There is no final reduction of the singular to the specific, in other words. Theory is metaphorical and autobiographical, but it is not *only* metaphorical and autobiographical. Our theories might well be on their way, through subtraction, to universality, but that movement has an unfinal quality to it that demands marking in writing. In conclusion, we can say that the folding of discourse into strange shapes to which Derrida refers demands formal innovation, linguistic experimentation, and what is a kind of theoretical autobiography or autobiographical theory; in terms of politics, it demands new and radically unpredictable forms of organization. Postcolonial theory is an exemplary instance of these two apparently discrete levels of description in that it constantly demonstrates the imbrication of these two levels. Instead of being an instance of a theory, postcolonial theoretical autobiography escapes any theoretical system; however, it always returns to system, even though that return is not simply a confirmation of system.

In this way, postcolonial autobiographical theory provides us with a clear example of the workings of the *quasi-transcendental.* If, of course, no theory (or indeed Theory in general) is able to account for autobiography (every instance of autobiographical writing, or the category itself), it should also be pointed out that autobiography as a category is itself unable to account for every theory (or indeed Theory in general). To the extent that this book has claimed a privileged explanatory capacity for this category, I seem to have elevated it to something like a transcendental position, allowing the argument that theories are absolutely determined by autobiographical situation or position. However, as an explanation of its power, such a demonstration or determination will always be inadequate, as the category of autobiography would then be occupying the position that it is supposedly explaining. It therefore follows that Theory (at least, some theories – but then, maybe the kind that enable or enjoin us to think about the transcendental) remains privileged because it foregrounds the complexity of such a transcendental explanatory category. Accordingly, although autobiography can be powerful in its capacity to situate theoretical frameworks (if not indeed explain them away), it can never be the final word in that the autobiographical is simply never enough of an explanation. That is to say that autobiographical contextualization is governed by the same laws structuring contextualization as such: meaning is context-bound, but context is boundless. This structure can be described in several ways borrowed from the work of Derrida, but perhaps most helpfully, I am arguing in conclusion, through the idea of the quasi-transcendental. According to this logic, my argument should not be taken to imply that Derrida accounts for or explains away all the texts I have discussed. For that again would be to place 'Derrida' (as a shorthand for some kind of theory of deconstruction as method or technique) in a transcendental position: his work may well occupy that position, but only to the extent that it enables us to think about the insaturable quality of context, including the context it itself provides.

References

1. Hallward, 'The Singular and the Specific: Recent French philosophy', *Radical Philosophy* 99 (January/February 2000), p.7; repeated in *Absolutely Postcolonial: Writing Between the Singular and the Specific* (Manchester: Manchester University Press, 2001), p.21.
2. Wittgenstein, *Tractatus-Logico-Philosophicus*, trans. David Pears and Brian McGuinness (London: RKP, 1974), p.86.
3. See Žižek, 'Multiculturalism, or, The Cultural Logic of Multinational Capitalism', *New Left Review* 225 (Sept–Oct 1997), pp.28–51.
4. Badiou, *Ethics*, trans. Peter Hallward (London: Verso, 2001), p.25. Further refs. to E in the text.
5. Badiou, *Infinite Thought*, trans. and ed. by Oliver Felthem and Justin Clemens (London: Verso, 2003), p.93.
6. Hallward, *Absolutely Postcolonial: Writing Between the Singular and the Specific* (Manchester: Manchester University Press, 2001), p.48. Further refs. to AP in the text.
7. Robert J. C. Young, *Postcolonialism: an historical introduction* (Oxford: Blackwell, 2001), p.8.
8. As discussed by, for example, Paul Gilroy, in *There Ain't No Black in the Union Jack* [Routledge Classics Ed.] (New York and London: Routledge, 2002), eg. p.268.
9. Hardt and Negri, *Empire* (Cambridge MA: Harvard University Press, 2000), p.19.
10. Žižek, *Organs Without Bodies* (New York and London: Routledge, 2003), p.xi.
11. Deleuze, *Nietzsche and Philosophy*, trans. H. Tomlinson, (London: Athlone Press, 1983), p.21.
12. In the postcolonial context, see for example Robert J. C. Young's *Colonial Desire: Hybridity in Theory, Culture and Race* (New York and London: Routledge, 1995), pp.168–169.
13. Hallward, *Out of this World: Deleuze and the philosophy of creation* (London: Verso, 2006), p.162.
14. See *Difference and Repetition*, trans. P. Patton (Minneapolis: University of Minnesota Press, 1994): 'A single and same voice for the whole thousand-voiced multiple, a single and same Ocean for all the drops, a single clamor of Being for all beings' (p.304).
15. Deleuze and Guattari, *A Thousand Plateaus: Capitalism and Schizophrenia*, trans. B. Massumi (Minneapolis: University of Minnesota Press, 1987), p.254.
16. Hallward, *Out of this World: Deleuze and the philosophy of creation* pp.162–3.
17. Hallward, *Badiou: A Subject to Truth* (Minneapolis: University of Minnesota Press, 2003), p.322.
18. Glissant, *Poetics of Relation*, trans. B.Wing (Ann Arbor, MI: University of Michigan Press, 1997), p.11.
19. Glissant, *Poetics of Relation*, pp.20–21.

20. Derrida, *Monolingualism of the Other; or, The Prosthesis of Origin,* trans. P. Mensah (Stanford: Stanford University Press, 1998).
21. Indeed, Glissant puts emphasis on proverb and aphorism as adequate forms; in this context, then, we might remember the way Deleuze values Nietzsche's use of aphorism, a form requiring explicit *valuation.*
22. Derrida, 'From Restricted to General Economy: A Hegelianism without Reserve' in *Writing & Difference* trans. A. Bass (Chicago: Chicago University Press, 1978), pp.251–277.
23. Derrida, 'From Restricted to General Economy: A Hegelianism without Reserve', pp.252–53.
24. Derrida, *Monolingualism of the Other; or, The Prosthesis of Origin,* trans. P. Mensah (Stanford: Stanford University Press, 1998), p.1. In quotation marks in the original, which is hesitantly dialogical. Further refs. to MO in the text.
25. Derrida makes an early dismissive reference to, 'playing the card of the exile' (p.5), a dismissal which evidently could not be straightforwardly generalized.
26. Hiddleston, 'Derrida, Autobiography and Postcoloniality', *French Cultural Studies,* 16(3), p.297.
27. Derrida writes that, 'I therefore venture to present myself to you here, *ecce homo,* in parody, as the exemplary Franco-Maghrebian' (p.19).
28. Derrida, *Spurs: Nietzsche's Styles* trans. B. Harlow (Chicago: Chicago University Press, 1979).
29. See again the 'Chinese prejudice' to which Derrida refers in *Of Grammatology,* trans. G.C. Spivak (Baltimore: Johns Hopkins University Press, 1976), e.g. p.80.
30. As already mentioned, there is an opening Édouard Glissant epigraph referring to the 'anti-humanism' of the revision of *le domesticage par la langue française.*
31. Derrida, *Specters of Marx: the State of the Debt, the Work of Mourning, and the New International* trans. P. Kamuf (New York and London: Routledge, 1994), p.75.
32. See *Monolingualism,* p.42, for France as *spectral,* 'A place of fantasy.'

7 Bibliography

Afzal–Khan, Fawzia and Kalpana Seshadri–Crooks (eds.) (2000) *The Pre–Occupation of Postcolonial Studies*, Durham, Duke University Press.

Ahmad, Aijaz (1992) *In Theory: Classes, Nations, Literatures*, London, Verso.

– – (1995) 'Postcolonialism: What's in a Name?' in Román de la Capra, E. Ann Kaplan and Michael Sprinker (eds.) *Late Imperial Culture*, London, Verso, pp.11–32.

– – (1995) 'The politics of literary postcoloniality', *Race and Class* 36(3), pp.1–20.

Al–Kassim, Dina (2002) 'The Face of Foreclosure', *Interventions* 4(2), pp.168–174.

Anderson, Linda (2001) *Autobiography*, London, Routledge.

Ang, Ien (1994) 'On Not Speaking Chinese', *New Formations* 24, pp1–18.

Ansell–Pearson, Keith, Benita Parry and Judith Squires (eds.) (1997) *Cultural Readings of Imperialism: Edward Said and the Gravity of History*, London, Lawrence and Wishart.

Araeen, Rasheed (2000) 'A New Beginning: Beyond Postcolonial Cultural Theory and Identity Politics', *Third Text* 50 (Spring 2000), pp3–20.

Ashcroft, Bill and Pal Ahluwalia (2001) *Edward Said*, London, Routledge.

Auerbach, Erich (1953) *Mimesis: The Representation of Reality in Western Literature*, trans. W.R. Trask, Princeton, Princeton University Press.

Badiou, Alain (1999) *Manifesto for Philosophy*, translated, edited, and with an introduction by Norman Madarasz, New York, SUNY Press.

– – (2003) *Infinite Thought: Truth and the Return to Philosophy*, translated and edited by Oliver Feltham and Justin Clemens, New York and London, Continuum.

– – (2004) *Theoretical Writings*, edited and translated by Ray Brassier and Alberto Toscano, New York and London, Continuum.

Barker, Jason (2002) *Alain Badiou: A Critical Introduction*, London, Pluto Press.

Barnett, Stuart (ed.) (1998) *Hegel After Derrida*, London, Routledge.

Barthes, Roland (1972) *Critical Essays*, trans. R. Howard, Evanston, Northwestern University Press.

– – (1977) *Roland Barthes by Roland Barthes*, trans. R. Howard, London, Macmillan.

– – (1977) *Image–Music–Text*, selected and translated by S. Heath, London, Fontana.

– – (1982) Susan Sontag (ed.) *A Barthes Reader*, London, Jonathan Cape.

– – (1982) *Camera Lucida*, trans. R. Howard, London, Jonathan Cape.

– – (1982) *Empire of Signs*, trans. R. Howard, New York, Hill and Wang.

Beasley–Murray, Jon (1997) 'So Here Comes a Book That Makes Everything Easy: Towards a Theory of Intellectual History in the Field of Intellectual Production', *Angelaki* 2(3), pp.125–46.

Bennington, Geoffrey with Jacques Derrida (1993) *Jacques Derrida*, trans. G. Bennington, Chicago, Chicago University Press.

– – (2000) *Interrupting Derrida*, London, Routledge.

Bernasconi, Robert (1992) 'No More Stories, Good or Bad: de Man's Criticisms of Derrida on Rousseau', in David Wood (ed.) *Derrida: A Critical Reader*, Oxford, Blackwell, pp.137–166.

– – (1997) 'Philosophy's Paradoxical Parochialism' in Keith Ansell–Pearson, Benita Parry and Judith Squires (eds.) *Cultural Readings of Imperialism*, London, Lawrence and Wishart, pp.212–226.

– – (1998) 'Hegel at the Court of the Ashanti', in Stuart Barnett (ed.) *Hegel After Derrida*, London, Routledge, pp.41–63.

Berry, Philippa (1998) 'Kristeva's Feminist Refiguring of the Gift', in Phillip Blond (ed.) *Post–Secular Philosophy: between philosophy and theology*, London, Routledge, pp.318–333.

Besemeres, Mary (2002) *Translating One's Self*, Bern, Peter Lang.

Bhabha, Homi (1990) 'DissemiNation: time, narrative, and the margins of the modern nation' in Bhabha (ed.) *Nation and Narration*, London, Routledge, pp.291–323.

– – (1994) *The Location of Culture*, London, Routledge.

– – (1994) 'Anxious Nations, Nervous States' in Joan Copjec (ed.) *Supposing the Subject*, London, Verso, pp.201–217.

– – (1995) 'In a Spirit of Calm Violence', in Gyan Prakash (ed.) *After Colonialism: Imperial Histories and Postcolonial Displacements*, Princeton, Princeton University Press, pp.326–344.

– – (1995) 'Freedom's Basis in the Indeterminate', in John Rajchman (ed.) *The Identity in Question*, London, Routledge, pp.47–62.

– – (1996) 'Day by Day...With Frantz Fanon', in Alan Read (ed.) *The Fact of Blackness: Frantz Fanon and Visual Representation*, Seattle, Bay Press, pp.186–205.

– – (1996) 'Aura and Agora: On Negotiating Rapture and Speaking Between' in Richard Francis (ed.) *Negotiating Rapture. The Power of Art to Transform Lives*, Chicago, Museum of Contemporary Art, pp.8–16.

– – (1996) 'Unpacking my library...again', in Iain Chambers and Lydia Curti (eds.) *The Postcolonial Question*, London, Routledge, pp.199–211.

– – (1997) "Fireflies Caught in Molasses': Questions of Cultural Translation', in Rosalind Krauss *et al* (eds.) *October: The Second Decade, 1986–1996*, Cambridge, MA., MIT Press, pp.211–22.

– – (1998) 'On the Irremovable Strangeness of Being Different', *PMLA* 113(1), pp.34–39.

– – (1998) 'Culture's In Between', in David Bennett (ed.) *Multicultural States: Rethinking difference and identity*, London, Routledge, pp.29–47.

– – (1998) 'Anish Kapoor: Making Emptiness', in *Anish Kapoor*, London, Hayward Gallery, pp.11–41.

– – (1998) 'Joking Aside: The Idea of a Self–Critical Community', in Bryan Cheyette and Laura Marcus (eds.) *Modernity, Culture and 'the Jew'*, Cambridge, Polity Press, pp.xv–xx.

– – (2000) 'On Minorities: Cultural Rights', *Radical Philosophy* 100 (March/April 2000), pp.3–6.

Bhatt, Chetan (2000) 'Primordial Being: Enlightenment, Schopenhauer and the Indian Subject of Postcolonial Theory', *Radical Philosophy* 100, pp.28–41.

Birla, Ritu (2002) 'History and the Critique of Postcolonial Reason: Limits, Secret, Value', *Interventions* 4(2), pp.175–185.

Boehmer, Elleke (1998) 'Post–Colonial Literary Studies: A Neo–Orientalism?' in C.C. Barfoot and Theo d'Haen(eds.) *Oriental Prospects: Western literature and the lure of the East*, Amsterdam, Rodopi, pp.241–256.

Bové, Paul (1981) 'Mendacious Innocents, or The Modern Genealogist as Conscientious Intellectual: Nietzsche, Foucault, Said' *boundary 2* (9–10), pp.359–87.

Boyne, Roy (1990) *Foucault and Derrida: the other side of reason*, London, Unwin Hyman.

Braidotti, Rosi (1991) *Patterns of Dissonance: A study of women in contemporary philosophy*, Cambridge, Polity Press.

– – (1994) *Nomadic Subjects: Embodiment and Sexual Difference in Contemporary Feminist Theory*, New York, Columbia University Press.

Brennan, Timothy (2000) 'The Illusion of a Future: *Orientalism* as Travelling Theory', *Critical Inquiry* 26(3), pp.558–583.

Brinkler–Gabler, Gisela and Sidonie Smith (eds.) (1997) *Writing New Identities: Gender, Nation, and Immigration in Contemporary Europe*, Minneapolis, University of Minnesota Press.

Burke, Seán (ed.) (1995) *Authorship: From Plato to the Postmodern–A Reader*, Edinburgh, Edinburgh University Press.

– – (1998) *The Death and Return of the Author: Criticism and Subjectivity in Barthes, Foucault and Derrida* [2nd Ed.], Edinburgh, Edinburgh University Press.

Butler, Judith (1997) *The Psychic Life of Power: theories in subjection*, Stanford, Stanford University Press.

– – (2003) 'Values of Difficulty' in Jonathan Culler and Kevin Lamb (eds.) *Just Being Difficult: Academic Writing in the Public Arena*, Stanford, Stanford University Press, pp.199–215.

Caesar, Terry (1992) *Conspiring with Forms: life in academic texts*, Athens, Georgia University Press.

– – (1998) *Writing in Disguise: Academic Life in Subordination*, Athens, Ohio University Press.

Carey-Webb, Allen (1998) *Making Subject(s): Literature and the Emergence of National Identity*, New York and London, Taylor and Francis.

Cavarero, Adrianna (2000) *Relating Narratives: Storytelling and Selfhood*, trans. Paul A. Kottman, London and New York, Routledge.

Chambers, Iain (1994) 'Exposure, abeyance and dislocation: Some comments on Benita Parry's discussion of Homi Bhabha's *The Location of Culture*', *Third Text* 31, pp.108–110.

Childs, Peter and Patrick Williams (1996) *An Introduction to Post-colonial Theory*, London, Prentice Hall.

Chow, Rey (1993) *Writing diaspora: tactics of intervention in contemporary cultural studies*, Bloomington, Indiana University Press.

– – (1998) *Ethics after idealism: theory, culture, ethnicity, reading*, Bloomington, Indiana University Press.

– – (1998) 'The postcolonial difference: lessons in cultural legitimation', *Postcolonial Studies* 1(2), pp.161–70.

– – (2003; 1994) 'Where Have All the Natives Gone?' in Reina Lewis and Sara Mills (eds.) *Feminist Postcolonial Theory: A Reader*, Edinburgh, Edinburgh University Press, pp.324–349.

– – (2003) 'The Resistance of Theory; or, The Worth of Agony' in Jonathan Culler and Kevin Lamb (eds.) *Just Being Difficult: Academic Writing in the Public Arena*, Stanford, Stanford University Press, pp.95–105.

Chrisman, Laura and Patrick Williams (eds.) (1994) *Colonial Discourse and Post-Colonial Theory: A Reader*, London, Harvester Wheatsheaf.

Chrisman, Laura (1997) 'Questioning Robert Young's post-colonial criticism', *Critical Inquiry* 11(1), pp.39–45.

– – (1998) 'Imperial Space, Imperial Place: Theories of Empire and Culture in Frederic Jameson, Edward Said, and Gayatri Spivak', *New Formations* 34, pp.53–69.

Christian, Barbara (1990; 1996) 'The Race for Theory' in Padmina Mongia (ed.) *Contemporary Postcolonial Theory: A Reader*, London, Hodder Arnold, pp.149–157.

Cixous, Hélène (1994) Susan Sellers (ed.), *The Hélène Cixous Reader*, London, Routledge.

– – (1998) *Stigmata: Escaping Texts*, trans. E. Prenowitz *et al*, London, Routledge.

– – (2000) 'Hélène Cixous in conversation with Sophia Phoca', *Wasafiri* 31, pp.9–13.

– – and Mireille Calle–Gruber (1997), *Rootprints: Memory and life writing*, trans. E. Prenowitz, London, Routledge.

Clifford, James (1988) *The Predicament of Culture: Twentieth-Century Ethnography, Literature, and Art*, Cambridge, MA, Harvard University Press.

– – (1997) *Routes: Travel and Translation in the Late Twentieth Century*, Cambridge, MA, Harvard University Press.

Cochran, Terry (1998) 'The Matter of Language', *boundary 2* 25(2) (Summer 1998), pp.71–94.

Confino, Alon (2000) 'Remembering Talbiyah: On Edward Said's *Out of Place*', *Israel Studies* 5(2), pp.182–198.

Conrad, Peter (1978) 'The Imperial Imagination', *New Statesman* 26 Jan. 1979, pp.117–18.

– – (1993) 'Empires of the Senseless', *The Observer* 7.2.93, p.55.

Coombes, Anne E. (1994) 'The recalcitrant object: culture contact and the question of hybridity' in Francis Barker *et al* (eds.) *Colonial Discourse/ Postcolonial Theory*, Manchester, Manchester University Press., pp.89–114.

Critchley, Simon (1996) 'Prolegomena to Any Post-Deconstructive Subjectivity', in Critchley and Peter Dews (eds.) *Deconstructive Subjectivities*, New York, SUNY Press, pp.13–46.

– – (1999) *Ethics-Politics-Subjectivity: Essays on Derrida, Levinas and Contemporary French Thought*, London, Verso.

Culler, Jonathan (2003) 'Bad Writing and Good Philosophy' in Jonathan Culler and Kevin Lamb (eds.) *Just Being Difficult: Academic Writing in the Public Arena*, Stanford, Stanford University Press, pp.43–57.

Davies, Gloria (1998) 'Professing postcoloniality: the perils of cultural legitimation', *Postcolonial Studies* 1(2), pp.171–82.

De Man, Paul (1982) *Allegories of Reading*, New Haven, Yale University Press.

– – (1984) *The Rhetoric of Romanticism*, New York, Columbia University Press.

Deleuze, Gilles (1983; 1962) *Nietzsche and Philosophy* trans. Hugh Tomlinson, London, Athlone Press.

– – and Félix Guattari (1987; 1980) *A Thousand Plateaus: Capitalism and Schizophrenia*, trans. Brian Massumi, Minneapolis, University of Minnesota Press.

Derrida, Jacques (1973) *Speech and Phenomena and other essays on Husserl's theory of signs*, trans. D.B. Allison, Evanston, Northwestern University Press.

– – (1976) *Of Grammatology*, trans. G.C. Spivak, Baltimore, Johns Hopkins University Press.

– – (1978) *Writing and Difference*, trans. A. Bass, Chicago, Chicago University Press.

– – (1978) *Spurs: Nietzsche's Styles*, trans. B. Harlow, Chicago, Chicago University Press.

– – (1981) *Dissemination*, trans. B. Johnson, London, Athlone Press.

– – (1981) *Positions*, trans. A. Bass, London, Athlone Press.

– – (1982) *Margins: Of Philosophy*, trans. A. Bass, London, Harvester Wheatsheaf.

– – (1986) *Glas*, trans. J. P. Leavey, Jr. and R. Rand, Lincoln, University of Nebraska Press.

– – (1987) *The Post Card: From Socrates to Freud and Beyond*, trans. A. Bass, Chicago, Chicago University Press.

– – (1987) *The Truth in Painting*, trans. G. Bennington and I. McLeod, Chicago, Chicago University Press.

– – (1987) 'The Laws of Reflection: Nelson Mandela, In Admiration', trans. M.–A. Caws and I. Lorenz in Derrida and Mustapha Tlili (eds.) *For Mandela*, New York, Henry Holt, pp.13–42.

– – (1988) *Limited Inc*, trans. S. Weber, Evanston, Northwestern University Press.

– – (1988) *The Ear of the Other: Otobiography, Transference, Translation*, trans. P. Kamuf, Lincoln and London, University of Nebraska Press.

– – (1989) 'Psyche: Inventions of the Other' trans. C. Porter in Lindsay Waters and Wlad Godzich (ed.s) *Reading De Man Reading*, Minneapolis, Minnesota University Press, pp.25–66.

– – (1992) Derek Attridge (ed.) *Acts of Literature*, London, Routledge.

– – (1992) 'Onto-Theology of National–Humanism (Prolegomena to a Hypothesis)', *Oxford Literary Review* 14(1–2), pp.3–23.

– – (1992) *The Other Heading: Reflections on Today's Europe*, trans. P.-A. Brault and M. B. Naas, Indianapolis, Indiana University Press.

– – (1994) '"To Do Justice to Freud": The History of Madness in the Age of Psychoanalysis', *Critical Inquiry* 20 (Winter 1994), pp.226–66.

– – (1994) *Specters of Marx: The State of the Debt, the Work of Mourning, and the New International*, trans. P. Kamuf, London, Routledge.

– – (1996) *Archive Fever: A Freudian Impression*, trans. E. Prenowitz, Chicago, Chicago University Press.

– – (1997) '"Perhaps or Maybe", Jacques Derrida in conversation with Alexander Garcia Düttmann, ICA, 8 March 1996', *PLI* Vol. 6(Summer 1997), pp.1–18.

– – (1997) *Politics of Friendship*, trans. G. Collins, London, Verso.

– – (1998) *Monolingualism of the Other; or, the Prosthesis of Origin*, trans. P. Mensah, Stanford, Stanford University Press.

– – (1999) 'Marx & Sons' in Michael Sprinker (ed.) *Ghostly Dermarcations*, London, Verso, pp.213–269.

– – (2001) *The Work of Mourning*, trans. by Pascale-Anne Brault and Michael Naas, Chicago, University of Chicago Press.

– – (2005) *Paper Machine*, trans. by Rachel Bowlby, Stanford, Stanford University Press.

Descombes, Vincent (1987) 'Je m'en Foucault', *London Review of Books* 5.3.87, pp.20–21.

Dirlik, Arif (1994) 'The Postcolonial Aura: Third World Criticism in the Age of Global Capitalism', *Critical Inquiry* 20 (Winter 1994), pp.328–356.

Djebar, Assia (2003) 'Writing in the Language of the Other' in Isabella de Courtivron (ed.) *Lives in Translation: Bilingual Writers on Identity and Creativity*, London, Palgrave Macmillan, pp.19–27.

Doring, Tobias (2002) *Caribbean-English Passages: Intertextuality in a postcolonial tradition*, London and New York, Routledge.

Douglas, Mary (1984) *Purity and Danger: An Analysis of the Concepts of Pollution and Taboo*, London, Routledge.

During, Simon (1998) 'Postcolonialism and globalisation: a dialectical relation after all?', *Postcolonial Studies* 1(1), pp.31–47.

Eagleton, Terry (1988) 'Capitalism, Modernism and Postmodernism' in David Lodge (ed.) *Modernism Criticism and Theory: A Reader*, London, Longman, pp.385–397.

– – (1990) *The Ideology of the Aesthetic*, Oxford, Blackwell.

– – (1998) 'Postcolonialism and 'Postcolonialism'', *Interventions* 1(1), pp.24–26.

– – (1999) 'In the Gaudy Supermarket', *London Review of Books* 13.5.99.

– – (2000) 'The Estate Agent', *London Review of Books* 2.3.00.

– – (2001) 'Welcome to Blarneyworld', *The Guardian* 27.10.01.

– – (2002) *The Gatekeeper*, New York, St. Martin's Press.

– – (2002) *Sweet Violence: the Idea of the Tragic*, Oxford, Blackwell.

– – (2003) *After Theory*, New York, Basic Books.

– – (2003) *Figures of Dissent: Critical Essays on Fish, Spivak, Žižek and Others*, London, Verso.

Eakin, Paul John (1992) *Touching the World: Reference in Autobiography*, Princeton, Princeton University Press.

Easthope, Antony (1998) 'Bhabha, hybridity and identity', *Textual Practice* 12(2), pp.341–348.

Edwards, Brent Hayes (2003) 'Selvedge Salvage', *Cultural Studies* (Jan 2003) 17(1), pp.27–41.

Egan, Susanna (1999) *Mirror Talk: Genres of Crisis in Contemporary Autobiography*, Chapel Hill, University of North Carolina Press.

Eze, Emmanuel Chukwudi (1997) 'The Color of Reason: The Idea of 'Race' in Kant's Anthropology' in Eze (ed.) *Postcolonial African Philosophy: A Critical Reader*, Oxford, Blackwell, pp.103–140.

Fabian, Johannes (1983) *Time and the Other: How Anthropology Constitutes its Object*, New York, Columbia University Press.

– – (1990) 'Presence and Representation: The Other and Anthropological Writing', *Critical Inquiry* 16 (Summer 1990), pp.753–772.

Fanon, Frantz (1952; 1986) *Black Skin, White Masks*, trans. C.L. Markmann, London, Pluto Press.

– – (1961; 1967) *The Wretched of the Earth*, trans. C. Farrington, London, Penguin.

– – (1970) *Toward the African Revolution: Political Essays*, trans. H. Chevalier, New York, Grove Press.

– – (1988) *A Dying Colonialism*, trans. H. Chevalier, New York, Grove Press.

Forrester, John (1990) *The Seductions of Psychoanalysis: Freud, Lacan, and Derrida*, Cambridge, Cambridge University Press.

Forster, Michael (1993) 'Hegel's dialectical method' in F.C. Beiser (ed.) *The Cambridge Companion to Hegel*, Cambridge, Cambridge University Press, pp.130–163.

Foucault, Michel (1967) *Madness and Civilization. A History of Insanity in the Age of Reason*, trans. R. Howard, London, Tavistock.

– – (1970) *The Order of Things. An Archaeology of the Human Sciences* , trans. A.S. Smith, London, Tavistock.

– – (1972) *Histoire de la folie à l'âge classique*, Paris, Editions Gallimard.

– – (1972) *The Archaeology of Knowledge*, trans. A.S. Smith, London, Tavistock.

– – (1977) *Language, Counter–Memory, Practice: Selected Essays and Interviews*, trans. D.F. Bouchard and S. Simon, London, Cornell University Press.

– – (1978) *The History of Sexuality Volume One: An Introduction*, trans. R. Hurley, London, Penguin.

– – (1979) 'My Body, This Paper, This Fire', trans. G. Bennington, *Oxford Literary Review* 4(1), pp.9–28.

– – (1981) 'The Order of Discourse' in Robert Young (ed.) *Untying the Text: A Post–Structuralist Reader*, London, Routledge.

– – (1984) Paul Rabinow (ed.) *The Foucault Reader*, London, Penguin.

– – (1986) 'Of Other Spaces', trans. Jay Miskowiec, *Diacritics* 16 (Spring 1986), pp.22–27

– – (1988) Lawrence D. Kritzman (ed.) *Politics, Philosophy, Culture*, London, Routledge.

– – (1997) Paul Rabinow (ed.) *Ethics, Subjectivity and Truth*, London, Allen Lane.

– – (1998) *Aesthetics, Method, and Epistemology*, London, Allen Lane.

Freud, Sigmund (1990; 1919) 'The 'Uncanny' in *The Penguin Freud Vol.14: Art and Literature*, London, Penguin.

– – (1991; 1901) *The Psychopathology of Everyday Life, The Penguin Freud Vol.5*, London, Penguin.

Fuss, Diana (1994) 'Interior Colonies: Frantz Fanon and the Politics of Identification', *Diacritics* 24(2–3), pp.20–42.

Gallop, Jane (2002) *Anecdotal Theory*, Durham and London, Duke University Press.

Gasché, Rodolphe (1986) *The Tain of the Mirror: Derrida and the Philosophy of Reflection*, Cambridge, MA, Harvard University Press.

– – (1994) *Inventions of Difference: On Jacques Derrida*, Cambridge, MA., Harvard University Press.

Gates, Henry Louis (1991) 'Critical Fanonism', *Critical Inquiry* 17 (Spring 1991), pp.457–470.

– – (1995) 'Europe, African Art and the Uncanny' in Tom Phillips (ed.) *Africa: the Art of a Continent*, London, Royal Academy of Arts, pp.27–28.

– – (1995) *Colored People*, London, Penguin.

Geertz, Clifford (1973) *The Interpretation of Cultures*, New York, Basic Books.

– – (1988) *Work and Lives: the Anthropologist as Author*, Oxford, Blackwell.

Gellner, Ernest (1993) 'The mightier pen?', *Times Literary Supplement* 19.2.93, pp.3–4.

Gilmore, Leigh (1994) *Autobiographics: A Feminist Theory of Women's Self-Representation*, Ithaca and London, Cornell University Press.

– – (2001) *The Limits of Autobiography: Trauma and Testimony*, Ithaca and London, Cornell University Press.

Gilroy, Paul (2000) *Between Camps: Race, Identity and Nationalism at the End of the Colour Line* , London, Allen Lane.

– – (2002) *There Ain't No Black in the Union Jack* [Routledge Classics Ed.], New York and London, Routledge.

Goodman, Daniel (1997) 'The Cultural Politics of Postcolonialism', *New Formations* 31, pp.107–18.

Gordon, Colin (1990) '*Histoire de la Folie*: An Unknown Book by Michel Foucault' in *History of the Human Sciences* 1990, vol.3, pp.3–26.

Gordon, Lewis R. (1995) *Fanon and the Crisis of European Man: An Essay on Philosophy and the Human Sciences*, London, Routledge.

Gregg, Melissa (2006) *Cultural Studies' Affective Voices*, New York, Palgrave Macmillan.

Griffiths, Gareth (1994) 'The Myth of Authenticity: Representation, discourse and social practice' in Chris Tiffin and Alan Lawson(eds.) *De-Scribing Empire: Post-colonialism and textuality*, London, Routledge, pp.70–85.

Guðmundsdóttir, Gunnþórunn (2003) *Borderlines: Autobiography and Fiction in Postmodern Life Writing*, Amsterdam, Rodopi.

Guha, Ranajit (1997) 'Not at Home in Empire', *Critical Inquiry* 23(3), pp.482–293

Guzzoni, Ute (1996) 'Do We Still Want to be Subjects?' in Simon Critchley and Peter Dews (eds.) *Deconstructive Subjectivities*, New York, SUNY Press, pp.201–216.

Hall, Donald E. (2004) *Subjectivity*, London and New York, Routledge.

Hall, Stuart (1994; 1990) 'Cultural Identity and Diaspora', in Patrick Williams and Laura Chrisman (eds.) *Colonial Discourse and Post-colonial Theory: A Reader*, London, Harvester Wheatsheaf, pp.392–401.

– – (1996) 'The After–life of Frantz Fanon: Why Fanon? Why Now? Why *Black Skin, White Masks*?' in Alan Read (ed.) *The Fact of Blackness: Frantz Fanon and Visual Representation*, Seattle, Bay Press, pp.12–37.

– – (1996) 'When Was "The Postcolonial"? Thinking at the Limit' in Chambers, I. and Curti, L. (eds.) *The Postcolonial Question*, London, Routledge, pp.242–260.

– – (1996) David Morley and Kuan–Hsing Chen(eds.) *Stuart Hall: Critical Dialogues in Cultural Studies*, London, Routledge.

– – (1997) 'Culture and Power', *Radical Philosophy* 86, pp.24–41.

Hallward, Peter (2000) 'The Singular and the Specific: Recent French philosophy', *Radical Philosophy* 99 (January/February 2000), pp.6–18.

– – (2001) *Absolutely Postcolonial: Writing Between the Singular and the Specific*, Manchester, Manchester University Press.

– – (2003) *Badiou: A Subject to Truth*, Minneapolis, University of Minnesota Press.

– – (2004) (ed.) *Think Again: Alain Badiou and the Future of Philosophy*, New York and London, Continuum.

Haraway, Donna (1991) *Simians, Cyborgs, and Women: the Reinvention of Nature*, London, Free Association Books.

Harbord, Janet (2002) 'Platitudes of everyday life' in Jan Campbell and Janet Harbord (eds.) *Temporalities, Autobiography and Everyday Life*, Manchester, Manchester University Press, pp.21–34.

Harding, Sandra (2004) 'Rethinking Standpoint Epistemology: What Is 'Strong Objectivity'?' in Harding (ed.) *The Feminist Standpoint Theory Reader: Intellectual and Political Controversies*, London and New York, Routledge, pp.127–140.

Hart, William (2000) *Edward Said and the Religious Effects of Culture*, Cambridge, Cambridge University Press.

Harvey, Irene E. (1992) 'Derrida and the Issues of Exemplarity' in David Wood (ed.) *Derrida: A Critical Reader*, Oxford, Blackwell, pp.193–217.

Hassan, Ihab (1997) 'Counterpoints: Nationalism, Colonialism, Multiculturalism, etc., in Personal Perspective', *Third Text* 41 (Winter 1997–98), pp.3–14.

Hegel, G.W.F. (1956) *The Philosophy of History*, trans. J. Sibree, New York, Dover Press.

– – (1975) *Lectures on the Philosophy of World History. Introduction: Reason in History*, trans. H.B. Nisbet, Cambridge, Cambridge University Press.

– – (1975) *Hegel's Aesthetics – Lectures on Fine Art*, trans. T.M. Knox, Oxford, Oxford University Press.

– – (1994) *Phenomenology of Spirit Selections*, trans. Howard P. Kainz, Pennsylvania, Pennsylvania State University Press.

– – (1996) *Lectures on the History of Philosophy. Volume one*, trans. E.S. Haldane and F. H. Simon, London, Routledge & Kegan Paul.

Hesford, Wendy S. (1999) *Framing Identities: Autobiography and the Politics of Pedagogy*, Minneapolis, University of Minnesota Press.

Hiddleston, Jane (2005) 'Derrida, Autobiography, and Postcoloniality', *French Cultural Studies* 16(3), pp.291–304.

Hitchcock, Peter (1994) 'The Othering of Cultural Studies' in *Third Text* 25, pp.11–20.

Hobson, Marian (1998) *Jacques Derrida: Opening Lines*, London, Routledge.

Holden, Philip (2005) 'Other Modernities: National Autobiography and Globalization', *Biography* 28(1), pp.89–103.

hooks, bell (1997) 'Revolutionary Black Women: Making Ourselves Subject' in Moore–Gilbert *et al* (eds.) *Postcolonial Criticism*, London, Longman, pp.215–233.

– – (1997) *Bone Black*, London, Women's Press.

– – (1998) *Wounds of Passion*, London, Women's Press.

– – (2004) 'Choosing the Margin as a Space of Radical Openness' in Sandra Harding (ed.) *The Feminist Standpoint Theory Reader: Intellectual and Political Controversies*, London and New York, Routledge, pp.153–159.

Howe, Stephen (1998) *Afrocentrism: Mythical Pasts and Imagined Homes*, London, Verso.

Huddart, David (2001) 'Making an example of Spivak', *Angelaki* 6(1), pp.35–46.

– – (2004) 'Postcolonial Piracy', *Critical Survey* 16.2 (2004), pp.7–27.

Hunter, Lynette (1999) *Critiques of Knowing: Situated Textualities in Science, Computing and the Arts*, London and New York, Routledge.

Innes, C.L. (2000) 'Review of Gayatri Chakravorty Spivak's *A Critique of Postcolonial Reason*', *Wasafiri* 31 (Spring 2000), pp.67–69.

Jameson, Frederic (1986) 'Third-World Literature in the Era of Multinational Capitalism', *Social Text* 15, 65–88.

– – (1990) *Postmodernism, or, The Cultural Logic of Late Capitalism*, London, Verso.

Jarratt, Susan C. (1995) 'In excess: radical extensions of neopragmatism' in Steven Mailloux (ed.) *Rhetoric, Sophistry, Pragmatism*, Cambridge, Cambridge University Press., pp.206–227.

Jay, Paul (1984) *Being in the Text: Self-Representation from Wordsworth to Roland Barthes*, London, Cornell University Press.

Johnson, Barbara (1987) *A World of Difference*, Baltimore, Johns Hopkins University Press.

Kamuf, Peggy (1999) 'The Experience of Deconstruction', *Angelaki* 4(3), pp.3–14.

Kant, Immanuel (1987) *Critique of Judgment*, trans. W.S. Pluhar, Indianapolis, Hackett.

– – (1991) *Selections from the Political Writings*, Cambridge, Cambridge University Press.

Kellman, Steven G. (2000) *The Translingual Imagination*, Lincoln and London, University of Nebraska Press.

Kennedy, Valerie (2000) *Edward Said*, Oxford, Blackwell.

Kristeva, Julia (1977) *About Chinese Women*, trans. A. Barrows, London, Marion Boyars.

– – (1984) 'Women's Time' in Toril Moi (ed.) *The Kristeva Reader*, Oxford, Blackwell, pp.188–211.

– – (1984) *Powers of Horror: An Essay on Abjection,* trans. L.S. Roudiez, New York, Columbia University Press.

– – (1994) *Strangers to Ourselves,* trans. L.S. Roudiez, London, Harvester Wheatsheaf.

– – (1998) 'Dialogue with Julia Kristeva', *Parallax* 8, pp.5–16.

– – (2000) *Crisis of the European Subject,* trans. S. Fairfield, New York, Other Press.

LaCapra, Dominick (1985) *History and Criticism,* London, Cornell University Press.

Landry, Donna and Gerald MacLean (eds.) (1996) *The Spivak Reader,* London, Routledge.

Lawrence, Tim (1998) 'Edward Said, Late Style and the Aesthetic of Exile', *Third Text* 38, pp.15–24.

Lazarus, Neil (1999) *Nationalism and Cultural Practice in the Postcolonial World,* Cambridge, Cambridge University Press.

Lejeune, Philippe (1989) *On Autobiography,* trans. K. Leary, Minneapolis, Minnesota University Press.

Lévi-Strauss, Claude (1966) *The Savage Mind,* trans. from the French, London, Weidenfeld & Nicholson.

– – (1973) *Tristes Tropiques,* trans. J. and D. Weightman, London, Jonathan Cape.

Lévinas, Emmanuel (1987) *Collected Philosophical Papers,* trans. A. Lingis, Dordrecht, Martinus Nijhoff.

Lim, Shirley Geok–Lim (2003) 'The Im/Possibility of Life–Writing in Two Languages' in Isabella de Courtivron (ed.) *Lives in Translation: Bilingual Writers on Identity and Creativity,* London, Palgrave Macmillan, pp.39–47.

Lindqvist, Sven (1996) *'Exterminate All the Brutes',* trans. J. Tate, London, Granta.

Lionnet, Françoise (1995) *Postcolonial Representations: Women, Literature, Identity,* Ithaca and London, Cornell University Press.

Loomba, Ania (1991) 'Overworlding the Third World', *Oxford Literary Review* 13, pp.164–192.

Luca, Ioana (2006) 'Edward Said's *Lieux de Mémoire: Out of Place* and the Politics of Autobiography', *Social Text* 87, 24(2) (Summer 2006), pp.125–144.

Lyotard, Jean–François (1991) *The Inhuman: reflections on time,* trans. G. Bennington and R. Bowlby, Cambridge, Polity Press.

– – (1993) *Political Writings,* trans. B. Readings and K. P. Geiman, Minneapolis, Minnesota University Press.

– – (1994) *Lessons on the analytic of the sublime,* trans. E. Rottenberg, Stanford, Stanford University Press.

McClintock, Anne (1992) 'The Angel of Progress: Pitfalls of the Term 'Post-colonialism", *Social Text* 31/32 (Spring 1992), pp.1–15.

MacKenzie, John (1995) *Orientalism: History, Theory and the Arts,* Manchester, Manchester University Press.

McNay, Lois (1994) *Foucault: A Critical Introduction,* Cambridge, Polity Press.

David Macey (1997) 'Fanon at seventy', *Radical Philosophy* 84 (July/Aug 1997), pp.41–43.

– – (1997) 'Fanon out of context', *Radical Philosophy* 86 (Nov/Dec 1997), pp.53.

– – (1999) 'Fanon, Phenomenology, Race', *Radical Philosophy* 95 (May/June 1999), pp.8–16.

Malouf, Amin (2000) *On Identity* trans. B. Bray, London, Harvill.

Marcus, Laura (1994) *Auto/biographical Discourses: Theory, Criticism, Practice,* Manchester, Manchester University Press.

Memmi, Albert (1965) *The Colonizer and the Colonized*, trans. H. Greenfeld, London, Earthscan.

— — (2000) *Racism* trans. S. Martinot, Minneapolis, Minnesota University Press.

Miller, Dan (1991) 'Privacy and Pleasure: Edward Said on Music', http://www.iath.virginia.edu/pmc/text–only/issue.991/review-3.991

Miller, J. Hillis (1976) 'Beginning with a text', *Diacritics* 6(3), pp.2–7.

Miller, James (1993) *The Passion of Michel Foucault*, London, Flamingo.

Miller, Nancy K. (1991) *Getting Personal: Feminist Occasions and Other Aurobiographical Acts*, London, Routledge.

Moore–Gilbert, Bart (1997) *Postcolonial Theory: Contexts, Practices, Politics*, London, Verso.

— —, Gareth Stanton and Willy Maley (eds.) (1997) *Postcolonial Criticism*, London, Longman.

— — (2005) 'Western Autobiography and Colonial Discourse: the Case of Rousseau's 'Orientalism'', *Social Identities* 11(4) (July 2005), pp.301–314.

Morley, David (2000) *Home Territories: Media, Mobility and Identity*, London, Routledge.

Morrissey, Lee (1999) 'Derrida, Algeria, and 'Structure, Sign, and Play'', http://jefferson.village.virginia.edu/pmc/text–only/issue.199/9.2morrisey.txt

Morton, Stephen (1999) 'Postcolonialism and Spectrality: Political Deferral and Ethical Singularity in the Writing of Gayatri Chakravorty Spivak', *Interventions* 1(4), pp.605–620.

— — (2003) *Gayatri Chakravorty Spivak*, London and New York, Routledge.

Mouffe, Chantal (ed.) (1996) *Deconstruction and Pragmatism*, London, Routledge.

Mowitt, John (1998) 'Strangers in Analysis: Nationalism and the Talking Cure', *Parallax* 8, pp. 45–64.

Mufti, Aamir R. (1998) 'Auerbach in Istanbul: Edward Said, Secular Criticism, and the Question of Minority Culture', *Critical Inquiry* 25 (Autumn 1998), pp.95–125.

Mukherjee, Arun (1998) *Postcolonialism: My Living*, Toronto, TSAR.

Nietzsche, Friedrich (1979) *Philosophy and Truth: Selections from Nietzsche's Notebooks of the early 1870's*, trans. D. Breazeale, New Jersey, Humanities Press International.

— — (1996) *On the Genealogy of Morals*, trans. D. Smith, Oxford, Oxford University Press.

Norris, Christopher (1996) *Reclaiming Truth: Contribution to a Critique of Cultural Relativism*, London, Lawrence & Wishart.

Okely, Judith and Helen Callaway (eds.) (1992) *Anthropology and Autobiography*, London, Routledge.

Olney, James (1998) *Memory and Narrative: the Weave of Life-Writing*, Chicago, Chicago University Press.

Papastergiadis, Nicos (1996) 'Ambivalence in Cultural Theory: Reading Homi Bhabha's *Dissemi-Nation*' in J.C. Hawley (ed.) *Writing the Nation*, Amsterdam, Rodopi., pp.176–193.

— — (1998) *The Turbulence of Migration: Globalization, Deterritorialization, Hybridity*, Cambridge, Polity Press.

Parker, David (2005) 'Inhabiting Multiple Worlds: Auto/Biography in an (Anti-) Global Age', *Biography* 28(1) (Winter 2005), pp.v–xv.

— — (2007) *The Self in Moral Space: Life Narrative and the Good*, Ithaca, Cornell University Press.

Parker, Kenneth (1995) 'Very Like a Whale: Post–Colonialism Between Canonicities and Ethnicities', *Social Identities* 1(1), pp.155–174.

Parry, Benita (1987) 'Problems in Current Theories of Colonial Discourse', *Oxford Literary Review* 9(1–2), pp.27–58.

– – (1992) 'Overlapping Territories and Intertwined Histories: Edward Said's Post-colonial Cosmopolitanism' in Sprinker, M. (ed.) *Edward Said: A Critical Reader*, Oxford, Blackwell., pp.19–47.

– – (1994) 'Signs of Our Times: Discussion of Homi Bhabha's *The Location of Culture*' in *Third Text* 28/29, pp.5–24.

– – (1998) 'Post–Colonial Ambiguity', *New Formations* 33, pp.149–53.

Pels, Dick (2004) 'Strange Standpoints, or How to Define the Situation for Situated Knowledge' in Sandra Harding (ed.) *The Feminist Standpoint Theory Reader: Intellectual and Political Controversies*, London and New York, Routledge, pp.273–289.

Penney, James (1998) 'Uncanny Foreigners: Does the Subaltern Speak Through Julia Kristeva?' in Christopher Lane (ed.) *The Psychoanalysis of Race*, New York, Columbia University Press, pp.120–138.

Pepper, Thomas (1997) *Singularities: Extremes of Theory in the Twentieth Century*, Cambridge, Cambridge University Press.

Pyle, Forest (2002) '"By a Certain Subreption": Gayatri Spivak and the "Lever" of the Aesthetic', *Interventions* 4(2), pp.186–190.

Quayson, Ato (2000) *Postcolonialism: Theory, Practice or Process?*, Cambridge, Polity Press.

Rai, Amit S. (1998) '"Thus Spake the Subaltern...": Postcolonial Criticism and the Scene of Desire', in Christopher Lane (ed.) *The Psychoanalysis of Race*, New York, Columbia University Press, pp.91–119.

Rapaport, Herman (2002) *Later Derrida: Reading the Recent Work*, New York and London, Routledge.

Readings, Bill (1996) *The University in Ruins*, Cambridge, MA, Harvard University Press.

Rich, Adrienne (2003; 1984) 'Notes Toward a Politics of Location' in Reina Lewis and Sara Mills (eds.) *Feminist Postcolonial Theory: A Reader*, Edinburgh, Edinburgh University Press, pp.29–42.

Robbins, Bruce *et al.* (1994) 'Edward Said's *Culture and Imperialism*: a symposium', *Social Text* 40, pp.1–24.

– – (1997) 'Cosmopolitanism and Boredom', *Radical Philosophy* 85, 28–32.

– – (1997) 'Secularism, Elitism, Progress and Other Transgressions: On Edward Said's 'Voyage In" in Keith Ansell–Pearson *et al* (eds.) *Cultural Readings of Imperialism: Edward Said and the Gravity of History*, London, Lawrence & Wishart, pp.74–86.

– – (2003) 'Soul Making: Gayatri Spivak on Upward Mobility', *Cultural Studies* (Jan 2003) 17(1), pp.1–26.

Robbins, Jill (1995) 'Circumcising Confession: Derrida, Autobiography, Judaism', *Diacritics* 25(4), pp.20–38.

Robinson, Cedric (1993) 'The appropriation of Frantz Fanon', *Race and Class* 35(1), pp.79–91.

Rooney, Caroline (2000) *African Literature, Animism, and Politics*, London, Routledge.

Rose, Jacqueline (2005) *The Question of Zion*, Princeton, Princeton University Press.

Royle, Nicholas (1995) *After Derrida*, Manchester, Manchester University Press.

– – (ed.) (2000) *Deconstructions: a user's guide*, New York, Palgrave.

Rupprecht, Anita (2002) 'Making the difference: postcolonial theory and the politics of memory' in Jan Campbell and Janet Harbord (eds.) *Temporalities, Autobiography and Everyday Life*, Manchester, Manchester University Press, pp.35–52.

Said, Edward W. (1966) *Joseph Conrad and the Fiction of Autobiography*, Cambridge, MA, Harvard University Press.

– – (1972) 'Michel Foucault as an Intellectual Imagination', *boundary 2* 1(1), pp.1–36.

– – (1975) *Beginnings: Intention and Method*, New York, Columbia University Press.

– – (1978; 1995) *Orientalism: Western Conceptions of the Orient*, London, Penguin.

– – (1978) 'The Problem of Textuality: Two Exemplary Positions' in *Critical Inquiry* 4(4), pp.673–714.

– – (1986) 'Foucault and the Imagination of Power' in David C. Hoy (ed.) *Foucault: A Critical Reader*, Oxford, Blackwell, pp.149–155.

– – (1991) *Musical Elaborations*, London, Vintage.

– – (1993) *Culture and Imperialism*, London, Vintage.

– – (1994) *Representations of the Intellectual*, London, Vintage.

– – (1995) *Peace and its discontents*, London, Vintage.

– – (1996) 'Orientalism and After' in Peter Osborne (ed.) *A Critical Sense: Interviews with Intellectuals*, London, Routledge., pp.65–88.

– – (1996) 'On Jean Genet's Late Works' in J. Ellen Gainor (ed.) *Imperialism and Culture*, London, Routledge, pp.231–242.

– – (1998) 'In Conversation with Neeladri Bhattacharya, Suvir Kaul and Ania Loomba, New Delhi, 16 December 1997', *Interventions* 1(1), pp.81–96.

– – (1998) 'Edward Said talks to Jacqueline Rose', *Critical Quarterly* 40(1), pp.72–89.

– – (1999) 'Defamation, Zionist–Style', http://www.ahram.org.eg/weekly/1999/444/op2.htr

– – (1999) *Out of Place: A Memoir*, London, Granta.

– – (2000) *Reflections on Exile and Other Essays*, Cambridge, MA, Harvard University Press.

– – (2000) 'Presidential Address 1999: Humanism and Heroism' *PMLA* 115(3) (May 2000), pp.285–291.

– – (2000) 'Diary', *London Review of Books* 1 June 2000, pp.43–44.

– – (2000) 'Losers in the games', *The Guardian* May 20 2000, pp.2–3.

– – (2000) 'A truly fragile identity', http://www.ahram.org.eg/weekly/2000/474/op2.htm

– – (2000) 'Invention, Memory, and Place' *Critical Inquiry* 26 (Winter 2000), pp.175–92.

– – (2000) 'My right of return', http://www3.haaretz.co.il/scripts/print.asp?id=89666

– – (2002) (edited and with an introduction by Gauri Viswanathan) *Power, Politics, and Culture*, New York, Pantheon Books.

– – (2006) *On Late Style*, London, Bloomsbury.

– – and Jean Mohr (1986) *After the Last Sky: Palestinian Lives*, London, Faber and Faber.

San Juan Jr., E. (2002) *Racism and Cultural Studies: Critiques of Multiculturalist Ideology and the Politics of Difference*, Durham and London, Duke University Press.

Sanders, Mark (2002) 'Representation: Reading–Otherwise', *Interventions* 4(2), pp.198–204.

Sandoval, Chela (2004) 'U.S. Third World Feminism: the Theory and Method of Differential Oppositional Consciousness' in Sandra Harding (ed.) *The Feminist Standpoint Theory Reader: Intellectual and Political Controversies*, London and New York, Routledge, pp.195–209.

Schaffer, Kay and Sidonie Smith (2004) *Human Rights and Narrated Lives: the Ethics of Recognition*, New York, Palgrave Macmillan.

Schwarz, Bill (1996) 'Conquerors of Truth: Reflections on Postcolonial Theory' in Bill Schwarz (ed.) *The Expansion of England*, London, Routledge, pp.9–31.

Shohat, Ella (1992) 'Notes on the "Post–Colonial" *Social Text* 31/32, pp.99–113.

Simpson, David (1996) 'Speaking Personally: the Culture of Autobiographical Criticism' in H. Aram Veeser (ed.) *Confessions of the Critics*, London and New York, Routledge, pp.82–94.

– – (2002) *Situatedness, or, why we keep saying where we're coming from*, Durham, Duke University Press.

Slemon, Stephen (1994) 'The Scramble for Post–Colonialism' in Tiffin and Lawson (eds.) *De-Scribing Empire: Postcolonialism and Textuality*, London, Routledge, pp.15–32.

Smith, Robert (1995) *Derrida and Autobiography*, Cambridge, Cambridge University Press.

Smith, Sidonie (1990) 'Self, Subject, and Resistance: Marginalities and Twentieth–Century Autobiographical Practice', *Tulsa Studies in Women's Literature* 9(1) (Spring 1990), pp.11–24.

– – Smith, Sidonie and Julia Watson (eds.) (1992) *De/Colonizing the Subject: The Politics of Gender in Women's Autobiography*, Minneapolis, University of Minnesota Press.

– – Smith, Sidonie and Julia Watson (eds.) (1996) *Getting a Life: Everyday Uses of Autobiography*, Minneapolis, University of Minnesota Press.

– – Smith, Sidonie and Julia Watson (2001) *Reading Autobiography: A Guide for Interpreting Life Narratives*, Minneapolis, University of Minnesota Press.

Spivak, Gayatri Chakravorty (1987) *In Other Worlds: Essays in Cultural Politics*, London, Routledge.

– – (1987) 'Speculations on reading Marx: after reading Derrida' in Derek Attridge, Geoff Bennington and Robert Young (eds.) *Post-Structuralism and the Question of History*, Cambridge, Cambridge University Press, pp.30–62.

– – (1989) 'Who Claims Alterity?' in Barbara Kruger and Phil Mariani (eds.) *Remaking History*, Seattle, Bay Press, pp.269–292.

– – (1990) Sarah Harasym (ed.) *The Post-Colonial Critic: Interviews, Strategies, Dialogues*, London, Routledge.

– – (1993) *Outside in the Teaching Machine*, London, Routledge.

– – (1994) 'Can the Subaltern Speak?' in Patrick Williams and Laura Chrisman (eds.) *Colonial Discourse and Postcolonial Theory: A Reader*, New York, Columbia University Press.

– – (1995) 'Ghostwriting', *Diacritics* 25(2), pp.65–84.

– – (1996) 'Lives' in H. Aram Veeser (ed.) *Confessions of the Critics*, London, Routledge, pp.205–220.

– – (1997) 'Displacement and the Discourse of Woman' in Nancy J. Holland (ed.) *Feminist Interpretations of Jacques Derrida*, Pennsylvania, Pennsylvania University Press, pp.43–71.

– – (1998) 'Three Women's Texts and Circumfession' in *Postcolonialism and Autobiography*, Amsterdam, Rodopi, pp.7–22.

– – (1999) *A Critique of Postcolonial Reason: Toward a History of the Vanishing Present*, Cambridge, MA, Harvard University Press.

– – (2000) 'Translation as Culture', *Parallax* 14, pp.13–24.

– – (2000) 'Deconstruction and Cultural Studies' in Nicholas Royle (ed.) *Deconstructions: a user's guide*, New York, Palgrave, pp.14–43.

– – (2002) 'Response: Panel of Papers on *Critique of Postcolonial Reason*', *Interventions* 4(2), pp.205–211.

– – (2002) 'A Conversation with Gayatri Chakravorty Spivak: Politics and the Imagination', *Signs: Journal of Women in Culture and Society*, 28(2), pp.609–624.

– – (2003) 'The Politics of the Production of Knowledge: An Interview with Gayatri Chakravorty Spivak' in Jonathan Culler and Kevin Lamb (eds.) *Just Being Difficult: Academic Writing in the Public Arena*, Stanford, Stanford University Press, pp.181–198.

– – (2005) 'Scattered speculations on the subaltern and the popular', *Postcolonial Studies* 8(4),pp. 475–486.

– – (2005) 'Thinking about Edward Said: Pages from a Memoir' in Homi Bhabha and W. J. T. Mitchell (eds.) *Edward Said: Continuing the Conversation*, Chicago, Chicago University Press, pp.157–162.

Sprinker, Michael (1980) 'Fictions of the Self: The End of Autobiography' in James Olney (ed.) *Autobiography: Essays Theoretical and Critical*, Princeton, Princeton University Press, pp.321–342.

– – (ed.) (1992) *Edward Said: A Critical Reader*, Oxford, Blackwell.

– – (ed.) (1999) *Ghostly Demarcations: on Jacques Derrida's 'Spectres of Marx'*, London, Verso.

Still, Judith (2004) 'Language as Hospitality: Revisiting Intertextuality via Monolingualism of the Other', *Paragraph* 27(1) (March 2004), pp.113–127.

Sturrock, John (1993) *The Language of Autobiography: Studies in the First Person Singular*, Cambridge, Cambridge University Press.

Suleri, Sara (1991) *Meatless Days*, London, Flamingo.

Swindells, Julia (ed.) (1995) *The Uses of Autobiography*, London, Taylor and Francis.

Swindells Julia (2000) 'First Person Suspect, or, the Enemy Within…' in Alison Donnell and Pauline Polkey (eds.) *Representing Lives: Women and Auto/biography*, Basingstoke, Macmillan, pp.33–42.

Taussig, Michael (1987) *Shamanism, Colonialism, and the Wild Man: A Study in Terror in Healing*, Chicago, Chicago University Press.

– – (1989) 'Terror As Usual: Walter Benjamin's Theory of History As A State of Siege', *Social Text* 22, 3–20.

– – (1993) *Mimesis and Alterity: A Particular History of the Senses*, New York and London, Routledge.

Taylor, Charles (1990) *Sources of the Self*, Cambridge, MA, Harvard University Press.

Trinh, T. Minh-ha (1989) *Woman, Native, Other: Writing Postcoloniality and Feminism*, Indianapolis, Indiana University Press.

Trotter, David (1999) 'Fanon's Nausea', *Parallax* 5(2), pp.32–50.

Varadharajan, Asha (1995) *Exotic Parodies: Subjectivity in Adorno, Said, and Spivak*, Minneapolis, University of Minnesota Press.

Veeser, H. Aram (ed.) (1996) *Confessions of the Critics*, London, Routledge.

Venn, Couze (1996) 'History Lessons: Formation of Subjects, (Post)colonialism, and an Other Project' in Bill Schwarz (ed.) *The Expansion of England*, London, Routledge, pp.32–59.

Vergès, Françoise (1996) 'To Cure and to Free: The Fanonian Project of "Decolonized Psychiatry" in Lewis R. Gordon *et al.* (eds.) *Fanon: A Critical Reader*, Oxford, Blackwell, pp.85–99.

– – (1997) 'Creole Skin, Black Mask: Fanon and Disavowal', *Critical Inquiry* 23(3), pp.578–595.

– – (1999) 'Colonising Citizenship', *Radical Philosophy* 95, pp.3–7.

Waters, Lindsay (1998) 'In Responses Begins Responsibility: Music and Emotion', *boundary 2* 25(2), pp.95–116.

Weiner, Justus Reid (1999) '"My Beautiful Old House" and Other Fabrications by Edward Said', http://www.commentarymagazine.com/9909/weiner.html

White, Robert (1998) 'The Deformity of Theory in Psychoanalysis', *Angelaki* 3(1), pp.171–186.

Whitlock, Gillian (2000) *The Intimate Empire: Reading Women's Autobiography*, London and New York, Cassell.

– – (2007) *Soft Weapons: Autobiography in Transit*, Chicago and London, University of Chicago Press.

Williams, Patrick (1996) "No Direction Home?' – Futures for Post–Colonial Studies', *Wasafiri* 23 (Spring 1996), pp.6–8.

Wills, David (1995) *Prosthesis*, Stanford, Stanford University Press.

Wittgenstein, Ludwig (1974) *Tractatus-Logico-Philosophicus*, translated by David Pears and Brian McGuinness, London, RKP.

Wood, David (1997) 'Identity and Violence' in Keith Ansell–Pearson, Benita Parry and Judith Squires (eds.) *Cultural Readings of Imperialism*, London, Lawrence & Wishart, pp.194–211.

Wood, Nancy (1998) 'Remembering the Jews of Algeria', *Parallax* 4(2), pp.169–183.

Robert, Young (1990) *White Mythologies: Writing History and the West*, London, Routledge.

– – (1994) 'Egypt in America: *Black Athena*, Racism and Colonial Discourse' in Ali Rattansi and Sallie Westwood (eds.) *Racism, Modernity and Identity: On the Western Front*, Cambridge, Polity Press, pp.150–169.

– – (1995) 'Foucault on Race and Colonialism', *New Formations* 25, pp.57–65.

– – (1995) *Colonial Desire: Hybridity in Theory, Culture and Race*, London, Routledge.

– – (1996) 'The Dialectics of Cultural Criticism', *Angelaki* 2(2), pp.9–24.

– – (1997) 'Response to Laura Chrisman', *Textual Practice* 11(1), pp.47–49.

– – (2000) 'Deconstruction and the Postcolonial' in Nicholas Royle (ed.) *Deconstructions: a user's guide*, New York, Palgrave, pp.187–210.

Žižek, Slavoj (1997) *The Plague of Fantasies*, London, Verso.

– – 'Multiculturalism, or, The Cultural Logic of Multinational Capitalism', *New Left Review* 225 (Sept–Oct 1997) pp.28–51.

– – (1998) 'Cogito as a Shibboleth' in Žižek (ed.) *Cogito and the Unconscious* Durham, Duke University Press, pp.1–8.

– – (2003) *Organs Without Bodies* New York and London, Routledge.

Index